BURY ME STANDING

Isabel Fonseca was educated at Columbia University and Oxford University. She was an assistant editor at the *Times Literary Supplement* and she edited *Soho Square*. She has written for a wide range of publications including the *Independent*, *Vogue*, *The Nation* and *The Wall Street Journal*. She lives in London.

'In Isabel Fonseca's wonderful book...the human beings behind these neglected stories come vividly to life...Her book is an unforgettable testament to a people whose stories have remained buried far too long'
Mail on Sunday

'*Bury Me Standing* [is] the superb and unique documentation and history, the vivid and scholarly, the passionate and disciplined, the excruciatingly fair account of a people close to me. The Gypsies and I have waited for this book'
Yehudi Menuhin

'Isabel Fonseca has written a compelling book about the Gypsies of Eastern Europe and has given a fascinating account of the lives they are living at the present time...I found this a most lively, thought-provoking and compelling book, which anyone who reads it will enjoy enormously'
Barbara Cartland,
Literary Review

'*Bury Me Standing* is the best of history-cum-travel book: conscientious, unhurried and full of odd bits of knowledge'
Daily Telegraph

'Illuminating...Ms Fonseca is as impressive for intrepid reporting as she is for analytical scholarship...A captivating portrait'
New York Times

'Many books have been written about post-communist Europe, but none displays such selfless commitment to its subject as *Bury Me Standing*'
Wall Street Journal

'A vivid, intelligent and compassionate portrait of a forgotten people, written with considerable insight and humour'
Telegraph Weekend Magazine

Isabel Fonseca

BURY ME STANDING
The Gypsies and Their Journey

VINTAGE

Published by Vintage 1996

6   8   10   9   7

Copyright © Isabel Fonseca 1995

The right of Isabel Fonseca to be identified as the author
of this work has been asserted by her in accordance
with the Copyright, Designs and Patents Act, 1988.

First published in Great Britain by
Chatto & Windus Ltd, 1995

Vintage
Random House, 20 Vauxhall Bridge Road, London SW1V 2SA

Random House Australia (Pty) Limited
16 Dalmore Drive, Scoresby, Victoria 3179, Australia

Random House New Zealand Limited
18 Poland Road, Glenfield
Auckland 10, New Zealand

Random House South Africa (Pty) Limited
Endulini, 5a Jubilee Road, Parktown 2193, South Africa

Random House UK Limited Reg. No. 954009

A CIP catalogue record for this book
is available from the British Library

ISBN 0 09 974021 4

Papers used by Random House UK Limited
are natural, recyclable products made from wood grown in
sustainable forests. The manufacturing processes conform to
the environmental regulations of the country of origin

Printed and bound in Great Britain by
Cox & Wyman Ltd, Reading, Berkshire

To my brother Bruno

1958–1994

ACKNOWLEDGMENTS

This book is the result of many visits, long and short, to East Central Europe—to Albania, Bulgaria, the former Czechoslovakia, Germany, Moldova, Poland, Romania, and the former Yugoslavia—between 1991 and 1995. I would like to thank (more or less alphabetically) Igor Antip, David Binder, Holly Cartner, Marcel Courtiade, the Duka family, Rajko Djurić, Moris Farhi, Edmund Fawcett, Angus Fraser, Andreas Freudenberg, Nicolae Gheorghe, Gabrielle Glaser, Ian Hancock, Herbert Heuss, Milena Hübschmannová, Elena Marushiakova and Vesselin Popov, Pete Mercer, Luminitsa Mihai, Sybil Milton, Andrzej Mirga, David Mulcahy, Ljumnja Osmani, Carol Silverman, Jeremy Sutton-Hibbert, Martine Tassy, Corin Trandofir, Rachel Tritt, Ted Zang, and Ina Zoon. Larry Watts and Livia Plaks of the Project on Ethnic Relations were also helpful.

I am especially indebted to Donald Kenrick, co-author of the pioneering study *The Destiny of Europe's Gypsies*. Over four years he patiently responded to my ideas and impressions and finally he read the whole book in manuscript. And I am grateful to Mick Imlah, Richard Cornuelle, John Ryle, Martin Amis, and Michael Glazebrook, who also read and improved this book in typescript.

In the text I have changed some names. I have not always given surnames. Often these were not volunteered for various reasons.

I changed people's names if they asked not to be identified and also if I thought that they didn't really understand that their stories might be read by strangers. I never concealed my notes, or the likelihood that I would reproduce and publish them, but this is one of the dilemmas of writing about a largely illiterate people: What could such declarations of intent mean to many of the illiterate, and isolated, Roma I met? I apologize to anyone mentioned by name who would have preferred anonymity.

CONTENTS

Map of East Central Europe

Bury Me Standing

Out of the Mouth of Papusza:
A Cautionary Tale

Her real name was Bronisława Wajs, but she is known by her Gypsy name, Papusza: "Doll." Papusza was one of the greatest Gypsy singers and poets ever and, for a while, one of the most celebrated. She lived all her life in Poland, and when she died in 1987 nobody noticed.

Like most Polish Gypsies, Papusza's family was nomadic—part of a great *kumpania*, or band of families, traveling with horses and in caravans, with the men at the front and the women and children following behind in open carts. Some of the richer families had elaborately carved hard-top caravans with narrow glass windows, sometimes diamond-shaped and set in painted wood frames. There might be as many as twenty caravans in the *kumpania*. Men, women, children, horses, carts, dogs: until the mid-1960s they moved along, down from Vilnius, through the eastern forests of Volhynia (where thousands of Polish Gypsies waited out the war), crossing into the Tatra mountains in the south. On the road, the silhouette of the Polska Roma would sometimes include the shapes of bears, their living, dancing livelihood. But Papusza's people were harpists, and from the northern Lithuanian towns to the eastern Tatras they hauled the great stringed instruments, upright over the wagons like sails.

While it traveled, the *kumpania* maintained contact with other convoys of the same clan moving along separate routes. They would leave signs at crossroads—a bunch of twigs tied with a red rag, a branch broken in a particular way, a notched bone—the signs called *shpera* among the Polish Gypsies (and *patrin*, or leaf, everywhere else, from Kosovo to Peterborough). Fearing the devil's spawn, villagers stayed clear of these markers.

This is how Papusza learned to read and write. When the *kumpania* stopped for more than a day or two—and even nomadic families usu-

ally had winter digs somewhere—she would bring to a likely villager a
stolen chicken in exchange for lessons. For more chickens she acquired
books, a secret library beneath the harps. Even today, around three-
quarters of Gypsy women are illiterate. When Papusza was growing up
in the 1920s, literacy among Gypsies was almost unknown, and when
she was caught reading she was beaten and her books and magazines
were destroyed. Equally intolerable to her family was her desire, when
the time came, to go with the blackest-eyed teenage boy in the *kumpania*.
At fifteen she was married by arrangement to an old and revered
harpist, Dionizy Wajs. It was a good marriage, and she was very
unhappy. She bore no children. She began to sing.

Whatever Papusza lacked in companionship or lost in love, in
Dionizy Wajs she at least found an accompanist. Drawing from the
great Gypsy tradition of improvised storytelling, and from short simple folk songs, she composed long ballads—part song, part poem,
spontaneously "enacted." Like most Gypsy songs, Papusza's were
wringing laments of poverty, impossible love, and, later, yearning for a
lost freedom. Like most Gypsy songs, they were equally plangent in
tone and in subject: they spoke of rootlessness and the *lungo drom*, or
long road, of no particular place to go—and of no turning back.

Papusza lost more than a hundred members of her family during
the war. But even this was not the tragedy that would shape her. She
wrote at a critical moment in her people's history, in Poland and
(unknown to her) everywhere else: one life—life along the *lungo drom*,
life on the road—was coming to an end and nothing recognizable or
tolerable looked like taking its place.

> *O Lord, where should I go?*
> *What can I do?*
> *Where can I find*
> *Legends and songs?*
> *I do not go to the forest,*
> *I meet with no rivers.*
> *O forest, my father,*
> *My black father!*
>
> *The time of the wandering Gypsies*
> *Has long passed. But I see them,*
> *They are bright,*
> *Strong and clear like water.*

> *You can hear it*
> *Wandering*
> *when it wishes to speak.*
>
> *But poor thing it has no speech. . . .*
>
> *. . . the water does not look behind.*
> *It flees, runs farther away,*
> *Where eyes will not see her,*
> *The water that wanders.*

Nostalgia is the essence of Gypsy song, and seems always to have been. But nostalgia for what? *Nostos* is the Greek for "a return home"; the Gypsies have no home, and, perhaps uniquely among peoples, they have no dream of a homeland. Utopia—*ou topos*—means "no place." Nostalgia for utopia: a return home to no place. *O lungo drom.* The long road.

Perhaps it is the yearning itself which is celebrated, even a yearning for a past one never had (the most powerful kind). Such yearning is the impetus to travel. But the nostalgia of Gypsy song is weighted with fatalism. "The crack of Doom / is coming soon. / Let it come, / It doesn't matter," goes the refrain of a Serbian Gypsy song.

Many of Papusza's song-poems fit into this tradition: through hundreds of refinements and retellings, they are mostly faceless, highly stylized distillations of collective experience. You find a few Gypsy Antigones—girls mourning their dead brothers—and sons, far from home or in prison, missing their mothers. Everyone has a brother. Everyone has a mother. Everyone has a tragedy. It is impossible to tell the origin or era of most songs by their words, because they speak of the universal and unchanging *čačimos*—truth—of a people living as best they can, outside history.

The collective *oeuvre* of the handful of Romany poets working today attests to an unresolved tension between a loyalty to lore and the individual's slightly guilty attempt to map out his or her own experience. Forty years ago, Papusza had already made the complete progression from the collective and the abstract to a private, minutely observed world.

Her great songs, which she sometimes just called "Song Out of the Head of Papusza," are in her own singular voice, a style that for the most part is still unheard of in Gypsy culture. Papusza wrote and sang

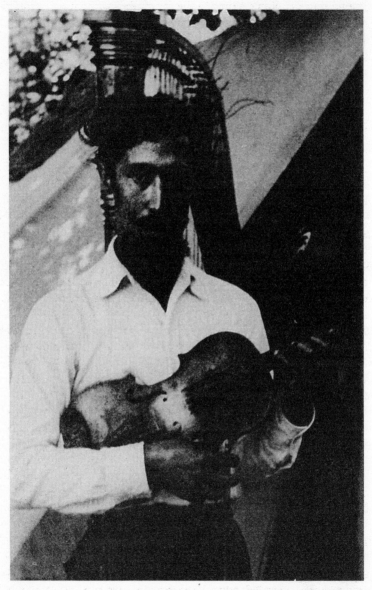

Karol Siwak, a fiddler from Papusza's kumpania, 1949

of specific incidents and places. She bore witness. A long autobiographical ballad about hiding in the forests during the war is simply called "Bloody Tears: What We Went Through Under the Germans in Volhynia in the Years 43 and 44." She wrote not just about her own people, and of the vague threat of the *gadjikano* (non-Gypsy) world; she also wrote of the Jews with whom her people shared forests and fate; she wrote of "Ashfitz."

By chance, in the summer of 1949, the Polish poet Jerzy Ficowski saw Papusza sing and immediately recognized her talent. He began collecting and transcribing the stories that she had painstakingly copied out in Romani, written phonetically in the Polish alphabet. In October of 1950 several of Papusza's poems appeared in a magazine called *Problemy*, alongside an interview with Ficowski by the distinguished Polish poet Julian Tuwim. There is talk of the ills of "wandering," and the piece ends with a Romani translation of the Communist "Internationale." The author of what is still the most important book on Polish Gypsies, Ficowski became an adviser on "the Gypsy question." The first edition of his book (1953) includes a chapter called "The Right Way," which—though omitted in subsequent editions and perhaps included only as a condition of publication—gave his backing to the government policy of settlement for the fewer than fifteen thousand Polish Gypsies who had survived the war. Ficowski cites Papusza herself as an ideal, and suggests her poems might be used for propaganda purposes among Gypsies. "Her greatest period of poetry writing was around 1950," Ficowski noted, "soon after she abandoned the nomadic way of life." Despite the fact that her poems constitute an elegy for that life—not so much abandoned as confiscated—Ficowski, in his role as an apologist for the government policy of compulsory sedentarization, asserted that she was "a participant and mouthpiece" for these changes.

The new socialist government in postwar Poland aspired to build a nationally and ethnically homogeneous state. Although the Gypsies accounted for about .005 percent of the population, "the Gypsy problem" was labeled an "important state task," and an Office for Gypsy Affairs was established under the jurisdiction of the Ministry of Internal Affairs—that is, the police. It was in operation until 1989.

In 1952 a broad program to enforce the settlement of Gypsies also came into effect: it was known as the Great Halt (although that goal was not achieved in Poland until the late 1970s, when travel, at least in caravans, was finally stopped). The plan belonged to the feverish fashion for "productivization," which, with its well-intended welfare provisions, in fact imposed a new culture of dependency on the Gypsies, who had always opposed it. Similar legislation would be adopted in Czechoslovakia (1958), in Bulgaria (1958), and in Romania (1962), as the vogue for forced assimilation gathered momentum. Meanwhile in the West, the opposite legislative trend, one enforcing nomadism, was emerging, though by the late 1960s settlement was the goal everywhere. In the England and Wales of 1960, for example, legislation kept Gypsies on the move—in fact, they were only "legal" while in motion. But within a decade the reverse was true, as the 1968 Caravan Sites Act aimed to settle Gypsies (partially by a technique of population control known as "designation," in which whole large areas of the country were declared off-limits to Travelers).

Reformers through time, Ficowski included, no doubt believed that such measures would greatly improve the difficult lives of Gypsies: education was the only hope for the emancipation of these people who lived "outside history"; and settlement would bring education.

But no one has ever thought to ask the Gypsies themselves. And accordingly all attempts at assimilation have failed. Ficowski, unlike policymakers less close to the source, did "refer" to the Gypsies he had come to know: above all to Papusza. And within two months of the appearance of her poems in *Problemy*, a pack of Gypsy "envoys" visited Papusza, and threatened her.

Papusza was soon identified among Gypsies as a culprit in the campaign to cancel their traditional way of life. Her stature as a poet and singer, and the love for her people expressed in decades of work, meant nothing. Papusza had done something unforgivable: she had collaborated with a *gadjo*.

> No one understands me,
> Only the forest and the river.
> That of which I speak
> Has all, all passed away,
> Everything has gone with it—
> And those years of youth.

Papusza had indeed been misunderstood—and used—by both sides. She tried desperately to reclaim the authorship of her own ideas, her songs. She rushed from her home in southern Silesia to the Polish Writers Union in Warsaw, begging for someone to intervene. She was refused. She went to Ossolineum, the publishing house that was preparing Ficowski's book, including her poems, for imminent publication. No one could understand her. Was she unhappy about the translations? Were there final revisions to be made? Papusza returned home and burned all her work—some three hundred poems—which, with Ficowski's enthusiastic encouragement, she had begun to commit to paper. Then she wrote him a letter, begging him to stop publication, though even the letter showed her resignation, the essential fatalism of Gypsy song. If you print these songs I shall be skinned alive, she wrote, my people shall be naked against the elements. But who knows, maybe I will grow another skin, maybe one more beautiful.

After the publication of the poems Papusza was put on trial. She was called before the highest authority among the Polish Roma, the Baro Shero, Big Head, or elder. After little deliberation, she was proclaimed *mahrime* (or *magherdi* among Polish Roma), unclean: the punishment was irreversible exclusion from the group. She spent eight months in a Silesian psychiatric hospital; then, for the next thirty-four years until her death in 1987, she lived alone and in isolation (perhaps wishing to avoid further harm, even Ficowski broke contact with her). She was shunned by her own generation and unknown to the next. She became her name: a doll, mute and discarded. Except for a brief spell in the late 1960s, when she burst out with a few of her best poems, Papusza never sang again.

In a revised edition of his great book *The Gypsies in Poland*, published in 1984, Ficowski reviews the results of the Big Halt campaign. "Gypsies no longer lead a nomadic life, and the number of illiterates has considerably fallen." But even these gains were limited because Gypsy girls marry at the age of twelve or thirteen, and because "in the very few cases where individuals are properly educated, they usually tend to leave the Gypsy community." The results were disastrous: "Opposition to the traveling of the Gypsy craftsmen, who had taken their tinsmithing or blacksmithing into the uttermost corners of the country, began gradually to bring about the disappearance of . . . most of the traditional Gypsy skills." And finally, "after the loss of opportunities to practice traditional professions, [for many Gypsies] the main source of livelihood became preying on the rest of society." Now there really was

Papusza, 1949

something to be nostalgic about. Wisdom comes too late. The owl of Minerva flies at dusk.

That a crude demographic experiment ended in rootlessness and squalor is neither surprising nor disputed; the corralling of words, however, may have had the opposite result. The language (and increasingly the written language) is the cornerstone of modern Gypsy identity and emancipation.

Poland, 1963

There are no words in Romani proper for "to write" or "to read." Gypsies borrow from other languages to describe these activities. Or else, and more revealingly, they use other Romani words. *Chin,* or "cut" (as in carve), means "to write." The verb "to read" is *gin,* which means "to count." But the common expression is *dav opre: dav opre* means "I give upwards," and so the phrase may be translated "I read aloud." It does not describe reading to oneself; this is not something Gypsies generally do. Similarly, *drabarav,* a version of "I read" used by Macedonian Gypsies, traditionally means to read in the specific sense of telling fortunes from the palm of the hand. And in Albania, Gypsies may say *gilabav* for "I read," though it primarily means "I sing."

A *gilabno* is a singer *or* a reader; a *drabarno* (or more often a female *drabarni*) is a reader and a fortune-teller but also a herb-dealer, which is to say a healer. These are recent innovations; they show what the written language means to an historically illiterate people. And it is to Ficowski's Papusza that all these singer-readers must look first.

Ficowski's efforts, like Papusza's, have not been repaid with gratitude. Sophisticated Polish Gypsies, such as the ethnographer Andrzej Mirga (who has revived Papusza since her death in a film and in a series of concerts, including performances by the New York Metropolitan Opera), recognize the importance of Ficowski's scholarly work, but still regard him as a traitor.

The Gypsies' rejection of the government proposals—and of Papusza herself—did not stem from any primeval "will to freedom." So soon after the war, many Gypsies had vivid memories of interviews with *gadje.* The Nazis were the most thorough of ethnographers. They collected more than thirty thousand Gypsy genealogies. They measured skulls, collected blood samples, and charted eye colors.

Today, the great majority of Gypsies know little or nothing of the elaborate and malicious documentation of a sizable group of their ancestors who happened to live in German territory; but this legacy nevertheless informs the living memory of Gypsies everywhere. The passionately held view of most Gypsies is still that *gadje* are dangerous, not to be trusted, and, in the interest of the survival of the group, they are to be avoided except for dealings in business. Indeed, in the most general sense, *gadje* are considered to be *mahrime:* polluted. To develop unnecessary relations with them is to risk contamination.

To be sure, in Poland, as elsewhere, more and more Gypsies and *gadje* are intermarrying but, as Andrzej Mirga—who is married to a *gadji*—pointed out, "our mothers are not happy about this trend." They needn't worry: instead of contributing to the disintegration of the group or to their assimilation into the world of the *gadjo,* intermarriage merely enlarges the stock. The children of such unions, like mulattos and mestizos everywhere, are considered by everyone to be Gypsies, just as they would have been classified by the Nazis.

The response of some regrettably powerful Gypsies to the Papusza/Ficowski collaboration perhaps reveals more about Gypsy life than the mass of data he diligently recorded. It unveils the most fundamental Gypsy value: that of "us against the world." Although the belief that they should remain a separate people is not based on a theological precept, this worldview, codified in hundreds of unwritten laws and superstitions enforcing symbolic purification, is not unlike that set forth in the Talmud: "Be deliberate in judging and raise up many disciples, and make a hedge for the Torah." Ever more pressed, Gypsies seek only to build up their hedge.

"You will never learn our language," a Gypsy activist—and teacher of Romani—proudly told me on a bus in Bucharest. He didn't mean that I had a wooden ear. "For every word you record in your little notebook, we have another one—a synonym, which we use and which you can never know. Oh, you might learn these; but you won't get how to use them, or what nuances they carry. We don't *want* you to know. You should've been born a Romany *chey* [girl]."

This teacher, one of the most prominent Romany nationalists, devotes fantastic energy to exposing and fighting anti-Gypsy racism. Still, on the bus he was reinforcing one of the oldest slanders: that Romani is not a proper language, but thieves' cant. The contradiction highlights a peculiar difficulty of the present-day Gypsy emancipation movement: clearly, and understandably, exoticism itself has been part of the hedge. (And so has humor: as in the Talmud, the layers of laws themselves constitute the hedge; among Gypsies, people who have participated in illicit sex, and so dipped themselves in lasting shame, are said to have "gone behind the hedge.")

But mimicry—or adaptation—has always existed alongside exoticism. Since 1989, the first Gypsy political parties have emerged, along with their first representatives: Members of Parliament, delegates to the UN. Gypsy poets now publish their work in Romani and in other languages. In Romania and in Macedonia there are Romany television programs produced by Roma; there is a first generation of Gypsy editors of newspapers and magazines (one of the best, edited by a Kosovan Rom out of Slovakia, is called *Patrin*—the old word for the signposts traveling Gypsies left for their traveling fellows). All of this is new; and the excitement is palpable. But one may also say, without disparagement, that beneath the surface things haven't changed. The arrival of democracy in no way signals a reordering of Gypsy traditions. The secret society continues. Its tangled underbrush of prohibitions—the Gypsy hedge—is intact.

Konferença, kongresso, parliamento: these are some of the most recent additions to the Romani language. It is true that, until 1989, Gypsies in the former Eastern bloc had not had much chance to use them. And these concepts remain alien, even antithetical, to the internal organization of the Gypsy people.

When they first appeared in Europe in the fourteenth century the Gypsies presented themselves as pilgrims and they told fortunes: two winning professions in a superstitious age. Their leaders called themselves Counts and Princes and Captains. These were not expressions of Gypsy values so much as further evidence of their (often underemployed) talent for adopting local moods and hierarchies in order to sustain their ever-precarious prestige. Us versus Them is a game which, for the time being, is still played in the language of the conquerors—or of the "host" society.

"Never ask questions and don't wear short skirts." That was the best advice I got before I set out. It came from an anthropologist who had done research among the Gypsies of Madrid. "Asking," he said, "is no way to get answers."

Fifteen years ago I traveled around Eastern Europe with my grandmother, who at age two had left her native Hungary in 1905. I remember stepping off the Orient Express in Budapest and wondering, "What are all these Indians doing here?" (That evening, and every other evening in Hungary, we recognized them as Gypsies, trios of Gypsies bowing their violins over our goulash.) During the revolutions of 1989 I wondered again about those "Indians." Though they were never mentioned in the papers, I had the idea that they would show the watching world what kind of democracies upheaval would bring to Eastern Europe.

Before I had actually met a Gypsy, I knew that there were twelve million of them living in diaspora all over the world, that perhaps eight million lived in Europe, mainly in Eastern Europe, and that they were the continent's largest minority. In a region with static and negative birthrates the Gypsies, I knew, were reproducing in intimidatingly large numbers. Their population was expected to double within seventeen years. Already they were being seized as the handiest scapegoats for *all* the ills of creaky communist societies in slow transition. I knew that hundreds of thousands of Gypsies had died in the Holocaust. Now again there were pogroms in Eastern Europe. Aware of the escalating violence they faced, Václav Havel had said that "the Gypsies are a litmus test not of democracy but of a civil society." It wasn't hard to see that the energies of nationalism would be excited by the particular difficulties the Gypsies presented to each bankrupt state. Gypsies are mostly illiterate, mostly unemployed, and mostly without proper housing. Their lives are about a third shorter than those of their countrymen. (And Eastern Europeans aren't the only vulnerable ones: 70 percent of Italian Gypsy families lose at least one child, while among Irish Travelers infant mortality is three times the national average.)

I knew all this. But I didn't know, for example, that Gypsies were offended by the sight of female knees. And I hadn't imagined that they might not *want* to repudiate all the slanders and vicious stereotypes, that they might not want to tell their story at all. "Never ask questions. . . ."

Gypsies lie. They lie a lot—more often and more inventively than other people. Not to each other, but to *gadje*. Still, malice is not intended. On the whole, lying is a cheerful affair. Embellishments are intended to give pleasure. People long to tell you what they imagine you want to hear. They want to amuse you; they want to amuse themselves; they want to show you a good time. This is beyond hospitality. This is art.

The liar—or, without being euphemistic, we can say the fabulist—may also believe that the revised version is *more* true. And so it may be: more true in the sense of more vivid. But lies of course are also designed to deceive. Indeed deception, the gentler the better, is considered a duty. "We don't *want* you to know," the teacher of Romani had said. And what he was really talking about was survival.

Relations between Gypsies and *gadje* have not always been as desperate as they are now. Some secrets have been common ones: there were many Gypsies in the Resistance during the Second World War. And before the advent of mixed marriage there were centuries of professional symbiosis—between, say, peasants and toolmakers. Yet their survival, over a millennium, has depended on secrecy: on disguise and misrepresentation, on keeping customs and ambitions hidden, on burying the past—on lying. The Gypsies have always been partisans.

When I returned from a month in Bulgaria or a summer in Albania, people at home would ask me if I had been accepted by the Gypsies among whom I'd stayed. I could say yes. I have been welcomed with bankrupting generosity. My honor has been defended by my Gypsy brothers, even when I didn't know it had been besmirched. I have felt completely safe among Gypsies. I have been called *chey*, or daughter, by my Gypsy mother. But I was never allowed to prepare food, to work, to contribute as a daughter would. In one community I wasn't even allowed to wash myself: that duty was delegated to the young women of the household. Most often I ate with the men, not with the women and children, who would pick over whatever we had left untouched. I knew that I would always remain a *gadji*, outside *their* history.

Secrets of course can only be kept by consensus and allegiance. For real or imagined collusion with the *gadje*, Papusza was condemned to a living death. The harsh law of the Gypsies—so cruelly at variance with the romantic stereotype of the Romany free spirit—prohibits emancipation of individuals in favor of preserving the group. And as so often a disastrous element of mimicry was at work: Papusza was called a nark, just as Gypsies have been dubbed agents and spies throughout their history in the West. In fact, "nark," British slang for stool pigeon, derives from the Romani word *nak*, or nose. The casting out of Papusza is an instance of the very demands for conformity more usually associated with *gadje*.

The miracle is that the Gypsies as a whole have resisted an assimilation which has always meant surrender. Papusza was herself sacrificed, but Papusza also survives—thanks to the *gadjo* Ficowski. Perhaps Papusza was already doomed, before she met him—doomed by childlessness, and by the very things that have come to seem liberating to a growing corps of Roma: by singing in her own voice and not just for the group; by writing things down.

ONE

The Dukas of Albania

Usually on my journeys in Eastern Europe I traveled alone and made friends along the way. But Albania was different. Albania was as remote and unknowable as Tibet, and I wanted a guide. I had to find "Marcel."

I had heard his name for years, but all I had been told about him was that he was a non-Gypsy who spoke Romani; that he had lived for many years in Albania; that he wore a long beard; and that he had no fixed address. Finally I caught up with him at a conference near Bratislava, though it might have been anywhere in the Balkans, where he lived at large. During a lunch break between sessions I approached the bearded delegate and asked him if he would go with me to Albania. Yes, that'd be all right, he said unsmilingly, barely glancing up from his schnitzel; we'd work out the details later. But later came and Marcel had gone.

A month passed before I found him again, in Paris. At his request we met on the Right Bank, outside the offices of LOT, the Polish airline. As soon as I spotted him, struggling with the zipper of his gray windcheater, I understood something of what the Roma world meant to him. Dressed all in gray, Marcel almost disappeared into the façade of the building. But the camouflage was incomplete: he looked poor, provincial, wrong. Up close, he looked permanently alarmed. His green eyes bulged in an even perimeter of white.

I took Marcel to lunch. I asked him to pick any place he liked. With all Paris before him, Marcel chose the dim upstairs cafeteria at Monoprix, the French equivalent of Woolworth's. Watching him wolf down the plate of boiled potatoes and the darkening mayonnaise salad that he'd selected, I saw that he felt at home here. It was very East European.

In fact Marcel was French; but in Eastern Europe, he wouldn't cut the shambolic figure I met near the Paris Opéra. Among the Roma, he was a personage; you could guess that there he swapped feeling like an outsider for actually being one, and strangeness made sense.

Though in general he preferred to talk about language, at the Monoprix Marcel told me about himself and his life among Gypsies; he began, as he began every conversation, with a raised finger and a correction. Marcel was *not*, as I had supposed, French at all, but *Occitanian*. The language, Occitan, of which he offered a sample, is a variety of Provençal and sounds like Catalan—the strident provincialism was certainly Catalonian in spirit. But Marcel was a pedant, and a rather cosmopolitan one.

His grandfather, he said, was from a traveling family—part of a group called the "Gringos"—signifying, here, not unwanted Americans but Greek-speaking Gypsies in Spain. Marcel *sounded* like a Frenchman, or rather he sounded like Peter Sellers, with his piquant, zestily accented English. "The family traveled and stopped at fairs to sell and repair sewing machines, while I stayed behind with my grandmother in the Massif Central." He told me that his father had been an organist, but that he had stopped playing when they settled and the old man had gone to work as a porter at the Clermont railway station.

As a teenager, Marcel had been a medical student at a provincial French university. In the early seventies he got into trouble for organizing hunger strikes against government cuts, and, disillusioned at nineteen, he left for Vojvodina, where he found work as a grape-picker and labored among Romanies for the first time.

By then he was already a brilliant linguist: Marcel knew Samoan, Hiri Motu (of Papua New Guinea), Maori, Tahitian. He could get by in Ajie (New Caledonian), and, of course, he spoke all the "ordinary" languages—French, English, Spanish, German, and passable Russian and Japanese. Figuring he was never going to get to the Loyalty Islands, or anywhere else in the South Pacific, Marcel turned his sights on the Balkans. His love for the region—and his vocation as a linguist—was settled when he traveled with a piglet under his shirt and was received everywhere as a bringer of good news.

"I stayed for some months in a monastery in Slovenia. With no money at all, I had no way of thanking the monks who had been so kind to me. After much thought I decided to give them the piglet, who, after all, was already something of a pig. They were very pleased. The abbot held him in his arms like a baby. I shall never forget it: *he could speak to it in its own language."* Even the memory left Marcel speechless with wonder and admiration.

When I asked him how he had ended up spending a decade in Albania, he explained without hesitation or irony: because he couldn't get a job anywhere else. The difficulty of the Albanian language had presented an irresistible challenge to Marcel, and once he had mastered it for himself he found that he had also become indispensable to the country's foreign embassies. Later, he was fired for smuggling out Gypsy refugees.

Marcel was one of a handful of specialists—linguists and social scientists—I met who devoted themselves to and completely identified with Gypsies. Some Gypsies called groupies *puyuria*—from the Romanian for "puppies" or "cubs" or "chicks"—if they were women (me, for instance). There were other, less affectionate terms, and a contempt sometimes showed itself, along with accusations that the *gadje* were profiting from Gypsy distress. Frustration came in part because Gypsies knew that they benefited from and sometimes depended on such relationships. It was an historic and strictly pragmatic arrangement: in exchange for practical help, the sympathetic *gadjo,* and his entire family, would be variously protected—no small service. The *gadjo's* contribution would include letter-writing and document-reading and acting as an intermediary with prejudiced authorities (in Marcel's case it was the Western ambassadors). In Tirana, Marcel was a star.

Marcel unambiguously identified himself as Rom. He spent his life going from Romany settlements to international conferences and, above all worked to promote the Romani language. Although he made a real contribution, in attempts to undermine his status within the movement other Gypsy activists occasionally "denounced" him as a *gadjo.* Denunciation was always the point; but what did it matter if the story of his Greek Gypsy ancestors *wasn't* true? Though Marcel devoted himself to their emancipation as an ethnic nation, he also availed himself of the common view that what constituted a Gypsy was his style of life. Marcel lived that life, or lived in its shadow.

Six weeks after our Paris meeting we shared a taxi. A taxi from Bulgaria to Albania: twelve hot hours across the memory of Yugoslavia. Like all border posts, the frontier near Struga in Macedonia is chaotic and dull, littered with a ragged population of shufflers, pushers, and peddlers, indolent and insolent, waiting for rejection and a long-familiar journey in the wrong direction. Approaching the border we found a convoy of massive, eighteen-wheel rigs (Italian, Swiss, German, Hungarian), which had been kept waiting for five days. Michele, a haggard driver from Treviso, supplied me with warm Cokes. "What's going on?" I asked him. Michele couldn't find words—he just sputtered with fatigue and rage and anxiety, the sweat and dust flying from his wagging head. Like a good Italian, Michele was anxious about food: with an open palm he indicated his baking truck, whose cargo—thousands of homely tins of EEC "Stewed Steak" ("75% animal product") and industrial drums of Italian sunflower oil—had been reheating for a week.

With ostentatious indifference to the queue, and to the customhouse's throbbing Turkish disco music, a half-dozen officials leaned against the wall and gazed dreamily out on a semibucolic, iron-red vista salted with small unshepherded goats. As for the others, their postures—legs apart, arms akimbo—told anyone who cared to see that a price had not yet been negotiated. Humanitarian aid is the number-one import of Europe's poorest nation. It is all donated gear, but nothing is free in Albania; everything coming in will be sold and resold several times, starting at the border.

We had all seen the pictures of Albanians festooning boats bound for Italy. Marcel even knew some of them. But no one in the queue, except Marcel, knew what to expect inside this country that no one was allowed to leave. So far, all we were confident of was that it was as hard for outsiders to get into Albania as it was for natives to get out.

At the very moment we were finally waved through, a small and toothless middle-aged Gypsy sidled up to me and tugged at my sleeve. She was bursting with some great joke. Suddenly serious, she shouted in Romani before disappearing: *"Te djivel o Tito, te djiven e Jugosloviage manusha!"*—"Long live Comrade Tito and long live the Yugoslav people!" Her comment was the only opinion offered by the locals—certainly by the local Gypsies—about the disintegrating country that we were stepping out of. The war was so close as to have become far: it was unmentionable.

Inside Albania, keeping a lookout for our ride, we walked for a while along the shore of the vast turquoise Lake Ohrid. There are no plastic spoons, no Coke cans, no scraps, no billboards, no beckonings of any kind. But immediately one felt that Albania was more than a tourist-free oasis between the ex-paradises of Greece and southern Italy. Or less. What you can't imagine before you get there is the emptiness. The land is so bad that even the trees come on one at a time, surrounded by more space than their spindliness can support. The particular beauty of Albania seems always to depend on isolation . . . A car came to a noisy halt under a cloud of dust: our lift. Out came the most disheveled pair of Gypsies I had ever seen. "This is Gimi" (pronounced "gimme"). A relieved Marcel indicated the rather shy-looking lank-haired driver in worryingly low-slung blue jeans: "And this is Nicu." Chubby, grinning, bare-chested Nicu was all hair, from the smoke track curling up the belly and bifurcating into ram's-horn flourishes about the breasts, to the whole of his matted cupid's head. I had never before seen facial cowlicks. Nicu's real name was Besnik, but the nickname which we hit on, and which he good-naturedly embraced, had more to do with the hair: Veshengo—literally, "Man of the Forest." Or Tarzan.

On the road, Vesh offered me my first Albanian cigarette. It was a Victory. On the brown packet, under a "V" and in the place where it usually says "Smoking causes fatal diseases," was written: "Keep Spirit High."

Kinostudio

THAT SUMMER I lived with Nicu's family, the Dukas, on the edge of Tirana, in the quarter known as Kinostudio, or Movieland. The Gypsies in Albania have been so isolated that they are only dimly aware of their millions of Romany brethren living in diaspora throughout the world. Still, the Roma of Kinostudio had more in common with those far-flung Gypsies than with their fellow Albanians, among whom they have lived for nearly six hundred years. They got along with their neighbors but they remained apart.

Ethnic strife was negligible here, because of the isolation and the long, hard years of repression and shortage which wore everyone out. But the healthy self-esteem of Gypsies was also due to tremendous solidarity; as in Macedonia but nowhere else, Albanian Gypsies were not the sediment at the bottom of the bottle. There were gradations of status among the four tribes of Gypsies; and, more important, there was another group in Albania which was worse off, namely the Jevgs—a small dark people, often to be seen begging in Tirana's squares.

The Dukas were one of the first families in the quarter, and they were Mechkari Gypsies, members of the largest of the four groups. Like all Albanian Gypsies the Dukas were notionally Muslim. They shared Kinostudio with their numberless hospitable cousins and cotribals, a few Gypsy families from another group—the Kabudji—and a handful of Albanians, a tiny minority, who were invisible rather than vilified. The patter of Kino was definitely Romani.

We arrived too late to meet the family: only Nicu's mother, Jeta (Albanian for "life," and pronounced "Yeta"), and Dritta, his broad-faced, sultry young wife, had waited up. Jeta was plump but compact and energetic. Though she looked much older than her forty-four years, her movements were springy and youthful. While her daughter-in-law yawned prettily, Jeta's whole body was turned to our weary needs. She swiftly produced a hot meal and drink, then scraped the crinkly gray hair back off her healthy nut-brown face, smoothed her skirt, and sat down. Face in hands, alert as morning, Jeta focused her small, bright brown eyes on me and waited, wondering who or what had mysteriously been brought to her.

The next day I met the rest—brothers and wives and babies. The women filed in one by one, inspecting me in bed, where I still lay at seven o'clock, in what locally constituted a lie-in. First came Liliana, the limping spinster sister, who hid her Cubist face (eyes on different planes, variously energetic facial muscles, the suspicion of a harelip) under shiny pelts of thick black Indian hair. Then came the *boria*, the daughters-in-law, as the three young wives of the Duka boys were called. Viollca and Mirella shyly advanced behind their own small sons, whom they pushed forward with a hand on each shoulder. The boys could only be their fathers' sons: chubby, pouty Mario was a miniature of Nicu, without the hair. Five-year-old Walther, with a bowl haircut, was all beauty, rubbery-limbed health, and bright eyes—like his father, Nuzi, the restless, high-voiced James Dean of Kinostudio, who got away with his endless primping and flexing through winsome self-mockery (such as the articulate use of eyebrows as a smoking aid). The last child was weepy Krenar, the undersized boy of Mirella and Artani, whose snotty terry-cloth romper hung low, the crotch grazing the floor and the trampled sock-feet trailing behind him. When he reached the bed, he burst into tears; and he was to remain damp and disgruntled pretty much for the rest of the summer. Krenar was known to all as Spiuni, short for *spiuni gjerman*, or German spy, on account of his blue eyes and blond hair. The Dukas had unconsciously appropriated, and inverted, two common myths about Gypsies: that all fair children among them are in fact abducted "Christian" children, and that Gypsies themselves were spies—supposedly for the Turks, and other enemies of Christendom.

After the little ones had touched my hair or some thread of my raiment, and the girls had put the burning question of Gypsy women everywhere—How many children do you have?—they filed out to get on with their chores: washing and carrying and cooking for the *boria;* smoking and cards and TV for the boys, whom I would meet later. It was unseemly for married men to be in a room with a woman in bed, even an outsider, to whom other rules didn't apply.

Artani, the only Duka with a job, went to work before first light. He collected the garbage of the capital, for which he was paid eight hundred leks, or eight dollars, a month. Artani didn't *say* he was paid eight hundred leks. He described his wage in terms of what it could buy that day: "I earn five kilos of meat a month." He went mainly for something to do, to walk into town in the cool dawn, to get away from Kinostudio.

Nicu slept in, and Nuzi sat moodily on the porch step, chewing an unlit Victory and patting his shoulder-length hair, waiting for Liliana to make his coffee. That was her job, and—ever since he lost his post at the Ministry of Vegetation—waiting for it was his. While Nicu didn't engage much with either younger brother, Nuzi found work in making fun of Artani. He ridiculed his terrible dress sense. And even these justifiable taunts—those oversized, top-stitched sponge-nylon flares *were* terrible—only showed the poverty of Nuzi. For to care about fashion in Albania, where you couldn't buy anything, was to plunge yourself into an unending torpor of deprivation and shame. Nuzi feigned disgust with Artani for selling his time for so little money; but the truth was that it was time that so burdened Nuzi. His old job, which had involved discouraging the ivy on innumerable Enver Hoxha statues, planting shrubs, mowing public grass, and generally keeping up appearances, was a properly civic expression of his natural primping proclivities; they had been a source of pride and health to Nuzi. Jeta, as any mother would be in a country of near-total unemployment, was more cut up about Nuzi's being sacked (gambling was mentioned) than even he was. The thing about Artani's job was not that he liked it, or earned a living at it, but that he had it.

Absent that first day were Bexhet (pronounced "Beh-jet"), Jeta's husband and the father of all, and Djivan, the ten-year-old son of Nicu and Dritta. Until suppertime, grandfather and grandson were away in the city of Berat, south of the Shkumbi River, visiting a couple and their nine-year-old daughter: the little girl to whom Djivan had just become engaged. Seeing my surprise, Jeta reassured me: "They won't be getting married for three or four years. What did you think? They're only kids."

Everywhere in the Balkans life felt unstable. But among the Roma one felt as they did: utterly safe, as in a family. For one thing, there was no intermarriage between Albanians and Gypsies in Kinostudio. Far from suggesting a demoralized culture, endogamy here seemed the mark of a buoyantly confident group, settled in their skin and not needing outsiders.

Kinostudio *was* a family—practically the whole neighborhood was related. Gimi, for example, was married to Mimi, one of Jeta's seven sisters. Within a day, the whole neighborhood knew I was there and that I was with the Dukas. I was chaperoned everywhere, partly because I was a woman and I was their ward. Before I gave up, I tried occasionally to slip out for a quick solitary stroll. No dice. Within minutes Nicu, Nuzi, or Artani, or a set of *boria*, would appear at my side.

Even at home I was never allowed to be alone: not ever (and not even to use the bathroom, but that was because there wasn't one). The Dukas did not share *gadjo* notions of or need for privacy. Or for quiet. The more and the noisier the better was their creed—one that I found to be universal among Roma. Their conception of a lone person was invariably a Rom who for some infraction had been recognized as *mahrime*, unclean, and had been excluded from the group. There was something wrong with you, some shame, if you had to be alone. The Gypsies have endured unimaginable hardships, but one could be sure that loneliness wasn't one of them.

Privacy of a kind was claimed in the way that all the Duka women might, as if by previous arrangement, just ignore all the Duka men for a period—and vice versa. Similarly, nobody spoke to a man in the morning before he had washed his face (the women had always been up for hours). They seemed really not to see someone who was not yet ready to be seen. Privacy came in the form of imaginary walls. (These walls didn't do it for me though. I became intransigently constipated, and remained that way for a month of mounting congestion and alarm.)

Kinostudio was built on and beyond the city garbage heap in the 1950s. The first Romanies who came to live here had previously occupied the cellars of houses in town. Ten families were evicted and moved to Kinostudio "temporarily." They built their own houses on empty promises of ownership from the town hall.

The Dukas lived in one of the first houses in the quarter, on the sloping dirt track that led up to the tarmacked road to town. The whole

Jeta and Bexhet Duka in the courtyard, Kinostudio, Tirana, 1992

settlement (like much of the capital) was unpaved, and in winter it became a river of mud. Like all the early houses of Kinostudio, it was a single-story, lime-slaked house, with a covered porch and a cement courtyard. Three barnacle rooms patched together from different materials (tin, board, cement) had been added on as one brother after another brought home his bride.

In the middle of the road was the communal well, and, beyond that, the bread place. It wasn't a bakery, but a queue. After a long and sociable wait—the bread line offered the neighborhood *boria* a rare chance to put down their pails and to gossip—you arrived at an unmarked hole in the wall. Sticking out from this paneless window were two arms: one took in the rumpled, filthy lek notes while the other (possibly it belonged to a different body) doled out the long, tall, still-warm loaves of bread: beige, or the more expensive white.

There were no shops in Kinostudio. Indeed, in all of Tirana there were hardly any stores you could walk *into*. There was the covered market for food, and the uncovered one for cheap rugs, plastic lamps, and cooking utensils down in the abandoned half-dug hole of a building site. In this gadget graveyard, Jeta inspected items which she wanted but considered inessential—a meat-grinder, an apron, Bulgarian face cream—and the next day I would return with one of the brothers and try to find and buy them. (An offer of rent had been indignantly refused; and so this subterfuge.)

Instead of stores, capitalism had so far brought only kiosks: movable prefab selling shacks where the customer had to rise on his toes to pay. Some of these specialized—like Shag, a booth we would pass on our way home from town, which sold religious paraphernalia, glass "evil eyes," and so on, but mainly crosses: wearable pendants, wall-hangers, plastic bedside stand-up Jesuses. Inside Kinostudio, shopping arrangements were more obviously impermanent, though more conducive to browsing and—because the vendors were Gypsies—to bargaining. A card table unfolded at a corner, a man squatting beside an overturned crate: these stalls were set up when and if there was anything to sell; and, as with similar stalls across the Balkans, anything might be on offer—batteries, toys, plastic shoes, socks, a paper fan, EC or UN canned food, single cigarettes, string.

The kids of Kino knew a few of the brand names that danced in heads all over the developing world: Coke, Kent, and Marlboro (cigarettes were scraps of the West that Albanians could aspire to owning; what was the point of knowing the names of American *cars*?). But in Kino these brand names had the same status value as the fake Western cigarettes such as Wenston (sic), Victory, Bond, Ronhill, Sher, and OK—which came from either Turkey or Iran. They were all ritzy goods because they were *not Albanian*. Beyond that it didn't much matter what they were or where they'd come from.

At the top of the road, the vegetable man sat in his cart amid the produce, which was usually just *domate* (tomatoes). Sometimes he had cherries and figs, but Jeta would never let me buy any: though they cost pennies, by local standards they were overpriced, and no one in Jeta's charge was going to get ripped off.

And there was Yolanda, the fat dark-brown woman who sat on a low wall by the post office, her calamine-colored stockings rolled down to the calf. She held a burlap sack of sunflower seeds between her knees, her palms flat on her thighs, fingers in, elbows up. When she got a customer, she would carefully measure out four wooden eggcupfuls and roll them into a newspaper cone. All over the neighborhood, people paused in their conversations to spit out the black husks, and children spat them at each other. Any place where queues formed—the bread line, say, or inside the post office—was marked by an ant trail of sunflower droppings. Yolanda's counterpart was the stick figure of Mr. Cashku, who sat within courting distance of her corpulence. He wore a tweed suit all through the scorching summer; and he sold lighter fluid, refilling through a tiny tin funnel the cheap plastic lighters that everyone seemed to have. Matches were not often for sale and nothing in Albania was disposable. Nothing but time.

Yolanda and Mr. Cashku had prime shop property: Kinostudio's post office was always packed. It was a place to pick up gossip, and to make phone calls (there were few private lines in Albania, and none in Kino). Sometimes the phone queue spilled out onto the steps; inside, it jammed to fill the space, with people waving bits of paper, calling out "Italia!" and "Gjermania!" They were hoping to place their calls before they reached the front and their turn to shout, for all to hear, into the single, early-model Bakelite telephone on the counter. Everyone seemed to have a relative who was a refugee. And it was clear just from their faces as they left the post office that Albanian mothers were not convinced that Westerners were showing proper appreciation of their boys.

So was it worse to be stuck in Albania or to be a refugee, stranded elsewhere? The consensus is clear. During more than a month in Albania, I didn't meet a single person who didn't want to leave. Their dreams of leaving were of different kinds, however. The Gypsies I met were anxious to take advantage of the new trade opportunities; they were impatient to bring back some of the outside world. The notion of severing oneself from the "family," and its rich pool of future partners in work and marriage, held little appeal.

Like many Gypsies, the Albanian *gadje* lived in disgust with their country; but they were also burdened by a sense of shame the Gypsies didn't share. They wanted to leave, and to leave off being Albanians. They wanted to "become Europeans." Unlike the Gypsies, whose allegiance was familial, and at the outer limit tribal but never national in the sense of aspiring to a territorial state, the Albanians I met were acutely aware of themselves as dud Europeans. Either way, everyone wanted out.

"Will you be my sponsor?" "Please, *please*, guarantee me." These are the things the sometimes menacing young men of Kino whispered if they ever managed to get me alone. These were not Albanian pickup lines. "Guarantee," like "no problem" (*ska problem* in Albanian), was one bit of English that everyone knew. It signaled a plea for rescue. For increasingly a native's only hope of escape was adoption: a foster Westerner had to be found who would be responsible for the Eastern ward, who would house and feed him, and post bail should he falter. This was a serious legal responsibility, and the vision of an apartment full of unemployed Albanian youths made it shamefully easy to say no.

Getting away: that was the point; there was not much thought about where one might actually go. Nuzi, who with Nicu walked me down to the post office one day, chose America. "Because it is rich and free." He laughed when I promised him that there were poor people in America. "And," he added, pressing his disadvantage, because "maybe Americans haven't heard of us." (A year after my stay, I learned that Nuzi had made it to Germany, as a member of a Gypsy musical ensemble. This was particularly pleasing news. I was sure that he had no musical leanings.)

All Eastern Europeans enjoy doom, but none so wittily as the Albanian Gypsies, who will offer, with upturned palms, the word "Albania" as an explanation for the unpaved streets in the capital, for the traffic fines one routinely receives for no vaguely guessable reason, for anything bureaucratic, poorly made, time-consuming, or sad.

But Nicu, the eldest son, wasn't going to let anything get him down. The post office was in the worst corner of Kinostudio: a scratchy unturfed patch of crumbling ten-story concrete apartment blocks.

These grim towers were built in 1965 for Hoxha's police force; but even they had rejected them, and so construction was abandoned, plumbing was never installed, and eventually the overflow from Kinostudio piled in. It looked like a slum. But where I saw the Projects, Nicu saw the future. This is where he hoped to buy an apartment for his own family, Dritta and Djivan and Mario. And when I stood next to him, listening to his plans (to repour the concrete floors, to paint and stencil the walls with flowers as Gypsies everywhere loved to do), little by little it stopped looking like a slum and simply became the neighborhood. Those children playing didn't look like doomy little criminals, once you knew their names. And there were no drugs. It was just poor, it was just Albania.

Sure, Nicu would have liked to get out, but he only wanted to make some money, to establish some trading partners and then come home. Turkey was the one place that occasionally extended visas to Albanians (former subjects, after all), and these were used over and over, razored out of one red vinyl passport and sewn into the next. Nicu had already been to "Stanbuli"—an excursion from which he returned as a figure of impossible glamour; and the transformation made his sultry wife, Dritta, even more unbearable to her sisters-in-law, the junior *boria*. He had plans, he was going into "import-export" (the latter half for the time being remained "undisclosed"); so far this had yielded stacks of circular aluminum Turkish floor ovens that, not yet sold out, formed a wall of articulated metallic columns in the Duka family courtyard.

Nicu had had a job in a textile factory. Boldly for someone from a neighborhood of near-total unemployment—there were 288 wholly unemployed families here—he quit. He wanted work, but like most Gypsies he had no use for regimented wage labor. The final blow came when they put him on night shift. He didn't want Dritta to be alone after dark (or he didn't want to be without her after dark). Above all, Nicu trusted that he could do better on his own—earn more money, have more freedom and more fun, and design a better future than he could in any job. And he was right.

Gimi's brother Arben, who was called Beno and was doing booming business in fabrics from Turkey, had invited Nicu into the firm. Or at least he had given him a corner of his truck. Once a month the truck would return from Stanbuli and the whole of Kinostudio would gather to finger and admire the new goods: bright bolts of cloth as tall as a man, elaborately flowery in accordance with Gypsy taste. All the houses and all the wives and daughters of Kino were upholstered in one or other of a couple of batches that had come off Beno's truck, giving the otherwise built-onto, shanty-accretive aspect of the place the uniform look of a camp. Nicu paid for a space in Beno's truck for his ovens, which had not *as yet* caught on: but Nicu was optimistic.

Trade was not a traditional profession for the Mechkari as it was for so many Gypsy groups (it is unusual that the Mechkari even said they had been agricultural workers for centuries). But still they were natural entrepreneurs. In Kinostudio there were a few fancy houses going up—a turret here, a balcony there—and they looked odd because there were no sidewalks or paved roads, just these mansions in the dirt. They belonged to Gypsies who were doing well in imports. In Albania, and all through the region, Gypsies were among the few who were going to seize the new opportunities and build their new houses, while the rest of the population looked on, envious, inert, tiredly enraged, and complaining.

Gypsies have no squeamishness about money: they talk about it freely, unboastfully displaying their wads. Jeta always had a bouquet of bills tacked under her bra strap (Gypsy women did not on the whole wear bras, and she seemed to sport hers mainly as a wallet). Nicu's encouraging prospects were greeted with joy, as they would have been by any parents. But still, among Gypsies, there was ambivalence about savings. I never once met a Gypsy with a personal bank account—though of course the banks are *gadjo* institutions.

Whatever his reasons, Nicu had hidden the money he'd saved to buy the new flat. And though everyone knew about it, it was not to be discussed.

I often slept in Nicu and Dritta's two-room "wing," on a Polish folding couch with Mario or Djivan or both. One morning before dawn, Nicu crashed around among a few of the Stanbuli stoves that he hadn't managed to fit into the courtyard. It was dark, but what I couldn't see I could hear. One by one he lifted off the circular ovens and restacked them. When he got to the bottom drum, he suddenly went gentle, and quietly settled it on the painted table in the middle of the room. He pulled off the lid and placed it on the chair. Only now did Nicu push up the sleeves of the tapered man's shirt that he'd slept in—the bright white of the shirt caught what light there was. He reached into the low vat and delicately unloaded something rectangular and heavier than bread—it might have been a brick. One, two, three bricks, neatly squared on the table each time. Four, five, six.

It was money. Bundles of money, each tied with a string; the money for the flat.

Dritta appeared with the laundry bag, now emptied, and held it open at Nicu's side. Like a thief with his newly acquired ingots, in the dark he deftly lowered all six loaves into it, three on the bottom, three on top. And the bag went behind the couch opposite mine, on which Marcel still snored. Dritta further camouflaged the loot with one of her many Day-Glo plastic fruit trees, and began her usual round of chores: water to boil for coffee, cups, tubs, and soap retrieved from their night spaces. Without a word passing between them, Nicu downed the shot of strong sweet coffee that Dritta handed him, exchanged the thimble-size cup for the money bag, and slipped into the courtyard and out the front gate.

That evening he returned with the deed for the flat, which also served as the only evidence of his having paid over his fortune, nearly one thousand dollars. Breathlessly he pushed it across the table towards Marcel, who sat phlegmatically behind his long beard like a pawnbroker. Nicu couldn't read the piece of paper: he literally didn't know what he had. The *deklerat* was handwritten in pencil on a piece of brown paper—the kind of paper that used to serve (extravagantly, it now seemed) as wrapping for bread—in an elaborately looped cursive script with extra loops at the tails of letters. In a rendition of a generic official document, there was even a circular seal drawn in a lower corner; the artist understood that those stamps were there for atmosphere. There was no mention of the sum, and no date.

A certain law of hospitality still held among Albanian Gypsies— though it had, inevitably, fallen from fashion elsewhere. This was the obligation of any Gypsy to offer welcome and material help to any other—ideally but not necessarily from the same group—who asked for it. Gypsies still depended on this when they traveled abroad. One evening in Kinostudio, Dilaver, a wiry, pockmarked brother of Gimi's recently returned from an expedition to Greece (even from Albania they managed somehow to move across borders), spoke in shocked tones for hours of the closed doors he had encountered. There was a time limit on how long you could prey on the hospitality of an unknown family in the group: some said three days, others told me seven. But within a Gypsy family, as in any family, obligations could be elastic, even unlimited. Not only was your enemy's enemy likely to be a relative, but your brother's crime was your own. During my weeks in Kino the law made a rare appearance. They arrested a Kabudji man for assault and robbery. He would be sentenced to a year in prison. However, as he had the only job in his extended family, and four children of his own, the family consulted itself and offered up a younger brother in his stead.

This happens among Gypsies all over the Balkans (though I had heard similar stories in Britain too), where collective punishment is not only directed towards Gypsies, but where responsibility, or shame, may be felt by them as a group. The practice proves the degree to which, for the authorities, Gypsies are all alike: any one of them will do. And the younger brother, did he mind? Not really. In many places imprisonment was a terrible fate, not for fear of stabbing or sodomy but because one was separated from the group and forced to live and eat among *gadje*, thereby risking all manner of contamination. Within the family, though, this sacrifice conferred honor, and among your peers time inside would be the equivalent of doing battle abroad. All the young men who had been in, and among Gypsies a sad many had, proudly displayed their blurry, blue razor-blade tattoos like war medals.

The rule of hospitality was a beautiful and thriving principle, but it could also be exploited. (When money came in, according to Michael Stewart, a Briton who lived with some Hungarian Gypsies, a common tactic was to spend it immediately on illiquid assets—heavy furniture.) Such communitarian codes had kept the Gypsies together for centuries, and had kept them poor.

It is certainly not the case that Gypsies attach no importance to possessions. Bexhet took extravagant care of his bicycle, and Nuzi dreamed like all young men of a fast car, of *any* car. Marriage came so early, for many before adolescence, that it seemed not to interfere with the usual yearnings and growth pains, which here might be perceived more as a midlife crisis. (The average Gypsy male in eastern Slovakia died before the age of forty.)

The difference was that these things—bikes and cars—were to be enjoyed, but also converted into profit. They were not just toys, and they were never regarded fetishistically; another bike or car would come along. Renewal and exchange were the only constants, reinforcing the belief among *gadje* that the possessions of Gypsies were all stolen goods. With regard to their rapid turnover of merchandise, Gypsies behaved more like rich Westerners than their poor counterparts in other countries. An aristocratic etiquette furthermore required that possessions be made to look easily acquired, in contrast to the non-Gypsy verities of hard work and frugality.

And so, when Nicu's fortune could no longer be concealed from neighbors, it was strenuously downplayed. Nicu falsely intimated that he had won it all in a crap game. And there was a certain prudence in this flourish of Gypsy style. What was abundant today would very likely be gone tomorrow.

Everybody Sees Only His Own Dish

FOOD. THOUGH THERE were no shortages in Albania during my visit, food—or meat—seemed to be the only subject of discussion, and the procuring and preparing of it busied three-quarters of the household for most of each day.

Just opposite the house, there was Mish Mas, or Meat Meat, the butcher's. (*Mish* is "meat" in Albanian; *mas* is "meat" in Romani.) Jeta didn't shop here, though. The proprietor of Mish Mas would jokingly beckon to her, and she would shout back, *"Xinav to mas!"*—"I am going to shit on your meat!" Wearing her most unforgiving grimace, she pronounced Mish Mas meat *bi-lacho*, no good, and so every day, cursing the local butcher, she would exchange her slippers for her "city shoes," the shiny black ones with heels, and walk three miles down to the covered market in town. There you could sniff and pinch the meat, and you could really haggle. Jeta knew how to haggle.

Her method involved disgusted jabbing of the various cuts of meat spread over the bloodied white tiles. Each poke was followed by a hoot or a cluck or merely a disappointed sigh. Such scrutiny of the meat seemed pointless because, at least to my untrained eye, it was all the same. It was certainly all sheep parts: brains, balls, guts, gut linings, organs and glands, whole skinned heads, and spindly joints. You could also buy the sheepskins from the butcher and hooves for stew, or perhaps for glue. Greasy, stringy ewe or ram—that was the only *mas* you could get, and we got it every day.

The same routine was played out over the vegetables, which Jeta didn't count as real food anyway, and over the raw green coffee beans, which were eyeballed individually as if they were emeralds. But the real passion was reserved for the mutton, which, once back home, would be washed and oiled and dressed like a king's feet—and certainly more assiduously than any of the children ever were. In such a poor country, putting meat on the table every day—more often than was now the practice in any developed country—was symbolically important. It could be a ploy for status, as living beyond one's means always could be; but for Jeta it meant strength and survival.

All over Central and Eastern Europe people had recent memories and occasional reminders of severe shortages (and for a while all the news from Albania seemed to be about food riots). In response to this continual threat, the *gadje* tended to hoard and the Gypsies to gorge.

The daily meal at the house of an Albanian family I came to know was meager—bean soup, perhaps, with a piece of fat floating in each bowl for calories: perfectly adequate, but in Jeta's eyes derisory. Still, she didn't shop for the future; she trusted in her ability to scour and bargain and come up with the goods, and to get them fresh, every day, however slack the money bra.

Marcel described the shopping practices of some Gypsies in other parts of the Balkans, and particularly of some Gypsy children. They would, he said, make the food unappealing to anyone else. Not only would they fondle everything, but simultaneously (and theatrically) they would scratch their own arms and scalps as if for lice, a routine that would stop the minute they had completed their purchase or had been sent on their way. Was this a racket? Marcel thought it as likely that these rapscallions were just having fun. They embodied the pragmatic Romany proverb *Te den, xa, te maren, de-nash!*: When you are given, eat, when you are beaten run away! For Jeta we could reserve the more philosophical saying *Sako peskero charo dikhel:* Everybody sees only his own dish. Jeta's children never indulged in such mischievousness but if they did she would certainly have smacked them, perhaps with her favorite and redundant warning, that *isi ili daba*—here there are also smacks.

Although it was not yet nine o'clock, it was already scorching when Jeta and I and a selection of urchins returned to Kinostudio, dragging lunch. (It was the one meal of the day, supplemented on either side by quantities of bread and jam.) No matter how hot it was, or how heavy the load, we always walked. Along the main road out of the city the buses were so infrequent that every stop looked like a demonstration—a demonstration being tear-gassed with exhaust fumes. There were hardly any private cars—before 1990 it was illegal to own one here—and so Albanians, most of whom had to travel great distances to shop, had to spend as much time waiting to travel. The pavements of popular routes were clogged with commuters. Old men in white felt fezzes squatted on their haunches along the whole lengths of some streets; families lunched and napped, waiting for a ride on a vacuum-packed bus. (No one collected tickets. No one dared.) There were nearly as many dead buses as running ones; abandoned along the main road, and stripped of any salable parts, these were now home to Tirana's large population of homeless children.

When we turned into the dirt track at the mouth of Kinostudio, restless kids would race up to greet us. Thirty-one-year-old Liliana would often be there, loping unevenly and unself-consciously along with the pack. She would take all the bags off us and, lurching from side to side, cheerfully haul them down to the house.

Watching her go one day, I paused to shake out my load-stiffened arms. Djivan and his pal Elvis hung back with me and, as we started down the hill, Djivan told me a riddle. "I have a sister who runs without legs and who whistles without a mouth. Who is she?" He beamed up at me, blew the black curls from his forehead, crossed his sun-browned arms, and waited for my reply. I scolded him for being so mean to his unfortunate sister and then Elvis came in with the right answer: "She is the *wind!*"

Next door to the Dukas was the school which all of the children had briefly attended—all, that is, except Liliana, who, with her disabilities ("caused by an old woman when she was a new-born"), was thought not to need any schooling. Nor would she qualify for marriage and motherhood. Lili was sweet-natured, patient, hard-working, and popular with all the children, who thought of her, because she was childlike but also because she was childless (and therefore not considered an adult female), as one of their own. She would have made an ideal *bori*. However, with her whiffly speech and her funny leg, Liliana was considered *dili:* mentally retarded, which she certainly was not. As is the case everywhere else in the premodern world, physical disability in Albania is still not distinguished from imbecility.

Another reason for "sparing" Liliana was perhaps that she would not have fetched much in the way of a bride-price, and would have been accorded a correspondingly low status by her husband's family. For Jeta and Bexhet, this fate had elements of a blessing: most Gypsies lost their daughters at the onset of puberty. "It is out of the question," Jeta said to me of her only daughter's prospects of marriage, no doubt wondering if I wasn't on the *dili* side myself. She spoke matter-of-factly, and in front of Lili, who showed no sign of hurt feelings. This mother's candor, which could seem brutal to an outsider, was typical of the Dukas, and indeed of all Gypsies I met. Among them it was recognized that truth in itself was not painful; only ignorance could bring suffering. Consequently, euphemism was eschewed—except in (strenuously avoided) reference to bodily functions of any kind.

Some afternoons I returned to town by car, with Marcel and Gimi. Marcel spent most of his time pursuing various unpromising projects, such as the setting up of a Gypsy-run collective to grow and export medicinal herbs. He was driven everywhere by Gimi, who after all had the profession *shofer* written in his passport, and who waited for hours in the baking car outside an embassy, an office, or a private house, while Marcel barked and fumed, trying to make phone calls and demanding things that he knew better than to hope for. Mainly he tried unsuccessfully to recover his scattered belongings which, since he had last been in Albania, had been sold by his Albanian friends, or otherwise "lost." Marcel involved more and more people in his searches, and no one, clearly, had anything better to do—certainly not work. (That summer unemployment simmered at around 70 percent.)

The impression of Marcel's stature created by his Gypsy retinue in Tirana—and in particular his manservant, Gimi, forever waiting in the car—was misleading in several ways. The real reason Gimi stayed outside when we stopped in at the house of Albanians was the food. Inevitably, and whatever the hour, our hosts would prepare a meal. It was impossible to decline the hospitality, but whereas for me it was at worst a nuisance, for Gimi it presented a danger. Gypsies everywhere do their best to avoid eating food prepared by *gadje,* which almost by definition is bound to be *mahrime.*

Marcel had no place of his own, in Albania or anywhere else, and never knew where he was going to be more than a few weeks, or days, before he got there. Nevertheless, his hysterical indignation over his stolen belongings—a few bits of furniture and a TV—was certainly at odds with his free-wheeling way of life. When the sun was highest in the sky, Marcel would wipe his naked head and ask himself how he could have been so stupid. His helpers, Gypsies and Albanians alike, would shrug and clasp their hands below downcast heads, not quite daring to ask him, Yes, how? If only I had left my things with the Dukas, or any of my other Gypsy friends, he'd say, they would still be here today. And it was true; the absolute loyalty of the Gypsies to anyone they'd accepted was not notable among the Albanians.

Gimi's full proper name was Palumb Furtuna—or Dove Storm. He was quietly wise and able to give any cliché the force of proverb—a common enough gift among a certain variety of Rom. His view of the corruption among Albanians, which *seemed* not to exist among the Albanian Roma, who kept to their own codes of honor and punishment, all came down to Enver Hoxha, the late dictator. "*Jekh dilo kerel but dile hai but dile keren dilimata,*" he said, resting his sweaty brow on the sun-softened driver's wheel—"One madman makes many madmen and many madmen makes madness. . . ."

Sitting and waiting with Gimi in the car, we watched the subtle and not so subtle violence of the street. "Now we have the culture of Italy," he commented, "but only the bad part." Chaos was more easily observable than crime—at Tirana's largest road intersection, at Skanderbeg Square, for example. Here hung the remains of the city's only four traffic lights, swinging from their loose wires like spent lanterns the day after a barn dance. Beneath the defunct lights, buses, a few cars, motorbikes, bicycles, and horse-drawn carts crossed the square along whichever route was most direct for each of them. There were a few policemen around, self-appointed traffic wardens, who themselves jaywalked back and forth across the square issuing tickets to whomever they chose, probably to whoever looked most likely to pay off their fines on the spot. There was no indication of how one might properly proceed, or what might constitute an offense. Gimi, a good driver, was routinely stopped (his, or Marcel's, car was a relatively smart affair: that is, one with all four original doors). He no longer bothered to ask why, resignedly referring to the fines (themselves arbitrary sums) as "tax." Plenty of motorists ought to have been pulled over but never were; they drove drunkenly, but in fact they simply didn't know how: this was all something new. There were car corpses at an unseemly number of corners, terrible tangled heaps, and they didn't look as though they had been put there in a municipal gesture of admonition.

There were also human wrecks, drunk and sober, parked everywhere on the side of the road, in the middle of the road. There was nowhere to go, and it was too much trouble, and too dangerous getting there. On the other hand, in a place where until last year the squares and boulevards were silent, empty, and ordered, traffic was still a novelty, an entertainment. People turned out to watch the traffic.

Gimi and I were among them. During one especially long wait for Marcel in a road leading out of Tirana, a trail of men passed by on foot. They carried rubber hoses, metal pipes, sticks, and garden tools. "Bandits," Gimi said, as I lowered my camera. But anyone in Albania may be a part-time "bandit," for such domestic weaponry is a common sight.

Albania has a great history of Corsican-style vendettas between the rival clans of the Gegs and the Tosks. Under Hoxha people were too terrified to fight, but blood feuds were soon to make a comeback. (Note that the local expression for "an eye for an eye" is *kokë për kokë*, a head for a head.) As is the case everywhere in the former Eastern bloc, the police are uncertain of their authority. Baffled by the concept of limited power, they generally prefer to do nothing and to live as best they can off the gratitude of thieves. The black-booted Italian soldiers who patrol Tirana's Skanderbeg Square and the Boulevard of Martyrs are charged with protecting foreign aid, not Albanian citizens. As a result, many unlikely Albanians, such as the scholarly family who shared their lardy bean soup, are arming themselves. That summer, there was a public hanging. Two brothers, both in their twenties, had slaughtered a family of five, including a seven-month-old baby, while trying to steal some money rumored to be hidden under the family's floorboards. Even the boys' parents thought the hanging was just.

Marcel had many Albanian friends. I liked one family in particular and early in my stay I went to their place often. They had books and quiet and they lived in town: it felt, at first, like refuge from the carnival of Kinostudio. Two old people, their two middle-aged sons, and two granddaughters shared three small rooms and a rose garden, from which the father would snip me a blossom each time I dropped by. The two thin daughters wanly moved bowls on and off the table. At nineteen and twenty, they had teeth like their ancient black-clad grandmother: few between them, and those remainders yellow-gray and flaking like elderly toenails. The girls moved as if to say they knew they had no future (this *was* the future), and to look at them, who could disagree? They had no vitality; they were not going to get out. Their grandfather sat cross-legged on the couch all day long, grinding coffee beans, and it seemed a fitting accompaniment. So the father kept his daughters, not because they were *dilia*, but because this was Albania: they were educated, kind girls, but there were no jobs, and no young man could afford a wife now; there was nothing their father could do for them. The family tortured themselves with the news: life was going on elsewhere. Even the war next door, in the former Yugoslovia, looked okay, like something *to do*.

I began to dread my visits, and soon I stopped going. As it turned out, the quiet I had been attracted to was a bitter lassitude and stunned resentment at life in Albania, past, present, and future. It was understandable but it made you relieved to be back in Kinostudio, where Solitude and her pensive handmaidens had no chance at all.

Women's Work

TWENTY-FIVE SQUARE feet of children, chickens, and clothes hanging out to dry: life for the Dukas took place in the courtyard. Especially the lives of the women. Apart from Jeta—and except for quick dashes for bread or butane for the outdoor cooking ring, and maybe, in the evening, a short after-work visit to a sister or a friend in the quarter—the women were not allowed out. In any case they were too busy.

There are many sources of advice on how to be a good *bori*, such as this proverb from Slovakia: *Ajsi bori lachi: xal bilondo, phenel londo*—"Such a daughter-in-law is good who eats unsalted food and says it is salted." Modesty and submissiveness were essential, to be sure, but in the main these girls *worked*. From around five-thirty in the morning, the day was a cycle of duties, with the burden falling on Viollca and Mirella, the younger wives. These women were never called by their names, or "wife" (*romni*), or any term of endearment by their husbands; nor were they called "mother" (*daj*) by their children. Everyone referred to them as the *boria*—the brides, or daughters-in-law—and indeed it was Jeta to whom they were answerable, not to their menfolk. So, despite the institution of male laziness, this really was a matriarchy. Only Jeta could inspire fear. That the men did nothing came very quickly to seem not so much a privilege as a relegation to child status.

The girls ignored my daily request to be woken up. I kept trying to program or dream myself into their rhythm, but the body did not want to get up before the sun did (and I really couldn't set my alarm clock, and wake all the children, just to watch the girls work). One night though, I'd slept badly and was still trying to settle down when the *boria* stirred in the dark and began their day. Viollca and Mirella (called Lela) got up before everyone else, including Dritta and including the *khania*, the hens. They moved silently about the courtyard, collecting wood from the tidy pile that they maintained along one inner wall of the courtyard. In the sooty light, they built their neat fire, always the same, neither too high nor too feeble. They bailed water from an old oil drum into cans, which they arranged among the burning logs. There was fuel, but it was expensive, and so it was reserved for Jeta's cooking. The *boria* had to build their fires from scratch.

While the water heated up, the girls gathered any vaguely soiled blankets, rugs, and clothes for washing. Each had her own work station in a different corner of the courtyard and there set up her long tin tub

The boria: *Lela and Viollca at work in the courtyard, with Elvis (left) and Djivan in Kinostudio, Tirana, 1992*

on an old wooden crate; then together they lifted each of the heavy slate washboards into the tubs. The tubs were thigh-high or lower, and so both girls scrubbed in a hunched, backbreaking position. My loudly whispered pleas to "bend from the knee" inspired an exchange of furtive, pitying giggles and glances.

Each broke off a hunk of soap from the Parmesan glacier in the storage cupboard and dropped it into her tub. (My own soap *bar* was an exotic item, regarded with skeptical wonder, as if it were a palm-top computer.) They poured in boiling water and swirled it around, beginning the real ritual: hours of trancelike, rhythmical rubbing, interrupted now by a stream of new demands—a hungry child, an insufficiently caffeinated father-in-law. And they really rubbed, with such vigor that they seemed to be trying to wring the color from every bit of soaking cloth. Washing—keeping clothes and houses and themselves clean—was the *boria*'s most important job. They worked in a competitive spirit, especially once Dritta made her appearance. And all of them had to be in mind of what they were washing: men's clothes and women's clothes were to be scrubbed separately, as were children's. Another tub was reserved for the kids themselves and another for dishes and pots. They had correspondingly designated towels or rags, and never transferred a bit of tide-worn soap, always hacking off a new hunk for each new task.

Dritta's superior status was due not only to her marriage to the eldest son, and her great age (she was twenty-six). She was from another group; she was a Kabudji. This should have worked against her, but clearly there were some benefits: she was much bigger than the other two, and much more confident, attractive in an earthbound, arcadian sort of way, like one of Picasso's thick-limbed, amphora-bearing peasant girls.

Nothing about Dritta was delicate. Her sense of fun consisted in annoying people. She would grab the other girls' breasts as a greeting, or as a punchline to one of her own jokes. This gesture was not exclusive to Dritta (the American anthropologist Anne Sutherland noted identical play among American Gypsies). Breasts are associated with babies rather than sex, and so the upper body is not of special interest or a source of shame. The lower body, by contrast, is considered highly dangerous from a pollution point of view; most Gypsy women wear long skirts, and even trousers are banned. But I never got used to the breast-pinching, which made her reach for mine all the more. Once, after an especially annoying round of such swipes, I kicked Dritta in the shin—not hard (I had bare feet), but in anger. After a sufficient blank-faced pause, a grimace spread over her face, and finally, like a child, she burst into fake tears, and of course, like an adult, I felt bad.

Dritta's antics irritated everyone except her husband, Nicu, and a few other not very secret admirers. She had the kind of mock-innocent sexuality that women disliked and that led men rather guiltily to laugh at her awful jokes and shameless impersonations, just to stay within her force field.

The Kabudji had a lower status than the Mechkari, probably because the Mechkari had been in Albania for hundreds of years longer. But among these Muslims a more proximate reason might have been the markedly sassier walk and brighter clothes of the Kabudji girls. When not under Jeta's eye, Dritta showed her true colors. One afternoon, she took me to visit her mother and sister, who had in tow two small children and a baby. On the fifth floor of the worst block in all Kinostudio, whose only window had caved in and gave dangerously out onto the street, the girls shrieked and gossiped and smoked cigarettes and danced, trying to outdo each other in pelvic rudeness.

They were drunk on their own rebelliousness, and they were egged on by their oily-haired squaw of a mother, who sat cross-legged on the floor, rhythmically clapping. None of them paid any attention to the toddlers, who wobbled perilously close to the wrecked window; they ignored the whimpering baby, who sat on the floor in a puddle of her own pee. It wasn't strange that the tiny girl didn't cry harder: she had clearly learned that wailing got you nowhere. They were rough with the kids when they got underfoot.

Sometimes one mistakes girls for grown women because they have children. Here one was reminded that these mothers were children themselves when they started to have them. (Dritta's beloved collection of plastic dolls, whose tiny outfits she occasionally slung in with the rest of the washing, should have been a clue.) But among the Gypsies teenage pregnancy wasn't like teenage pregnancy in the West. Rather it was expected and desired, and it happened within the context of a large group whose members were poised to carry out their supporting roles.

Jeta's sister Xhemile—Mimi, married to Gimi—that summer be-came, at thirty, a grandmother. Jeta and the *boria* and I were invited to inspect her. Before we crossed Kinostudio, Jeta had asked me if by any chance I was menstruating; if so, no visiting the ten-day-old baby. This was Dritta's reason for not coming along. They took precautions against pollution very seriously—for a menstruating woman was *mahrime* (though I suspect Dritta wasn't much interested in someone else's new baby anyway). The girl and the baby were camping out in Mimi's par-ents' house, while the grandparents, the *puri daj* and *puro dad*, stayed for the duration at Gimi's. It was common among Gypsies that three gener-ations would help each other out in this way.

The two tiny rooms were feverishly hot: they had a fire going in the middle of July, and dark-red fabric tacked over all the windows. How scandalized these women would have been by the English couple next door to me at home, who left their bundled baby out in the garden in really cold weather, "to make her hardy." The young mother, a sullen and anemic-looking girl of fourteen, sat quietly on a bed across the room, waiting with both feet on the floor, in case Mimi called for her. She would feed the baby and then go back to the cot and demurely sit, as if she had nothing to do with the fuss in the corner. And she hadn't, not much. Her job was feeding, and recuperation.

Mimi as a matter of course took over the care of the infant, of the washing and elaborate swaddling. Her mother, the *puri daj* whose house this was, could also have shown the girl how to take care of the baby. Mimi's mother was just fifty, but she was *old*: tired, hunched, and desiccated (*puri daj* means "old mother"). She preferred to leave the lessons to capable Mimi, and to sit out with the old men, smoking. (Only old women had the right to smoke, and they took a lot of pleasure in it, after years and years as cooks and cleaners and food-finders and mothers.) The *puri daj* kept her pipe and tobacco in her bra, now that she didn't have to concern herself with the household bank.

For the new mother there was a lot to learn. Baby's bath was followed by lengthy rubbings in home-brewed unguents and sprinklings of a saffron-yellow, curiously acrid powder. Then the infant was wrapped in a muslin envelope, so tightly that she could not move her arms and legs; the whole parcel, which was called the *kopanec*, was then fastened with pins and talismans to ward off "evil eyes." Mimi pulled a thread from the red scarf I wore—red is the color of good health and happiness—and tucked it into the envelope. Jeta supplied a handful of new lek notes and in they went.

The young mother couldn't much enjoy this confinement (she, like her baby, was off-limits for forty days). But she had a lot of support; she didn't really *need* to grow up. So long as a young *bori* was sufficiently submissive, and did all her chores, there was no reason for her to become an adult in any sense but the bodily one.

Babies were adored. They offered the opposite of *mahrime*—they purified. For example, a woman was not allowed to walk in front of an older man; it was considered disrespectful to the point of contamination. But with a babe in arms you could walk where you pleased. Babies received constant and careful attention: they were wrapped and unwrapped and washed and dusted and oiled and wrapped back up again so much that, it seemed to me, they never got any peace. But once they were walking they became the responsibility of older kids, and they became part of the crowd scene, unspecified.

Gypsies were rough with their children (not their babies); or so I felt. They were always shooing them away, yelling at them, and smacking them, and the children didn't appear to be much bothered by any of it. It wasn't cruel or unusual; it wasn't frightening. Even play was rough, such as Jeta's constant yanking and tweaking of all the little boys' penises. They simply had a different style, and mostly it was okay: the kids were tougher than ours too, they *had* to be (*o chavorro na biandola dandencar*, the saying goes—"the child is not born with teeth"), and there was no shortage of love and attention and assurance of membership in the great Gypsy congregation.

At Dritta's mother's, however, something else was at work. Jeta wasn't just being a snob when she spoke ill of the Kabudji. They, or this family, lived by a different standard, or without one, and so they were a threat to the rest. On Dritta's part it was pure delinquency, for she knew better: she didn't allow her own children to witness this scene and would never have behaved this way in Jeta's courtyard. I wondered why she let me see her like this. To show her independence, I suppose; to mock and to challenge anything I might take for universal and had earnestly recorded under *"boria* life" in my notebook. Her spirit came most of all from the fact that, unlike everyone besides O Babo (Pop— that is, Bexhet) and the children, Dritta was truly happy: she loved her man, she was a sister to her two sons, and she coasted above the demands and the remorseless vigilance that so often felled the two younger *boria*. In fact both of the other two were prettier than Dritta, but they didn't know it and therefore neither did anyone else. Dritta was pleased with herself—wasn't I pleased with her too? she seemed always to be asking, proudly grabbing at her own pony buttocks, not really interested in the confirmation. Dritta's free time was often spent in the company of her own face. She had a much-prized mirror, hardly bigger than a compact and set in a ring of pink plastic petals.

One morning at around five, Dritta in clogs banged over to the couch where I slept with little Mario. Not minding if we watched but paying us no attention, she went to work. Out from under us came her private cigar box, a treasury of single earrings, gum-machine bracelets, and bobby pins, a few grubby lipsticks, curlers, ribbons, eye kohl, thread, a tin of powdered henna, a photograph of a famous Turkish singer clipped from a magazine, and, her deepest secret, a small jar of skin-whitening paste. Dritta set the fashion trends, and without her resources in paint—for she was a typical big sister in her rigorous refusal to lend anything—the other girls did their best to keep up.

Courtyard life was not fun, really, for any of them. They were indentured servants, stuck there, hardly allowed out, and with no place of their own inside (a drawer here, a stowed box there). Jeta was their boss, but Bexhet was their cross. They never so much as looked his way. This seemed, when sides had subtly to be taken, out of deference to Jeta, but it was also modesty, or anyway came in its guise. It was unseemly for a young wife to have much to do with her *sastro*, or father-in-law, in whose house she had to live; even to look directly into his eyes might imply impropriety—which naturally would have been shame and endless trouble for the girl only, whose fault it would by definition be.

On rare occasions when there was no work to be done, Lela and Viollca would go into one of their rooms and blockade the door.

They'd crank up the disco music on Nuzi's blaster and have their own little dancing party. All over Eastern Europe girls still mostly danced together and not with men, but in the Duka household even this was not really allowed. A couple of times I was dragged into this all-girl club and made to boogy American-style, which produced great hoots and yelps (and within no time they could both do the hustle). Lela showed me her stilettos, old but unused, with smooth vinyl soles and metal heels like umbrella tips. After I had admired them she wrapped them back up in rags and hid them in a suitcase, pushed far under the bed. She was of course not allowed to wear these shoes but derived illicit pleasure from having them stowed in their hiding place.

Normally so inert, in her own room Viollca was witty. The injustices of Dritta were a rich theme. She'd stomp her tiny feet in a mock tantrum, green eyes flashing. And then she would do a perfectly exaggerated impression of Dritta, her butt caught in the door.

After one such session there was a commotion in the room which I was baffled by—as if a bat had flown through and only I had missed it. The girls' horror came from the discovery that Bexhet was *on the premises*. These young mothers lunged simultaneously to muffle the music box and ricocheting off each other flew to the bed, where they sat primly, hands in their laps, heads down, and holding their breath until his voice could no longer be heard.

Those two worked pretty much in tandem: it was a natural form of protection (against Dritta, against loneliness). They wore dresses made from the same bolt of bright-yellow flowered material, whereas Dritta had made hers in red. It was the same pattern, both off the back of Beno's Stanbuli truck; there wasn't much choice in Albania, but the difference in color was significant, a demarcation which underlined Dritta's far greater glamour.

The rancor among the *boria* was a good work-aid. Each shredded shirt and towel was wrung within an inch of its life, practically dry, and, all along the four permanently stretched clotheslines, the rags were arranged, as artfully as possible, transforming the courtyard into a pleasing labyrinth of dripping kelims and clothes (underwear, and women's kit in general, was tucked away, hidden under others or placed out of the likely sight-path of men).

By seven or so the children were up and, like the hens and the puppies and Papín the goose, in danger of entering the main room and waking O Babo. It was the job of the *boria* to prevent this. They continually waved their rags and brooms and hissed at the animals; the children were silenced with fat slices of the hot brown bread thickly spread with chunky fig jam.

The *boria* hauled logs and built a new fire, this one to be good and hot for Jeta's return from market. The girls might prepare *mariki*, a sweet, layered, pizza-shaped pastry made from flour, powdered milk, sugar, and lard, whenever all of these ingredients happened to be available. But Jeta was the senior cook and the only shopper. Jeta alone handled the sheep, ripping off the skin with her hands if the butcher had neglected to perform this service. She alone chopped the meat into small pieces with her special cleaver.

The longest part of the preparation was given over to more obsessive washing, this time of the meat. Jeta soaked and scrubbed that hacked-up mutton just as the younger women scrubbed blue jeans. Every once in a while she would yell out for *pani nevi!*—fresh water!— and the old would be poured out, marking the start of another round of scrubbing. All of these steps were complicated and protracted by the superstitions that had to be observed along the way. (Jeta spat on her broom. Why? Because she had swept under my feet. If I do not, she continued, seeing the first answer had not got through, your children will remain bald all their lives, stupid.)

Hosing down the courtyard was a good job: animals and children scattered satisfyingly when the tubfuls of spent suds reclaimed the yard, the littlest one, Spiuni, jogging unsteadily away and shrieking happily through his tears as the water caught his heels. Everything had to be washed: the ground, the steps, the walls. Inside the houses too.

Nobody, and certainly not the women, considered it remotely unfair that they did all the work. In addition to their regular tasks, all through the day they had to fit in those that the men continually made for them—for example, by using the floor as an ashtray. Nor in this closed world did they feel themselves to be victims. Quite the opposite: they had the comfort of having a clear role in a world of unemployment without end. It was the men, jobless and bored, who looked the worse off. This, I would find, was the norm among Roma everywhere—in Romania, Bulgaria, Czechoslovakia, Hungary, and even among the refugees from these places, stockpiled and snoozing in the train stations of Poland, on hold, while their women and children went out to beg. The disparity between the women and the men was much greater among the Roma than among the *gadje*, and in Albania it could not, I didn't think, be explained away by Islam.

They called themselves Muslim but the designation had a peculiar local significance. For one thing, after Albania's own "cultural revolution" in 1967, religion was vigorously outlawed in a way that it hadn't been in the rest of the region, where during most of the communist period religion was quietly tolerated. When I first asked if they were Muslims, Dritta turned to Nicu and asked: "What are we?" None of them had been in a mosque; no one prayed; there was no Koran on the premises. The men were circumcised, but there was no rush about it. Normally the operation took place when boys were about twelve, or just before puberty, though at fifty, I heard, O Babo was intact.

One dawn I was awoken by a mass visit from the boys: Mario, Walther, Spiuni, and a wild-eyed Djivan all scrambled into my bed as if for protection, perhaps thinking that as a guest whose wishes were never denied I could keep them there indefinitely. What were they so afraid of? Next door there were terrible child-screams. Elvis, Djivan's best friend, had gone under the knife.

It is commonly said that Gypsies are irreligious, adopting the going faith as it suits them, in the hopes of avoiding persecution and possibly of reaping whatever benefits membership might bring. This is true. For one thing, they have often been made to listen to sermons from outside the church. But the deeper reason is that among themselves they have no need of the religions of other nations. It was hard to say exactly what it meant to the Gypsies of Kinostudio to be Muslims, as they claimed. Their women were chaste and wore long skirts, but this was the code of "decent" Gypsies everywhere.

One of the reasons I wanted to go to Albania was to see how, or if, isolation distinguished the Roma here from their brethren on the outside. In matters of belief, at least, they were just like some Gypsies I knew in New Jersey. Whatever it had once been, Albania was not now a religious culture. It was a superstitious one, for Gypsies anyway, and their spiritual life consisted of a mixture of animism, Deism, fear of ghostly ancestors, and imported religion—which is what Islam was. It is clear from the fact that personal responsibility is an unknown cultural value here that formal religion, and especially monotheism, has made no impact. The *absence* of formal religion was significant, though, for what has flourished in its place is a powerful sense of tribe.

But the Gypsies do have fervently held beliefs. These come from the group, and not from an unseen power, and they are as strictly and unquestioningly honored as those of the most zealous fundamentalist. These beliefs are the tightly woven taboos and forms which guard against contamination—of the group, the person, the reputation. They constitute Romipen—"Gypsyhood"—and they are the key to the unusual ability of Gypsies everywhere to endure persecution and drastic change of many kinds and remain Rom. Relations between *gadje* and Gypsies are highly regulated and restricted, as are relations between Gypsy men and women—and the burden for keeping such customs falls mainly on the women. The parts of the body are symbolically cordoned off from each other; washing and language have a rich symbolic value that goes far beyond getting out the dirt and getting the salt passed, and these codes exist among Gypsies from Tirana to Tyneside to Tulsa.

Lela and Viollca had the largest number of jobs and all the worst ones, and so I was sorry when I became one of their chores. They washed me every day, inside one of their rooms. Just as I was barred from doing any of the housework, I was not allowed to wash myself. They saw themselves not only as responsible for me as their guest, but responsible for and uniquely equipped to combat Albanian germs. There was no point in protesting.

As they did for the children, and for themselves in the secrecy of first dawn, they boiled water, and one poured from a can while the other lathered me up and down. They were efficient and sometimes rough in their scrubbing; frowning with concentration they ignored my whine when they got soap in my eyes. They showed nothing other than their usual desire to do a thorough job.

After I had got to know them, though, we had a lot of laughs, and both girls opened up. They were fascinated by my body, which, apart from being made up of the same basic female components and being about the same color, was totally unlike theirs. In common with most Gypsy women the *boria* were short—around five feet—and they had almost no indentation from armpit to thigh. They were narrow-hipped as boys, small-breasted and short in the legs. Their feet were ridiculously small. Both girls were unexpectedly hairy—unexpectedly, I suppose, according to the child analogue they presented.

It was my breasts that really intrigued them, though, as if they were boys experiencing their first close-up viewing. Without hesitation, they moved straight in to inspect. They poked and cautiously squeezed, and (sensing this might be going too far) very briefly they pinched. What were they doing? Did they think mine might even *feel* different from theirs?

The touching wasn't remotely sexual. It was part of a general stock-taking of everything about me that was different from them. Fascination and disbelief: they unself-consciously yanked their own breasts out of the tops of their dresses, and presented them as proof of my freakishness. These women were twelve and thirteen years younger than me, but never having worn bras and having breast-fed their sons for *years,* their breasts hung in yamlike triangular flaps, with slightly discolored tips for nipples. They were shyly earthbound, more tuber than sexual characteristic, strange and beautiful. The girls seemed to have stopped developing—rounding and blooming—before full womanhood, and then, still childlike and not fully realized, had begun their decline. Old girls: that's what the naked *boria* looked like.

Despite the inordinate amount of lather on the Duka premises, the children always looked like urchins. They started out clean but, like all kids who are allowed to play, they soon got dirty. Among many Gypsies the appearance of dirtiness was emphasized by the fact that their clothes, especially those of the more active children, were in shreds. For some reason Gypsies never mended; this was the case everywhere.

It might be assumed that people as poor as the majority of Gypsies would darn, stitch, and salvage, like the expertly patched peasants among whom they mostly lived. But whereas cleanliness, especially symbolic cleanliness, was supremely important, a tidy appearance simply wasn't. The girls were neat and they were expected to be, but they didn't bother to hem their dresses. A great many Gypsies, especially men, were interested in looking natty; at the same time children and adults were often to be seen in rags. Like Jeta, as she shopped for food, they had an instinctive trust that when the need arose the necessaries would be found.

The resistance to mending in Kino was the only trace of a custom among Gypsies, who had traditionally found that looking shabby could be useful: it could inspire fear in *gadje,* and therefore keep them at a respectful, or anyway fearful, distance. This could backfire, however. All xenophobia is at some point linked to a fear of dirt—disease and contamination as represented in dark skin, feces, and the night.

And a raggedy appearance could arouse pity, a sentiment properly reflected in their contempt. Gypsies laugh at the *gadje* who turn moist eyes on them, but they are happy to take their money. Certainly some beggars need to beg, but for many, especially among children, it is a sideline, a chance to pick up a little pocket money and simultaneously confirm one's proud isolation from the white donor. This attitude—though not necessarily the begging—is widely encouraged by adult Gypsies, who are understandably anxious that their children should neither mix with *gadje* nor be thin-skinned. The Gypsies of Tirana, in any case, didn't beg. This was left to the homeless children in the center of town, who belonged to that miserable group known as the Jevgs.

Clothes were not generally passed down—they didn't often survive their first owner and, more important, they could bring pollution. In many parts of the world the clothes of a Gypsy who dies are burned along with the rest of his or her few possessions. (There is a more convenient alternative: as the American sociologist Marlene Sway noted, urban Gypsies drop these items at the dry cleaners and never collect them.) Gypsies preferred new clothes, but in Kino I found a certain enthusiasm for the secondhand. When I left the Dukas I was finally traveling light. One by one, shirts, skirts, brushes, makeup, hair gadgets, and even shoes were pledged to the girls, and mainly of course to Dritta—not out of greater affection for her, but because she was the most determined, the greatest pest. (It was obvious that any attempt at an equitable distribution would be rectified after I'd gone.) Still, when the previous fall an American Pentecostal mission had given the Kino Gypsies a large batch of secondhand clothes, including much-needed winter coats, they promptly sold them.

Jeta's father, Sherif (just for example), like most traditional Gypsy men, wore a suit all the time, the same suit, no matter what the occasion or the weather. And he would wear that suit until it fell to pieces and had to be replaced. This habit flourished alongside the foppish tastes of many Gypsy men: they loved flash cuts and flapping lapels, in shiny, striped or stippled fabrics (young men picked fashionably off colors and wore them in winning, original combinations); they liked hats, wore watch fobs, mustaches, and lots of (gold) jewelry. When suits became shiny from wear and grease, so much the better. If they were rich, they picked the biggest cars—real pimpmobiles, whose two-tone paint jobs, diamonds-in-the-back, and custom features echo the gaudy caravans once used in Poland and still occasionally to be seen in Britain and France. In their brilliant sense of color and their taste for glitz, along with the necessary flair to carry it off, they resembled African Americans, with whom (in parts of what is now Romania) they also shared a history of prolonged enslavement by white men.

Also like black Americans, they suffered a common and slanderous stereotyping. They were supposed to be shiftless and work-shy. In fact, Gypsies everywhere are more energetic, if not always more industrious, than their neighbors; they have always had to be quick on their feet. Sure enough, they have mainly shunned regimented wage labor in favor of more independent and flexible kinds of work. The wall of Stanbuli ovens in that soapy courtyard in Kinostudio was a testament to this; here the word "shiftless" had to do with the consumer, or perhaps with the albatross ovens themselves.

Learning to Speak

IT IS NOT hard to see why linguists like Marcel are so fond of Romani. Jan Yoors was also intoxicated by the language—and by the life. At the age of twelve he left his bourgeois home in Antwerp and with his parents' permission traveled with a group of nomadic Lovara Gypsies. Yoors stayed with them on and off for six years; and when in 1940 it came time to leave them, he despaired:

> I would no longer express myself in the wild, archaic "Romanes," unfit for small talk. I would no longer use the forceful, poetic, plastic descriptions and ingenious parables of the Rom or indulge in the unrestrained intensity and fecundity of their language. Old Bidshika once told us the legend about the full moon's being dragged down to earth by the sheer intensity, weight and witchery of the Romany tongue. And it almost seemed that it could be true.

I had hoped that staying with a family would give me a chance to learn some Romani. But as a guest of the Dukas I was inhibited by the strict Roma etiquette. Each time I rose or tried to do something useful, I was ordered: *Besh!*—Sit! I was an honorary man in this respect and in others—such as eating with the boys, before the women and children. And so while the women worked, I sat, and I watched, and sketched, and wrote in my notebook. Reading was out of the question. Reading plain worried the Dukas. *So keres?*—What are you doing?—was the usual puzzled response to an upheld book. But as often I would be asked: *Chindilan?*—Are you fed up, weary?—as if any quiet, or stillness, was a sign of infirmity or depression. Like most nomadic or once-nomadic peoples, the Gypsies were not readers. Even literate Roma (a minority everywhere) are not readers.

Lili was not a *bori* and so she didn't do washing; she was charged with keeping all the pitchers and dozens of empty pop bottles brimming with fresh drinking water, and with roasting and grinding coffee. She often sat beside me in a mocha-scented cloud on the porch step, a tin tray of the blackened beans at her feet. And there was the polished brass grinder that she was hardly seen without; it wasn't much more than a long pepper mill inside which spoonfuls of brown dust were painstakingly produced. The children sat around eating their fig-spread bread, still stung with sleep and quiet, and I asked for words:

my "work." Luckily for me, my efforts to learn Romani became a family project and entertainment.

After a question, and sometimes, it seemed for a long time, after every *word* anyone said to me, I would have to ask: *So?*—What?—and hope for a good clue. *So* was unspecific enough to elicit a wide range of replies, all of them apparently very funny. The whole family, from little Spiuni to old man Sherif, fell about in tearful and helpless familial laughter. And the good mood ensured that my lesson would go on longer and be less guarded.

Disinforming inquisitive *gadje* has a long tradition. It is a serious self-preserving code among Gypsies that their customs, and even particular words, should not be made known to outsiders. It is also a time-honored source of fun. One of the earliest glossaries, collected from English Gypsies in 1776 at a Windsor fair by an antiquarian called Jacob Bryant, gives the word *ming* for "father." (*Minge* comes to British slang from the Romani, in which it has the same pronunciation and meaning: the female pudendum.)

Sometimes the Dukas' disinformation was accidental. In many cases each of them gave me Albanian words. Though bilingual, they themselves were often unable to distinguish between the two languages: it was just what they spoke. And the ways in which family members attempted to teach me (or even to reach me) at least told me something about them.

Lili was playful, as if she imagined the whole thing was just a children's game and that any minute I would be rattling along in Romani, chatting with the rest of the grown-ups. "Okay!" was the only word of English I managed to interest her in; otherwise she would just make a low gurgling noise and shake her head vigorously—a gesture that for all Albanians (as for Bulgarians) meant the opposite of what you imagined: yes.

Like many shy people, Artani, the youngest son, made exchanges even more excruciating for himself by talking very fast and intimately to his armpit, so that he always had to repeat himself. He seemed unable to accept that with all my worldly experience—I had, had I not, traveled all the way from America?—I couldn't understand them. And, like many others, if I understood one phrase, he would charge ahead, assuming that I had suddenly mastered the whole language. O Babo's solution was to translate difficult words into *Albanian:* I was a *gadji,* his logic seemed to go, so surely I spoke the language of the *gadje.* Tatoya, Jeta's beautiful, blushing sister, employed a technique as delicate as her features: instead of speaking she *mouthed* the words. And Kako, their hoarse old uncle who along with Sherif often visited our courtyard, attempted to convey the meaning of words just by shouting them.

Shkelgim, a young cousin, tried speaking to me in Romani with what he imagined was an American accent. I know this because he told me. I couldn't have guessed, even with the giveaway pelvis-thrusting, hair-combing Elvis gestures. Nicu was a great performer; indeed he only joined in when there was a crowd, and it was he who was the primary source of dirty jokes. He never stayed long, though, and having squeezed the most from one line or another he would shimmy his

A joke before dinner: Kako, Lela, Spiuni, Viollca, Marcel, Jeta, Liliana, and Nuzi on the front porch in Kinostudio, Tirana, 1992

shoulders, swivel his hips, shake his belly like a Turkish dancer before slipping out the front gate. This joking of Nicu's was cute and his brand was rare: not many Gypsy men would risk compromising their macho images, not even in jest.

Jeta tried to scold him. She called him *bengalo*, or devilish, but it was said with the gleaming pleasure reserved for those who make one laugh. She found it difficult to be stern with her first boy, whom she adored—as she publicly admitted with characteristic candor—just a smidgen more than the others. (And he did have great charm: cheap, childlike charm, unlike the moody, more subtle appeal of the middle son, Nuzi, or of the tender, tortured Artani.) Jeta's face could switch from horror-witch to granny bear in a second, alternately for the control and comfort of her grandchildren. Either way, no one, not even I, could mistake her meaning.

The Romani language has a small basic vocabulary—a limitation which forces the speaker to be resourceful. And so, for example, they say "ears" for "gills"; an earthquake is just described: *I phuv kheldias*—The earth danced. As in Turkish, there is one verb—*piav*—for both smoking and drinking (two crucially contiguous occupations); *chorro* stands for both "poor"—indigent—and "bad." There are no words for "danger" or "quiet" (though some Romani speakers use *strážno* and *mirnimos* respectively—recent borrowings from Slavic languages).

Donald Kenrick, a British linguist and Gypsiologist, took up the challenge of translating *Romeo and Juliet* into Romani for Pralipe, a Rom theater group from Skopje. In London he showed me some of his solutions for the balcony scene.

> *Romeo* But soft! What light through yonder window breaks?
> It is the East, and Juliet is the sun!
> Arise, fair sun, and kill the envious moon,
> Who is already sick and pale with grief
> That thou her maid art far more fair than she.
> Be not her maid, since she is envious.
> Her vestal livery is but sick and green,
> And none but fools do wear it. Cast it off.

> Romeo *Ach! Savo dud si andi kaja filiastra?*
> *O oriento si thai Juliet si o kham.*
> *Usti lacho kham kai mudarel o chomut,*
> *nasvalo thai parno si o chomut thai na mangel ke tu—leski*
> *kanduni—si po-lachi lestar.*
> *Lesko uribe si zeleno thai nasvalo*
> *sade o dinile uraven pes andre, chude le.*

This we retranslated as follows:

> *Romeo* Oh! what light is in that window?
> It is the east and Juliet is the sun.

> Arise good [or nice] sun and kill the moon
> Sick and white is the moon which doesn't want you
> Its servant is more beautiful than it.

(Donald couldn't find a word for "envious," so in the Romani version neither the moon nor the maid was going to be envious.)

> Its clothing is green [or blue] and sick
> Only fools dress themselves like that, throw them out.

Things got trickier. Farther into Romeo's speech we got to:

> I am too bold; 'tis not to me she speaks.
> Two of the fairest stars in all the heaven,
> Having some business, do entreat her eyes
> To twinkle in their spheres till they return.

Kenrick had come up with:

> *Na tromav. Na kerel mange duma.*
> *Dui lache cerhaia ando bodlipen*
> *si len buti averthane—mangen lake jakha*
> *te dudaren ando lengo than*
> *zi kai aven palpale.*

We ran this back into English:

> I do not dare. She is not speaking to me.
> Two good [or nice] stars in cloudy place [the cloudiness]
> They have work [or jobs] elsewhere—they want her eyes
> To give light in their place
> Until they come back.

Apparently the production was a great success and, last I heard, Pralipe had taken it on tour in Germany.

All languages are expanded and invigorated by loan words, but perhaps none so markedly as Romani. This is because its speakers have frequently crossed borders, and because a common language has not yet been fixed in writing. A store of mainly "domestic" words—those relating to home and hearth and mostly of Indian origin—has been retained over the centuries, and it is this which is shared by the speakers of the many dialects of Romani (there are around sixty in Europe alone), their notionally common language. More pervasive is the *spirit* of the language or that which it seems especially well suited to express—hyperbolic, gregarious, typically expressive of extreme emotion. Vivid usage is of paramount importance and original images are prized. The tale is never as important as the telling, and great storytellers are highly revered members of the community, tending to specialize in ghost stories, fairy tales, shaggy-dog yarns, or riddles.

With the simple addition of the ancient Indic suffix *pen*, like "hood" or "ness," one can create abstract nouns, such as Romipen, Gypsiness; or else such words may be borrowed from another language. But among Romani speakers these big-concept, encompassing words are not much needed. Without these generalities, the language flows like a good poem, rich in detail, in concrete images, and in fresh, inventive use of simple words. So, for "I love you," you got (as in Spanish) "I want you," but just as often "I eat you," or even "I eat your eyes." "I want to eat your face" (or "I want to eat your mouth": the word for both "face" and "mouth" is *muj*) is a request for a kiss.

The highly aspirated, raucously guttural vernacular is unusually expressive, especially when produced by an old, deep, and tobacco-stained voice. Although a new "political" language is emerging, Romani is generally phatic—that is to say, its function is to express sociability rather than to exchange ideas (which are likely to be shared already).

Jeta's style was typical. She was rude and funny, applying unexpected images to unlikely targets, and often conveying terror and irony at the same time. "Why can't a *gadji* make a good *bori*?" Jeta put the question seriously, following the jokey proposal in the courtyard that while they considered prospective brides for the ten-year-old Djivan, why not consider me? Because "A *gadji* wouldn't know how to take out her own eyes." Jeta's reply conveyed the primary meaning that, compared with a proper Gypsy girl, a *gadji* would lack the necessary training and sensibility for her role. But she also managed to convey that such a wife would be no fun, for the taking out of one's eyes was also a Romany expression for orgasm.

Considering how priggish Gypsies could be about sex and about the female body in any context, Jeta—with the license granted to a grandmother or, rather, to a woman past menstruating—was exceptionally ribald: "The salted ones, into the mud" was her kind of remark about women she didn't approve of. On the other hand, if a place was nice—say, the new coffee bar in town—she might say, "*O manusha khelaven tut*"—"The people make you dance." She would call out after the children, if they walked in front of her while she was talking to someone, interrupting her flow: "May I pee on your eyes?" or "Are your guts falling out?" (So that you didn't have time to go around?) Or, if she was really pressed, she might say: "*Te bisterdon tumare anava!*"— "May your names be forgotten!" Her style was one of mock fierceness, and everyone loved it.

I never met a Gypsy who didn't have a sweet tooth. Although salt, pepper, vinegar, and pickled foods are considered *baxtalo*, lucky, they like things *but guli*, very sweet, and were alarmed and revolted by my preference for the salty, or *bushalo* (sour). Sugar was a luxury in Albania, and Jeta may have thought my demurral was self-sacrificing, which she could not tolerate in a guest. Fed up one morning, she dumped a heap of sugar into the plain yogurt I was settling down to eat, shaking her head as if to say, Where did she grow up? What she actually said was: "If you put that yogurt up a pig's ass it would fly away." It was *that* sour.

She was also in the habit of adding the exclamation *Ma-sha-llah!* or "As God wills!" after everything. Jeta explained: "It is to let whoever you are talking to know that when you say that their newborn baby is such a darling cupcake you aren't really deep down in your heart saying may his brain dry up." It was also a useful precaution. "If you do not show that your heart is pure it is your own fault if something terrible happens." Ribald, rude, and, for ballast, unshakably superstitious.

Wit was the province of Kino women. The male idiom more often involved the ponderous intoning of statements of fact (or of ludicrous nonsense) to convey ancestral heft and the wisdom of proverbs. Kako, Jeta's hoarse old uncle, was a tireless intoner, always using this two-part formula: "Just as the mare beats the road, so the young wife wants the penis." And of course there would follow a sagacious nod.

The renowned linguistic aptitude of Gypsies the world over was not always apparent in Kinostudio. For an unlucky start, my name presented a difficulty. The problem was that *i* in Romani is the feminine article, as in *i daj*, "the mother," and it is much used, even with proper nouns, as is the masculine (O Kako). "Isabel" thus sounded to them like "the zabel," and so I became Zabella, Zabade, then Zabe, and finally just Za.

The days and weeks seemed to roll into one another—perhaps because I was never told words for the days of the week or for the months; and any inquiries I made were regarded as trick questions. If pressed, the children, and even the *boria*, had a lot of trouble, especially with the months. Seasons were easy. There were only two: summer and winter, the hot and the cold. No day was different from any other (and not because it was summer: only ten-year-old Djivan would be going back to school). None of the children knew how to tell the time; no one wore a watch (no one except Nuzi, who wore mine and took an unusual interest in time, which he was biding). The older adults did not know how to read, and the younger ones mouthed each syllable like children; nobody wrote with any confidence.

I received a letter from the Dukas a year after I had been to stay with them. It was a piece of card covered with their autographs, which were elderly and tremulous, or else childishly deliberate. Below, there were a few lines which were not in any language at all, but which gave the graphic sense of a letter, and that was the point.

There were no newspapers, no radio, and of course no books; the television was usually on, but was hardly ever watched; images flickered by like scenery out of a car window. And appropriately so; in outer Tirana you could only get lurid dramas from Sicily and crassly proselytizing soap operas sponsored by American church groups. Unlike most of the Albanians among whom they lived, the Gypsies knew nothing about what was going on in the world, and (again with the exception of Nuzi) showed no curiosity.

Sometimes, though, their restraint was due not to lack of curiosity but to tact. They were interested in family life: they asked after my brothers and sisters and parents and cousins as if they had actually met them. When there were no men around, we talked about childbearing and wifing . . . I turned thirty while I was with the Dukas. I had not been looking forward to that especially; but what for me amounted to a single sigh was for them a seriously sad, even a grave matter. When (on my first day) they discovered that at the age of twenty-nine I still hadn't had even *one*, the *puri daj*—herself a mother of ten—patted my wrist sympathetically: clearly I was barren. This explained why I had no husband either and, worst of all, why I was condemned to wander the world, to go to *Albania*, for Christ's sake, far from family and friends, to stay with *complete strangers*. It was hard to tell which part, from their

Beno's truck returns from "Stanbuli." Kinostudio, Tirana, 1992

point of view, was the greater trial. My presence among them could have no other explanation, it seemed, for everywhere Gypsies I met assumed this version of events and, not wishing to put me through a painful experience, gave me no chance to elaborate or explain. My life was a tragedy, they saw that, but it was one they could warm to, and they let me know it: after all, hadn't they in their past been "condemned" to wander the world? Hadn't they too been condemned to Albania? (Their weary objectivity about Albania was impressive, given that they had lived there all their lives. Not Albanians in their own minds, they were refreshingly free from the regional disease of ethnic patriotism.)

Dritta had no time for such reflections. She had other, more pressing concerns. Dritta was also the most difficult member of the family to communicate with, because her Kabudji dialect was more corrupted with Turkish words. And yet, with her unrivaled determination, she prevailed as a teacher. It was from her that I learned the language of *trampa*, or barter. The store of vocabulary included the words for blouse, skirt, comb, brush, lipstick, mascara, shoes, scarf, sponge, soap, ribbons, pins, hairband, and, learned up in self-defense, the words for ring, bracelet, earrings. . . . Dritta claimed she wanted to learn English; this was *trampa* after all, an exchange. And so I began: "What is your

name? My name is Zabe," and so on. She just laughed and made
mushy underwater word-noises. She sounded like my fourteen-
month-old nephew mimicking adult speech into the telephone, which
he used as a kind of mike.

Our lessons were difficult not only because we had no common linguistic ground but because so much about me was plain alien to her: if
you can't understand *actions*, the chances are you won't understand
speech. I was continually shocked by the isolation my strangeness
implied, and touched by the protective gestures it inspired. Once, I
crouched at a boiling kettle, poised to pour water over a teabag. Dritta
lunged for it, yanking the rectangular pouch out by its tail. "It will get
wet!" she scolded, patting the bag dry in the folds of her skirt. She had
never seen a teabag and had kindly been trying to rescue something that
she imagined was—what?—perhaps a perfuming sachet or *bouquet
garni* (though it is hard to imagine such fragrant ephemera making their
way to inner Albania). In a similar incident, O Babo, riding in the front
seat of Gimi's car, complained that it was horribly squalid and that
Gimi really should tidy it up. "What are all these ropes?" he asked irritably, attempting to tug the seatbelts from their sockets. Such safety
devices were a novelty in Albania—like private cars themselves.

Nothing, however, produced so much bemused interest as the
twice-daily ritual of Zabade brushing her teeth. This they found obsessive and weird, and before they were smacked away by their mothers
the boys would gingerly finger my toothbrush, touching the special
baby tool with the tentativeness they might have stroked a fledgling
that had dropped out of its nest.

The toilet was a hole in a cupboard with a swinging door on crazy
hinges; it banged but didn't shut. For a basin they had a depressed
drain at ground level, and on a ledge at waist height a can of water,
constantly topped up by Liliana. And so the brushing of teeth was a
public event. One of my nicknames was Dandi, from *dand*, tooth.
When the need made itself felt (about once a week), they brushed
theirs with a finger, generously coated with thick salt, or *lon*. And they
all had beautiful strong white teeth, as Gypsies, in sparkling contrast to
the rest of the local population, very often do—when, that is, they are
not obscured by decorative gold or silver or even two-tone caps.

O Babo's toilette was more popular still. Every morning Bexhet
stretched out his shaving ritual for as long as he could, as if hoping
each day to add a few seconds, perhaps even a minute, to his personal
best. For the children it was a great show. For O Babo it was a way of

filling the prodigious leisure in which Albania was incomparably rich. All the jobless men had to do it, and they did it with greater or lesser degrees of panache.

One by one, he would produce the implements from his locked trunk: a shaving brush, a shaving bowl with the soap stuck in it, the folding razor. Wearing his morning suit—striped pajama bottoms and a khaki military shirt—he would make three trips in and out of the house for these tools, holding each with a ten-fingered delicacy you might reserve for the handling of a small but perfectly preserved Minoan pot. After all the implements had been arranged along the courtyard ledge, which became barber's corner for a good part of each morning, Bexhet would make a final trip in for the *pièce de résistance*, his special cracked shaving mirror. Not wishing to lose any of the broken slivers, he moved in the comically stealthy steps of a cartoon thief, carrying the glass flat and out in front of him on an open palm, like a fresh-baked pie.

Bexhet's toilet set was spread in and around a sad little antler-shaped branch of the neighbor's tree. Though dead, the branch remained erect, a prisoner of the cement through which it had pushed in its sun-searching youth. In the antler's crook, Bexhet nestled his mirror with utmost concentration. He coaxed and jiggled it and tested his talent by letting go, two fingers at a time. He whispered soft, loving encouragement to his own shattered reflection: "Now don't you go and fall, little face. . . ." Fall it did though, two or three times a morning, and Bexhet caught it each time, when he was feeling frisky, with a clever backhand and a little victory cry, "*Eppah!*" or sometimes "*Oppah!*" before returning it to its V to try again.

Into Town

JETA WAS BITTER about her marriage which, she once explained, came about only because her grandfather was dying. "I want to see my granddaughters married before I go," he'd said. Bexhet was available, if not ideal (having got through three wives by the age of twenty-one), and that was that. Jeta was seldom sullen and never self-pitying—she didn't have time to be—but she had a strong and richly comic image of herself as one of the wronged. Still, Jeta believed in arranging the marriages of her own children: *that* wasn't the problem. The problem, she would tell you in loud whispers, was Bexhet. The real trouble, though, was that Jeta was far too intelligent for the life she ended up with, and smart enough to see it.

It was rare to find a *modern* malaise in a Gypsy woman; experience was generally too circumscribed. But Jeta was exceptionally bright. Unlike the cluckingly complacent Bexhet, she had been stirred, under Marcel's influence, to new considerations of the Roma struggle. Alone among her large family, she had inklings, and they imperiled her equilibrium, and her tolerance for life in Albania, let alone in Bexhet's courtyard.

One morning, when even I thought Bexhet's shaving routine was wearing a little thin, I took her off to go *ando foro*, into town. With no shopping mission, we walked and walked and she spoke about her life with a rare reflectiveness. For thirty years Jeta had carried out her daily chores with that same courtyard as her headquarters; she'd raised and married off her children. Even the marriages—normally a mother and grandmother's domain—had proved a disappointment and humiliation for Jeta; one son after another foiled her elaborate and expensive arrangements with a suitable girl's parents by eloping with or impregnating the bride of his own choice. She had never taken a vacation; she had never been away from Kinostudio for more than a day or two, and then only in service of her children—on a (futile) trip to the south, for instance, to audition a prospective wife.

We paused in front of a shop called *floket*. What's a *floket*? I asked, unable to guess from the bare storefront, through which one could see a leatherette dentist's chair and an old stuffed armchair raised on cinder blocks and facing the same wall. On the counter stood a rusted appliance, perhaps from the 1940s. It looked like an early-model blender: chrome and bullet-shaped and standing at about a foot and a half in height. But the odd machine sprouted a headful of cracked rubber-tube tentacles, each with a clip attachment at the end. A beauty parlor!

I dragged Jeta inside. Two tidy beauticians in white smocks stood beside their deep sink, their hands demurely crossed in front of them. They shrugged their shoulders apologetically. A handwritten sign on the wall advertised a *twalet complet*—manicure, pedicure, and make-over, for the equivalent of thirty cents—but unfortunately they had no tools: no nail files, no makeup. Sorry. The old appliance on the counter that we had spied through the window turned out to be a steam-powered curler-heating device, as confirmed by the few lead curlers with wire fasteners that lay around like spent ammunition. It hadn't worked in years. They did have a bit of shampoo, though, or some green detergent in an unmarked plastic bottle, and so I went in for a wash. I had been hoping to pamper Jeta at the *floket*. It wasn't much, but I was thrilled when she consented to have her hair washed—by a *gadji*, no less. Jeta was more relaxed than I had ever seen her, sitting in the dentist's chair and humming to herself, flicking disdainfully through Soviet beauty magazines from the early 1980s, while the two young beauticians rubbed our wet heads. Dinner would be late because of our escapade, and Jeta would have a screaming match with Bexhet, but she didn't care. I still have a lead hair-grip from the *floket*. It is oxidized and encrusted with mineral accretions as if it had been at the bottom of the sea for a hundred years; you can hardly guess its function.

Refreshed, we began to make our way home. We passed dozens of caved-in, burnt-out, ransacked, and abandoned ex-shops, right in the middle of Tirana. And then we arrived at the state maternity hospital. Jeta paused outside the gloomy, totalitarian-era edifice, and then took my hand and pulled me inside: never mind that we were late; this, clearly, was something I had to see. She charged past the desk and no one stopped to ask questions: Jeta moved like she *owned* the place. We walked down the long, dimly lit halls in silence.

The yellow-tiled walls, the ancient steel-tube beds, the unmuffled moans and vintage stench: this place had the feel of a nineteenth-century mental institution, with women wandering around in shredded, browning gowns, waiting in the halls, squatting on the floor. There were not enough beds. Only people about to give or actually giving birth or undergoing some kind of operation were in bed—six in a row, twelve to a room. Births, abortions, every screaming thing, happened just behind a screen from the other patients, and just yards away from the terrified women waiting their turn in the hall. At least the wards were not segregated, as they were in Slovakia: one room for Gypsy women, another for *gadja*.

We spoke to the resident obstetrician. Sometimes there was penicillin, sometimes not. There hadn't been any anesthestic for several months. Sonographs were unknown here, and there were only two incubators left—a third had been stolen the week before, along with all the hospital's refrigerators and the drugs they contained. The Ministry of Health itself had been gutted: they even took the staircase.

From a medical point of view, things were worse than they had ever been before, according to Dr. Viollca Tarc, who had been working these halls for eighteen years. Still, she was optimistic. Under Hoxha (whose pride was Albania's health care), contraceptives were illegal, and so were abortions; women therefore routinely performed their own, and *then* sought medical treatment. One in 978 died this way, at least of those who actually made it to the hospital. The majority had permanent pains and recurring infections, and many had such mangled works that they would never again be able to conceive.

Now doctors were allowed to perform the operation. However, as with nearly all the new freedoms of Eastern Europe (publishing, for example), what had once been prohibited by law was now rendered impossible through lack of equipment or supplies. So contraceptives were allowed but there weren't any; and though hospital abortions certainly were now safer, they weren't much less distressing.

On our way out we poked our heads into the laundry. In a tall vaulted room, lit only by the rays filtered through high, small-paned industrial windows, five women were bent in a row over low sinks, scrubbing sheets on washboards, just like the *boria* back home. In the middle of the room was an enormous cauldron over a ring of blue gas flames. They were cooking sheets. After a good scrub, a woman would hold the sheet up with both hands for inspection, and then she'd toss it back into the pot; with a rosy wooden pole she'd catch and pull up another one. There was blood everywhere. Not just the splashed-on bright blood of wounds and cuts, but female blood: dark, gelatinous, clotted. Those gouts of maroon were not going to wash out. Only a week before, there had been a shipment of new linen, a gift from the Swiss government, but it had been stolen within hours of its arrival.

Walking home, Jeta told me that she had had twenty-eight abortions (she used the third person: "Jeta had twenty-eight abortions").

She'd performed them herself with a boiled and doubled length of washline cable, followed most times by a "mop-up" at the state maternity hospital. I wondered where in the Duka household she might have done this; there wasn't even a tub big enough to hold a grown woman. Jeta was the kind of person you could ask, but I didn't.

Such horror stories are common enough in Eastern Europe, and, listening to Jeta, I began to reevaluate earlier accounts. The experiences of a Romanian friend, for instance, seemed comparatively breezy. In the Bucharest of Ceauşescu she had undergone two illegal abortions on her kitchen table, while her boyfriend guarded the door. But she had had a doctor—or anyway a nameless person in a stocking mask with holes cut for the eyes who was willing to perform the operation. She never had any proof that he was a doctor, but the jobs were done—the first for a bottle of whisky, the second for a carton of Kents.

The Zoo

THE FRAMED WEDDING portrait is a feature of almost every East or Central European household—rich or poor, Gypsy or *gadje*. The faces of the newly joined, just smaller than life-size, stare straight and solemnly out of the frame. The black-and-white busts (they are just heads and chests, never bodies) are usually rouged and browned by hand, and they seem always to be hung strangely high up, a foot below the ceiling and leaning out from the wall, as if the couple is not there to be seen but rather to observe, as if the only guardian over a couple, now a family, is its hopeful first idea of itself.

Jeta kept her wedding portrait on the wall, but she covered it over completely with snapshots of her children, of their children, of animals, and even just nature shots—trees, a river view. It was *him* she couldn't bear to see, handsome Bexhet, lording it over her.

Because modern photographic technology has not yet reached the East, these wedding portraits all look like turn-of-the-century frontier pictures (and in the case of many Gypsy portraits, like turn-of-the-century American Indians). You can see evidence of the long sitting in the stiff necks. There is nothing of the disposable Western snapshot—nothing "candid." But maybe the formal slow shot reveals more than the snap. Anyway it was impossible to take candid photographs of the Duka family—whenever they saw the black snout of my camera they immediately dropped what they were doing, held their arms stiffly at their sides and froze in unsmiling wedding-portrait poses. Like Gypsy children everywhere, the little Dukas and their friends would rush to form a short-lived lineup, which collapsed into a scrum of pushy starlets, each shoving and trampling over the littlest kids to get into the picture. Even if they looked through the viewfinder, they could not grasp that the camera's view was wider than the actual two inches of its "eye."

Nuzi and Viollca's picture hung over the doorway of the tiny built-on room they shared with their son, Walther. Viollca at thirteen looked like Viollca now, at eighteen: huge green eyes that were more cross than quizzical, hard-set into the middle of her square face; her painted lips seemed thin and black in the photograph. Nuzi was captured in a moment of swollen adolescent beauty that was now fairly well decompressed. The mouth was full and pouty; the raised right eyebrow was there but not yet fully or archly hoisted. A pretty-boy, a pinup: except for his vanity, in that portrait there was little of Nuzi now—Nuzi, the anxious dreamer.

All summer he wore the same pair of perfectly faded jeans—whitening evenly over the thighs and bleached at the crotch—and he rotated his shirts, careful always to fold back the cuffs to the same tan-line on the forearm. Nuzi looked athletic, but in fact he never lifted a

Dritta with her favorite plastic orange tree and one of her dolls. In the background are Lili, Viollca, and Lela. Kinostudio, Tirana, 1992

finger except to bring a cigarette to his sulking lips. He smoked and he hardly ate—not, one sensed, for lack of appetite, but because he was watching that perfect blue-jean fit. And he walked. Nuzi walked every day, for hours and hours, into town and around it, up and down and all through the sloping neglect of Hoxha Park. This wasn't for exercise either; it was for survival.

Alone among the Dukas, he was permanently restless. Nuzi was my great escape from the courtyard at Kinostudio; with him I covered the town. He wanted to make sure I understood him; he had a lot to get across. And so we developed a system. *Shnet pach!* is the Albanian equivalent of "Bless you!" said after a sneeze. "*Shnet?*" Nuzi would inquire, and, if I had understood, I'd reply with a triumphant "*Pach!*"

On a day of constant drizzle, we walked away from Tirana's Skanderbeg Square along the Boulevard of Martyrs and up towards Hoxha Park (which all the Dukas affectionately called Enver Park). Along the way we passed one of the capital's two hotels, the Dajti, with its out-of-scale columns looming in the best Stalinist style. Outside the hotel, on either side of the broad steps, two Gypsy boys in matching Michael Jackson T-shirts were voguing atop two vast white plinths, which had supported a bronze Lenin and a bronze Stalin until they were evicted the year before. Such blank spaces—great marble question marks— exist in every town square in Albania. Only one rider still rears above his pedestal. He is Albania's national hero, on Albania's national hero's horse: it is Gjergji Kastrioti, known to all as Skanderbeg. In the fifteenth century Skanderbeg briefly liberated parts of his homeland from Ottoman control. His small victories have earned him the lasting reverence of an unlucky populace, though they were succeeded by a further 450 years of the Turk.

Certain heroes from Latin America turn up in unlikely places, distributed abroad by their small countries' governments at a rate of about one statue for every ten citizens (the smaller the country, it seems, the more eager the gift). Bolívar, of course, but also Uruguay's Artigas, both of whom can be found, for example, in puny Emil Markov Park on the outskirts of Sofia, in Bulgaria. In Albania there is no such competition, no national-hero theme park. One has the impression that every Albanian cooperative, or block association (if there were such things), is the proud possessor of a Skanderbeg. In this avenue, the Boulevard of Martyrs, replicas of the rearing hero appear so frequently that they give the illusion of a military parade or gymkhana. There is only *one* martyr. And now more than ever his statues seem an appropriate symbol of his nation's paralyzed aspirations: mid-gallop, raring to go, forever riveted to the plinth.

The rain was coming down hard. Perhaps it was the combined talk of Skanderbeg and his horse that imbued Nuzi with the self-sacrificing determination to show me the Tirana zoo.

"Zoooo," said Nuzi. "*Shnet?*"

"*Pach:* zoo," I replied, and we pulled up our jackets into tents over our wet heads and climbed the nettled path in Hoxha Park. Like all parks this one had benches and, despite the rain, these benches were occupied by variously bedraggled or determinedly ponchoed couples who had come to the zoo grounds for petting. Nuzi remarked adamantly that I would find no Roma among these neckers. Like Artani on an earlier walk, he was continually generalizing about and defending Romany practices, mainly by way of favorable comparison with "Albanians." Artani had pointed scornfully to a "disko," as the sign said over the door of a sail-shaped sixties building that once housed the Hoxha Museum. "You would find not one Rom there," he sneered. "Why not?" I asked, thinking it might be fun to go with the brothers to Albania's first-ever discotheque. "A disco is for developed people," he said with finality, using some of the little Italian we shared to make sure I understood. I think he meant overdeveloped people— that is, rotten, jaded, and loose. So, no disco.

If the disco represented some circle of hell for the Duka boys, to my eye (and to my nostrils) the zoo was its molten heart. The disgraceful pavilion was death row for wildlife. Standing before it, collar firmly over nose, one could only wonder why all the animals hadn't been killed, as all Albanian laboratory animals had been by now, one researcher told me, for lack of food. He hadn't meant food to feed the rats and rabbits: the pink-eyed specimens had all been stolen and sold *as* food. The newspapers printed warnings about the rare cancers and viruses that these black-market Rodentia carried. Luckily Jeta stuck with the sheep.

Still, stunned curiosity impelled us forward. There was a bear-dog, and a lion-dog, with enough remaining fur-patches between them to quilt a chihuahua. The smallest hairless animals—and it was unclear what they were, or had once been—looked like large baby hamsters: pink tubes. A pair of eczema-stricken piglets were probably pumas when they first arrived in Hoxha Park. An X-ray tiger lay head-down and ill in one cage; next along was an ex-chimp, morosely bathing in a manky puddle below his little section of tree. There was a dead tortoise and something that looked like a hunk of pressed peat: was it an iguana? No, it was another dead tortoise, a naked one. Perhaps the keeper had made off with its valuable shell.

The birds didn't look as though they could fly, or walk, or even step out of the congealing egg-drop soup they all stood in and tried to pull loose from—the liquid was like chewing gum on your shoe sole. In contrast to their neighbors, the birds at least resembled some lightweight version of themselves. In the last cage there was an eagle, its Turkish trousers now several sizes too big, and the beak bunched and rippled into accordion ridges from some kind of beaky osteoporosis, so that it looked as though it had been punched, hard.

"The eagle," Nuzi told me, with unnecessary irony, "is our national bird."

On the way back to town, we ducked out of the now sluicing rain into the vast park café. All over Central Europe enormous eateries with uniformly slow and surly service are a reminder of the old regimes' grand contempt for overheads and profits. . . . It was empty except for me and Nuzi, a soaked pair of defeated petters, and a cluster of unchaperoned Gypsy children bobbing about a distant table. They had been dashing in and out of the rain through a broken plate-glass window, as a dare, it seemed: who could go through and not get cut? Though barely dressed, they seemed indifferent to the cold rain which streamed down their legs.

"They are not Roma," Nuzi asserted, pre-empting any insolent suggestion from me. Well then, who, or what, were these water babies?

"They are Jevgs," Nuzi explained in his most professorial tone, "and we call them *sir.*" *Sir* is Romani for garlic. And no, in no way were the Jevgs related to the Roma—*shnet?* he added, displeased with my skeptical expression.

The Jevgs were originally Egyptian slaves in the Turkish army, I read later, with special responsibility for the care of horses—a detail which suggests they might indeed have been Gypsies. As for the Egyptian tag, this seemed a standard way of disowning other tribes, for hadn't the Gypsies themselves been called Egyptians (thereby gaining the name Gypsy)? Some Jevgs were now keen to promote the Egyptian theory, just as Europe's earliest Gypsy visitors had found it useful to do. In 1990, a group of Jevgs in Macedonia consecrated a mosque of their own on Lake Ohrid: they invited the Egyptian ambassador and (to his embarrassed bewilderment) publicly proclaimed themselves a lost tribe of Egypt.

From the Dukas' point of view, all that mattered was that these guttersnipes—and they seemed mainly to be children, though even the adults one sometimes saw were small enough to qualify—were not Roma. The "proof" of this was that they did not speak Romani; and speaking Romani was the kernel of Gypsy identity.

Marcel, who was very knowledgeable not just about Balkan languages but about its ethnographics, later confirmed that the Jevgs probably *were* Gypsies, belonging to a group thought to have appeared in the region long before the Dukas' ancestors. Like other groups (the Ashkali and Mango in Montenegro, Kosovo, and Macedonia), they were Gypsies who had lost their language. Lack of documents about such fringe folk makes them vulnerable to anyone's version of history; and so while Gypsy activists may wish to recuperate these deracinated elements to bulk up the tribe, or as proof of the assimilationist crimes against their people, those who live on the same patch of ground are free to disown them. Like half-breeds, such groups are sometimes rejected with more hostility than are *gadje*, the primary "other" in the Rom imagination. All sentimentality among the Gypsies is reserved for song.

To Mbrostar

A WHOLE WEEK had passed since I visited the maternity hospital and the *floket* with Jeta, but O Babo's anger over our lateness still smoldered. He had forbidden her from accompanying Marcel, Gimi, and me on a day trip to visit some rural Gypsy communities, and relented only on the condition that he come along and that we "stop off" in the town of Mbrostar, hours away from where we were going, to pay a visit to his brother.

We set off with a packed lunch early the next morning and made a long climb through the calcite-white Dajti Mountains, passing under Skanderbeg's crumbling castle before arriving in Fushë-Krujë, where the poorest Gypsies I had ever seen were living in mud huts and twig shacks, some no bigger than appliance cartons. One or two houses at the front of the settlement were more substantial: lime-slaked, thick-walled, adobe-style structures, with the lumpy appearance of hand-molded clay. At the farthest end of the camp from the road there were families living in plastic bags. (Gypsy settlements often evolve in this way: the most presentable parlors make an impression at the front and conceal the real slums—subsections, with names like No-man's-land—at the rear.) Most of the people living in Fushë-Krujë had been laborers on a nearby farm. We could just make out the skeleton of its blown-out buildings—roofbeams against a cloudless sky.

Within a few minutes the whole population, some three hundred people, were pressing in around us, small children filling in the spaces between grown-ups' legs and under their arms. Just as there were always ravaged, beaten-down older people, and a couple of kids with minor disabilities like crossed eyes, there always seemed to be one outrageous beauty: an angel who would have been forced into indentured topmodeldom had she been found on a Paris bus; or a wavy-lipped, chisel-chinned, almond-eyed boy-warrior out of the *Iliad*, as beautiful as humans come.

The crowd quickly became oppressive. In rural settlements when the whole joint pressed up against you, you could become truly claustrophobic, trapped and crouching in the airless center. "*Ov yilo isi?*" Marcel asked, meaning "Is it okay?" (literally, "Is there heart here?"). An ancient toothless man in a grimy felt fez crawled out of his hutch—a twig cocoon with an artfully woven roof—to say that, yes, there was, except in winter when they had to "feed the rats." He laughed heartily at his joke, his Adam's apple bobbing hysterically and twanging the thick cords of his turkey neck. The oldest person on the site (though he had no idea how old), he told us that before they had come to work at the farm some thirty years before, his people had been traveling basket-weavers. And certainly a trace of the craft could be seen in his pitiful house, even though it was not tall enough for him to stand in or deep enough to lie down in without his feet sticking out. When he'd had enough of us he inched inside on the backs of his fists and we said goodbye to his feet.

Gimi—Palumb Furtuna—was normally tolerant and sensitive, but he had refused to enter the settlement, as had O Babo. From his car seat he told me that these Gypsies were in fact much richer than those in Kinostudio, but that they "didn't know how to live." It was a common—and in this case obviously false—view, but one normally held by struggling *gadje* who believed that all Gypsies hid sacks of gold coins in the folds of their filthy skirts.

We stopped at another village—Yzberish—which was poor but markedly less desolate. Here the Gypsies, who belonged to a group called the Chergari, carefully (and untypically) maintained fences of tethered branches; unlike most Roma, who greet intruders with deep suspicion or open hostility, they were friendly and relaxed, and they did not press in on us with complaints that they hoped we might pass on to "the government." Exceptionally elegant people, these Chergari were tall and dark as bitter chocolate, with long, thin faces and features and straight hair. And as in Fushë-Krujë they had no idea of the wider world of Gypsies, even of other groups in Albania (they were stunned when short, butterscotch-brown Jeta spoke to them in Romani. And she in turn was astonished that they understood). The Chergari had equally little grasp of their own history, about which they could tell us nothing (their name means "tent-dwellers," though they were tent-dwellers no longer). As for the present, there was little to be said: there was no work, and they lived on the eggs of their ducks and their chickens, supplemented by the sunflowers and apricots that grew everywhere around.

As we left Yzberish, an old woman, so thin that her cheekbones seemed to be pointing out of her face, hung on to my sleeve. She wanted to show me something. She reached into her apron pocket and produced a fuzzy scrap of white paper, no bigger than a gum wrapper, folded down to the size of a thumbnail. The others were already in the car, but I waited while she shakily unwrapped it. She held it up close to my eyes, and I saw nothing—maybe a *slight* smudge of dirt. I took it from her, and checked the other side. Nothing. Apart from the grubby crease marks it was blank. Disappointed, she retrieved and quickly refolded the slip and smuggled it back into her deep front pocket.

What had I failed to see? Written on that piece of paper, she claimed, was the telephone number of her son, a refugee in Italy. It probably had been once, written in pencil that had long since worn away. If she was illiterate, which seemed likely, and had never been able to *read* the characters, what she had seen there was already an abstraction. Anyway, I am sure that she did see and continued to see that telephone number. *"Te xav ka to biav,"* the old woman called after me as I climbed into the car: May I eat at your wedding.

I felt close to tears as we left and wished we could go back to Tirana. But we drove on, making our long way to Mbrostar. The land was empty. In the middle of nowhere we passed a new sign written in an old tongue. "Democracy is a struggle for progress," it read, "not a force of destabilization and destruction."

Albanians live with the abandoned: abandoned farms, forgotten fields, sagging sheds with blank windows; ghost towns. Miles on miles of sunflowers wilt and weep while everyone rushes to the city to buy the Italian government's sunflower oil that has ended up on Tirana's black market. In the open country there were goats but no people, as if the whole place had been evacuated—a notion given eerie plausibility by the spread of bunkers across the land.

Since the end of communism it is not just the repatriation of would-be refugees that confirms Albanians in their belief that the outside world is essentially inimical. The cluttering thousands of concrete domes that decorate the entire Albanian landscape serve as ungainly reminders. These curious igloos, found not only along the coast and on main roads but also, inexplicably, in remote fields, were the idea of Enver Hoxha. Hoxha distracted Albanians from tribal hatreds by uniting them in hatred of foreigners: all of them potential invaders. The bunkers certainly look ridiculous, but the slaughter of Muslims in nearby Bosnia (which Albanians, who are predominantly Muslim, showed little interest in) give them a certain point. By typical Albanian jest, however, the domes are so tiny that only toy—or boy—soldiers could use them for shelter. The bunkers in towns were used as toilets; here under the midsummer sun perhaps they supplied humanitarian shade.

Bexhet's urgent desire to see this "brother" was puzzling. In my first few days with the Dukas, O Babo had told me how he had *had* a brother who died—a story that he had repeated many times. Baby Bexhet had been persistently ill while his *binak*, or twin, had flourished and fattened and grown. One day his mother had to go into town and, not wanting to leave either one, took both babies with her. On the road she encountered a peasant woman who had no children. Seeing that his mother had two, the peasant woman demanded one, the healthy one. His mother of course told her to go to hell and so the peasant woman "gave the eye" to his baby twin. Two days later he was dead.

But to remind Bexhet of this tale now was to reduce him to histrionic tears for the continuing curse on his family. Although he told it weepily as a kind of fable, Bexhet seemed really to believe it. What gave the story its force was a truth about the way his people regarded their peasant neighbors. The story duplicated the typical *gadjo* myth about Gypsies and curses, and in both versions the iron proof of evil was the desire of the other to steal one's children.

Sure enough, Aziz Čiči (pronounced "cheechee"), whom we were to visit in Mbrostar, was not a brother but a cousin; Bexhet had used the term as a gesture of solidarity. That gesture, and even the tale of the sundered twins, became clear when the reason for our visit was revealed: Aziz Čiči had murdered a *gadjo* and next week would be going on trial.

What we'd already seen that day had the sadness to commit the most hardened social worker to silence; it was the anonymous misery of the whole impoverished world—a world which is always populated mainly by children. The tragedy at Mbrostar had a further, racial dimension: a crime had been distorted and deepened by the tension between the group and the surrounding, and larger, white community. It also showed the genuine inability of the Gypsies to avoid being, in *gadjo* terms, their own worst enemy.

We crossed Albania's biggest bridge, the suspension bridge whose image graces the ten-lek note. Not far off we found the house of Aziz Čiči, a white three-room structure perched over a railroad track. It was empty. The sunny rooms were bare, with only a few broken chairs to suggest any human occupation. A few broken chairs and a mournful female voice: in a back room, facing an open window with her back to us, an elderly woman knelt swaying in a trancelike movement that was the bodily expression of her plangent, somehow disembodied, dirge. It was a song to the *mulo*, the spirit of the dead. Had we come too late?

From next door a Romany family who knew Bexhet greeted us with relief and urged us inside. It was easy to overestimate the number of

people crammed into that little house—with the usual gallery of children's faces pressed against the window, and the awkward custom of
our hosts, who shook hands outside the house and then again when
we were inside the door. "God bless your legs," the husband said to
me, raising my hand as if to kiss it. I smiled weakly and stole a glance
at Marcel; when we had sat down (all five of us in a row on a cot) Marcel expanded: "God bless your legs for bringing you here."

The dead man, Fatos Gremi, was a well-known thief and widely
despised drunk; nevertheless, since the incident three months before,
the once well-integrated community had irremediably split in two. The
entire Rom population had been ostracized. No one could buy food at
the local shop; they were afraid to go out after dark. The stifling room-
ful of the desperate Aziz's friends, describing these events, all agreed so
far. But this extended family of Mechkari didn't need to be outcast in
order to feel it: the immediate family of Aziz, and to a lesser extent the
wider circle of family and close community, shared his shame. They
too were considered *mahrime*. Aziz's sister, for example, was in the village, but she did not join in this recapitulation and Bexhet didn't think
of going to see her; she was also his cousin but for the time being she
was as contaminated as her brother.

What actually happened on the day was the subject of the upcom-
ing trial, and in that room a matter of confused and surprisingly indifferent debate. The drunken Gremi had supposedly tossed rocks at
Aziz's window late one night (one said 7 p.m., another insisted on
midnight, a third suggested the hour before dawn). Terrified, Aziz had
then rushed to the door (in that crowded room one friend obliged us
with a sadly hampered pantomime) and fired a shot into the dark—
perhaps not so uncommon in Albania these days. But the bullet struck
and killed Fatos Gremi. Still more terrified, Aziz dragged the body into
the house.

Then he panicked. That night (the next morning / days later) he
and his wife sewed Gremi into a burlap sack, lugged him to the car,
drove to the ten-lek bridge, squeezed rocks in to fill the bag and rolled
him off the edge. But the river was low and the next morning Fatos
Gremi was an outcrop and Aziz Čiči was an outlaw.

None of those gathered there attempted to deny the crime in
Aziz's behalf, or to question the implications of his subsequent
actions (he had immediately decamped to the town of Pluk). Instead,
they offered competing versions of the timing and sequence, spiritedly

interrupting and attempting to outdo each other as if to say, "Wait up, how about *this?*"

They are all lying, I thought early on in our summit. And they're doing it just for fun. Then I began to understand. They had no sense of time (and were unbothered by such details as the impossibility of stealing off in the dark at five o'clock on a summer evening). But above all they did not regard the reconstruction of events as a project of memory. Instead, they told the story as they felt it to be at the moment of the recounting. In front of our eyes, as if for the first time, they were immersing themselves in the drama, conjuring up afresh the feelings that would fit such a terrible deed. The truest version for them—the winning version—was merely the most convincing or the most vivid. The heroic present was where they lived.

This impression was confirmed when Marcel attempted to explain to them what an appeal was, and how it might be possible to have sympathetic international observers at the trial (which was only a week away). In the middle of his unusually lucid explication, a chicken appeared in the narrow strip between our toes and those of the relatives in the chairs opposite. All of the Gypsies wriggled and giggled like children, as if someone had farted during a particularly portentous church sermon. And then with great and loud seriousness they all started talking about the chicken: where had it come from, who was its owner, whether they shouldn't just stick it in the pot before someone claimed it, whether those spots on its beak weren't evidence of a disease whose ravages someone began now flamboyantly to describe, another explaining with the flat precision of a tour guide that "the chicken plague" had been visiting various towns and villages in the region before making its way to Mbrostar. The conversation never returned to poor Aziz.

Fractured communication and a spontaneously theatrical approach to indisputably grave stuff was the norm among Gypsies everywhere: it was the spirit that made them attractive, but it was also what made them difficult neighbors. Marcel said they were incapable of establishing priorities. In fact their priorities were simply different priorities: value was assigned to all events equally but serially; what was going on at the moment—Aziz's trial, a stray chicken—had top billing. Neither event would have a lasting hold on them. Special fondness was attached to those incidents and persons with the greatest dramatic possibilities—that is, with a continuing, endlessly repeatable and improvable life in the imagination: memory of a kind.

Exhausted and anxious to be gone, we were nevertheless persuaded that it was too late to drive through the black countryside and the unlit, unfenced mountain roads to Tirana. And so we stayed, had a delicious chicken dinner, and passed a fitful night on mats laid out in the house of the condemned man. Bexhet, though, slept outside, so unwilling was he to linger in that unlucky place. It turned out that his anxiety was not to do with Aziz Čiči but with the old woman, Aziz's mother, whom we had first seen, from behind, as she intoned her wailing dirge. The oldest woman in the family and in the Mbrostar Roma community, she had a great deal of power. In matters of death and spirits she had more authority than her even more ancient husband.

The Mbrostar Gypsies, like most Gypsies, believe in and fear the *mule*. Though men appear to have all the authority, and do indeed wield it in secular life (deciding punishments for wayward members of the group, or dealing with *gadjo* officials), it is the women who possess the darkest and most forbidding powers. Their legitimacy resides in knowledge of spirits and medicinal cures, and ultimately in their ability to pollute men. Death, the final authority, is a man (Anne Sutherland noted), but only a woman can frighten him off.

It is not just the spirits who need worry, however. A woman can "pollute" a man just by throwing her skirts over his head, or even by threatening to do so—and thereby make him ritually unclean and in need of purification before other Gypsies can again associate with him. The woman has the power because she herself is innately *mahrime*—if she is married, which is to say sexually active. She must take elaborate precautions not to expose others to her "uncleanness." These well-defined codes of purity and contamination are the real universal language of Gypsies, understood if not always rigorously upheld in every district and dialect.

Old women have perhaps the best deal in Gypsy society. As women, they are invested with mystical powers. But because they are *old* women their sexuality is not a threat, and they cease having to observe many of the cleanliness rituals, eating and smoking as they do with the men. In direct contrast to Western women, who may feel great depression during menopause as their biological allure looks like waning, Gypsy women of a certain age gain status. By becoming physically more like men, they overcome the social inferiority of their sex. Old people are generally revered among Gypsies, and, for their deeper knowledge and experience, old Gypsy women, from Albania to the Americas, often have a lot of say in secular affairs as well.

It was unclear to me why Aziz's mother was singing these songs for the dead (she sure as hell wasn't singing for Fatos Gremi). Perhaps it was because of a fear among Gypsies that people who were deprived of the respect that comes only with old age—either by death or by disgrace such as Aziz's—were likely to become malevolent spirits. Perhaps, as mothers will, she was trying to make a deal for her son. Bexhet, in any case, was staying well clear of the *puri daj*, the old mother of Aziz.

Jeta had hardly ever been away from Kinostudio so long, and was anxious to make an early start. It was still dark when we left, and the journey was a dream of chalky mountains and vertiginous passes better left unobserved. I slept, and then feigned sleep, for the privacy it offered. The tarmac of the main road out of Tirana comes to an end at the entrance to Kinostudio; the familiar bumpy trail beneath the car told me we were home. As the car fell forward, lurching in and out of potholes like a wagon, all five of us inside bounced joylessly on the sticky seats. Then suddenly we stopped, the car's nose rubbing in the dust. We were stuck at a thirty-degree angle, in hundred-degree heat and a traffic jam.

As the dust settled, a pharaonic scene came into focus: a dozen bare-chested men, heaving the arm-thick twisted cable of a great pulley. Hanging from the inverted question mark of the cast-iron hook was the carcass of a dead horse, slung over a wide leather swing. The horse slid down, its legs still hooked over the leather strap, fetlocks frozen in a ghastly pose of prayer. And then it fell to the ground, its cataract-clouded, fishy blue eyes still open, heavier and more earthbound than it could ever have been in life.

The horse still glistened from sweat not yet dried; patches of fur stood up dully against the silky coat like back-brushed velvet. Hundreds of flies buzzed and tentatively dipped. There was a dark patch of ground and a shallow pit, dug by the horse, I guessed, in its last struggle for life.

Some of the men stood aside, cooling their cable-burned palms. A new shift had arranged itself on either side of the unwieldy animal; half of them pushed its bony haunches, while the other half pulled the stiff, spidery legs. Though I saw no wound, their hands and chests were smeared with black blood. Children ran up the dirt track from the neighborhood, dragging or pushing a range of other tools—planks and shovels and a wheelbarrow. Finally the pulley was winched and cranked and hoisted up as high as it could go, and the great fly-spattered beast was dumped into a waiting cart. From where I stood I couldn't see the men in the cart, just a row of clenched fists dug into the matted mane from the other side, tugging.

That evening and in the days that followed, the horse was never mentioned. In a protective gesture of unspoken but unmistakable admonition, Jeta silenced my inquiry—not, I inferred, because the animal had died gruesomely, but because of residual respect for an honored beast.

A few days before I left the Dukas and Albania, Nicu and Dritta and their boys moved out of Jeta's courtyard; their new apartment was ready. Over an afternoon a buoyant Dritta directed all the children and brothers back and forth in a two-way convoy, unpacking boxes in transit if they grew too heavy for the little body struggling beneath. Nicu and Nuzi shouldered the Polish couches. Liliana carried the painted table. Dritta beamed for onlookers. A place of their own: this was the biggest event of their lives. And of course Dritta was no longer a *bori*—she had properly become a *romni*, a wife. Normally this would come only when she had a *bori* of her own—that is, in a few years, when Djivan married the little girl from Berat. But Dritta had seized her chance; it was time to go.

Back home, the remaining *boria* feigned indifference and quietly got on with their chores. Dritta was gone, and Viollca and Nuzi, next in line, would soon move into their considerably bigger quarters. But even they were subdued: the courtyard was going to be a much quieter place. Bexhet was withdrawn as well, polishing his sparkling bicycle. And Jeta, unable to settle into her usual routine, set off on various invented errands. It wasn't her job to fetch water from the communal well, but that is where I saw her, perched on its ledge, a hand over one eye and the other tracking Dritta and Nicu as they made their last trip around that familiar corner, carrying between them a Stanbuli oven with Dritta's prized Day-Glo plastic orange tree potted in it. Jeta returned home with wet eyes and an empty bucket, yelling *nash!*—git!—at one of the hens that loitered in the courtyard gate.

TWO

Hindupen

Tᴇʟʟ ᴍᴇ," ʜᴇ asked. "Where do Roma come from?" On a scrap of Slovakian newspaper I made a pirate's map and sketched out the route of the exodus of the Gypsies from India a thousand years ago. "And we are *here*." I drew an X on my map, just left of center. X was Geza Kampuš's one-room house, halfway down the nameless main street of the Gypsy quarter of Krompachy, a town in eastern Slovakia, south of Poland, just west of the Ukrainian border, close to Romanian Transylvania and, until only a few generations ago, still a part of Hungary. We were sitting smack in the heart of Mitteleuropa—a place where people (Robert Maxwell, many American Gypsies, Andy Warhol's parents, my grandmother) tend to come from rather than go to. Krompachy, which used to have a functioning copper plant, where Geza used to work, isn't in any of the guidebooks. And though I had been there for a fortnight, I hesitated before staking my X. The frequent revision of borders hereabouts has meant, oddly, that only bodies of water appear as solid forms in the geographic imagination. Countries and capitals don't correspond to the map of the political imagination (Poland is the size of Germany; Prague is *west* of Vienna). I drew the borders of Central Europe as they are today; the rest of the map, the migration route, I left in the amorphous shapes of landmasses of the distant past.

The Gypsy migration has been likened to a fishbone spread over the map of Europe. If one included every group, or every imagined group, that peeled off in its own direction, perhaps that is how it would look. But I tried to keep it simple, with two main lines indicating the human trek: India to Persia to Armenia—and then a fork, to Syria and what would become Iraq in one direction, and in the other Byzantine Greece, the Balkans and on into Western Europe and the

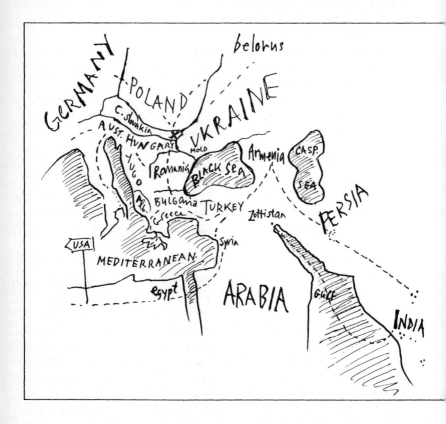

New World. Holding the X down with one finger, I turned the map towards Geza. He studied it, looked up, and smiled, apologetic but firm.

"It just doesn't fit," he said, leaning back and showing a half-octave of perfect ivories. "I'm sorry, but that just can't be right."

You might have guessed Geza's Indian origins. If you saw him on a Bombay bus or the London Underground, you wouldn't think twice: dark-skinned, well proportioned and delicate, with straight black hair and jet almond eyes, he was an Indian archetype. Even if he hadn't heard of India, and I guessed that he hadn't, Geza would have noticed that he was unlike his tall, white, round-shouldered Slovak neighbors, with their gray eyes and yellow teeth and tobacco mustaches. But it was a refreshing indication of how easy he was in his own skin that Geza didn't instinctively think that this land was *their* land.

"Well, what do *you* think?" I asked him, folding the map over. "Where do you think the Roma come from?"

Geza turned his palms up, opened his eyes wide, and pulled down the corners of his mouth—thoughtful again. After a while his smile flipped back up.

"Krompachy?" He raised his shoulders. "I don't know. I think we come from Krompachy." "And where are *you* from?" asked one of his daughters, who had been following our conversation. "America," I said, and she replied, "Oh, I've been there." "You *have*?" I asked. "Yes, that's just by Michalovce," she said, referring to a town about forty kilometers from Krompachy.

Perhaps Geza had asked me about the origins of his people to make small talk. I didn't meet many Gypsies who were interested in such matters; ancient history, for most, consisted of the earliest memory of the oldest living person among them. But I thought of Geza often in my travels, and I met him again and again. Over four years I visited dozens of Roma communities in the former Eastern bloc—in Albania, but also in Poland, Bulgaria, Czechoslovakia, Yugoslavia, Romania, Moldova, and Germany. Whether or not Gypsies spoke of national or ethnic identity, in Eastern Europe they were surrounded by people who seemed to talk of nothing else. And this not-knowing distinguished them, even if they were hardly conscious of it. It was, I came to believe, a defining attribute of Gypsy identity. If you couldn't say where you came from, you were nobody, and anyone could say anything about you.

But Geza's answer was a good one: home could be anywhere, and everywhere was home. Maybe beginnings didn't matter much. With their almost mythical presence, these were people who had always been around but had always had to begin again, wherever they found themselves. And getting there had always been a long, hard journey.

The Indian origin of the Gypsies has been known to scholars since the eighteenth century, when a few European linguists became aware of

Rom couple in Bohemia, holding their wedding
portrait, 1991

people in their midst who spoke an Oriental language. Istvan Vali, a Hungarian pastor, made the link in 1753, during a year at the University of Leiden. Vali had there met and interviewed three students from Malabar, on the southwestern coast of India. From them he compiled a lexicon of a thousand words (no record of this list remains), and when he returned to Hungary he found that the local Rom population understood them.

But for half their thousand-year migratory history there is hardly a useful mention of the Gypsies in contemporary accounts—and they never kept records of their own. Dark looks didn't suggest India as the original homeland in the minds of speculating early non-Gypsy chroniclers either, though "exotic" Eastern lands consistently came to mind. Since their first appearance in print—in the Persian chronicler Hamza al-Isfahani's *History of the Kings of the Earth* (950)—the Gypsies have been called many things, nearly all of them insults: Tartars, Heathens, Saracens, Greeks, Turks, Jews, Jats; Athingani, Atzinganoi, Romiti, Bohemians, "Fools Styled Greek Bohemians," Pharaoh's People, Egyptians, Luri, Zingari, Zigeuner, Zotts.

In his 1783 book *Die Zigeuner* (published in England as a *Dissertation on the Gipseys* in 1807), Heinrich Grellmann of Göttingen University gave an overview of the rich confusion abroad concerning the origins of the Gypsies.

> Because they were likewise called Gipseys (Cingani), they must immediately derive their origin from the Grecian heretics, called Athingans: then again they must have wandered from the African province formerly called Zeugitana. Another time they are supposed to be fugitives driven from the city Singara, in Mesopotamia, by Julian the Apostate: others again have transplanted them to Mount Caucasus, and made them Zochori; or to the Palus Maeotis, making them descendants from the Ziches. . . .
>
> Another brings them from Mauritania, and to corroborate his opinion by the name, calls them descendants of Chus. . . . Some people fancy they had heard that the Gipseys called themselves More, and often used the name *amori* among one another (not *amori*, but *Discha more*—Get out, Fellow!) and now they are Amorites! . . . They were sometimes torlaques (Mahometan monks, who, under pretense of holiness, are guilty of the most flagrant excesses), faquirs, or kalendars; sometimes the remains of Attila's Huns; at other times the Avari, who were vanquished by Charles the Great: then again Petschenegers, who played their last stake in the twelfth century; or perhaps a mixture of all kinds of rascally people gathered together, having collectively no certain country, as their name *Zigeuner* [as they generally have been called in Germany] indicates, signifying, "to wander up and down"; for which reason, it is said, our German ancestors determined every strolling vagrant Zichegan. . . .

Though not the only one to make the India connection, Grellmann was the first to apply rigorous philological analysis to the question of origins, leading the way in the new science that one historian has called "linguistic paleontology." Grellmann supplied a fifteen-page comparative catalogue of Romani words, along with their "Hindostan" (and English) equivalents, establishing a rate of agreement between them of about one in three, resolving for good any doubt about the provenance of Europe's Roma.

And then, as if to make the theory of exotic origins more compelling, Grellmann also helped to install Gypsy stereotypes: of wanton women, of carrion-eaters, and even of those among them who had a "relish for human flesh"—a slander which took more than a century to dislodge. In *Die Zigeuner* he gave generous space to contemporary reports of events the previous year (1782) in Hont County (then part of Hungary, now part of Slovakia). The case involved more than 150 Gypsies, forty-one of whom were tortured into confessions of cannibalism. Fifteen men were hanged, six broken on the wheel, two quartered, and eighteen women beheaded—before an investigation ordered by the Habsburg monarch Joseph II revealed that all of the supposed victims were still alive.

But the cannibalism libel stuck: as recently as 1929, in Slovakia, a band of Rom robbers was accused of eating their victims, and though the charge was dropped it continued to supply sensational headlines for weeks.

Early speculation by *gadje* on the homeland of the Gypsies came mainly in the form of Bible legends—all of them eye-of-the-beholder readings to which the Book has proved lastingly susceptible. And so it was said that the Gypsies were the cursed descendants of Cain, condemned to wander the world. (In Semitic languages—Hebrew, Aramaic, and others—*cain* means "blacksmith," perhaps the profession with which Gypsies are most closely associated.) "When thou tillest the ground, it shall not henceforth yield unto thee her strength; a fugitive and a vagabond shalt thou be in the earth" (Genesis 4:12). This text has been used as an explanation for the fact that Gypsies have never been much attracted to cultivation of the land—which they themselves may (disingenuously) refer to as their "curse." Speeches by contemporary Gypsy leaders very often kick off with a mention of the Biblical curse against their people. But such "proofs" mainly reveal how regrettable it is that the Gypsies do not have a Book of their own—although, according to another legend, they once did. I heard nothing of this kind in Albania but, according to a tale from Bulgaria, when God was handing out the different religions the Gypsies wrote theirs down on cabbage leaves, and before long the holy book was a donkey's dinner. Another weird tale of alimentary blasphemy comes from Romania:

The Gypsies built a church of stone and the Romanians built one of bacon and ham. The Gypsies haggled until the Romanians agreed to exchange buildings—and promptly ate their church. The Serbian version has the church made of cheese, and also offers an explanation for Gypsy begging: the reason Gypsies go from door to door looking for money, the fable says, is that the Serbs still owe them for their church; the beggars are only collecting what is their due.

The Gypsies themselves have no heroes. There are no myths of a great liberation, of the founding of the "nation," of a promised land. They have no Romulus and Remus, no wandering, battling Aeneas. They have no monuments or shrines, no anthem, no ruins. And no Book. Apart from just over a hundred words and phrases noted by three non-Gypsies in the sixteenth century, there are no samples of early spoken Romani. But they do have myths of ancestry and of migration. Or at any rate such myths have been attributed to them.

Like those of many other nations, the Gypsy tales lay claim to a Biblical lineage, however undistinguished. They tell of being condemned to wander for having denied succor to Joseph and Mary on their way out of Egypt; for having "told" Judas to betray Christ; for being descendants of the miscreants who murdered the children of Bethlehem (baby-killing always surfaces as the ultimate slander against the most hated groups; the Jews and the Gnostics were also accused of it); for having forged the nails used in the Crucifixion. These tales were spread even by the Gypsies themselves, perhaps to reinforce the myth of an Egyptian homeland that at first had seemed so useful.

The following tale, about the forger of Christ's nails, was recorded by Konrad Bercovici in Macedonia in the 1920s. Though this translation is not particularly evocative of the Gypsy manner of tale-telling, I cite it at length here. During most of the story not one Gypsy appears (and when he does he is a figure of last resort, an afterthought pitched up outside the gates of Jerusalem), but it is, in its various forms, perhaps the best-known of the early legends, and the only one which was occasionally recognized by Gypsies I met.

When the Roman jailers were given the person of Yeshua ben Miriam, whom the world later called Jesus, that they should crucify him, because he had talked ill of the Emperor of Rome, two soldiers were sent out to get four stout nails. For every man to be crucified, the soldiers were given eighty kreutzer to buy nails from some blacksmith. And so when these soldiers were given their eighty kreutzer with which to buy nails, they first tarried at an inn and spent half of the coppers drinking the sweet-sour wine the Greeks then sold in Jerusalem. It was late in the afternoon when they remembered the nails again, and they had to be back in the barracks by nightfall. . . .

Soon they stumbled out of the inn hastily, not altogether sober, and coming to the first blacksmith, they said to him loudly, so as to frighten him into doing the work even if there was not enough money to pay for the iron and the labour:

"Man, we want four big nails made right away, to crucify Yeshua ben Miriam with. . . ."

The blacksmith was an old Jew who had seen the long pale face and the light brown eyes of Yeshua ben Miriam, when he had once looked into his shop. So the man stepped out from behind the forge at which he had been working, and said:

"I will not forge nails to crucify Yeshua ben Miriam."

Then one of the soldiers put down the forty kreutzer and yelled loudly:

"Here is money to pay for them. We speak in the name of the Emperor!" And they held their lances close to the man. . . . The soldiers ran him through with their lances after setting his beard on fire.

The next blacksmith was a little farther away. It was getting on in the afternoon when they arrived there, so they told the man:

"Make us four stout nails and we shall pay you forty kreutzer for them."

"I can forge only four small nails for that price. I have a wife and children."

"Jew," the soldiers bellowed, "make us the nails and stop talking!" Then they set his beard on fire.

Frightened out of his wits, the Jew went to the forge and began to work on the nails. One of the soldiers, who tried to help at the forge, leaned forward and said:

"Make them good and strong, Jew; for at dawn we crucify Yeshua ben Miriam."

When that name was mentioned, the hand of the Jew remained poised high with the hammer. . . . "I cannot forge the nails you want to crucify Yeshua ben Miriam with," the Jew cried out, and stretched himself to his full height. "I cannot. I cannot."

Both soldiers, furiously, drunkenly, ran him through with their lances again and again.

The sun was low behind the hills and the soldiers were in great haste. They ran to a third blacksmith, a Syrian. They entered his shop while he was getting ready to leave off work for the day. Their lances were still dripping blood when they called to that man:

"Khalil, make us four stout nails, and here are forty kreutzer to pay for them. And be quick about it!"

The Syrian looked at the bloody lances and returned to his bellows. . . . The man cast his hammer aside. And he, too, was run through with the lances.

When I tried this story out on Gypsies in Macedonia, they corrected me at this point: "Khalil" was an Albanian, of course; and in Bulgaria he had become Todor—as in Todor Zhivkov, the former dictator.

Had the soldiers not drunk forty of the eighty kreutzer, they might have returned to the barracks and told what had happened, and thus saved Yeshua's life. But they were short of forty kreutzer, so they ran out of the gates of Jerusalem, where they met a Gypsy who had just pitched his tent and set up his anvil. The Romans ordered him to forge four stout nails, and put the forty kreutzer down.

The Gypsy put the money in his pocket first, and then set to work. When the first nail was finished, the soldiers put it in a bag. When the Gypsy had made another nail, they put it in the bag. And when the Gypsy had made the third nail, they put it in the bag. When the Gypsy began to forge the fourth nail, one of the soldiers said:

"Thank you, Gypsy. With these nails we will crucify Yeshua ben Miriam."

He had hardly finished speaking, when the trembling voices of the three blacksmiths who had been killed began to plead with the Gypsy not to make the nails. Night was falling. The soldiers were so scared that they ran away before the Gypsy had finished forging the last nail.

The Gypsy, glad that he had put the forty pieces of copper in his pocket before he had started work, finished the fourth nail. Having finished the fourth nail, he waited for it to grow cold. He poured water upon the hot iron but the water sizzled off, and the iron remained as hot and red as it had been when held between the tongs in the fire. So he poured some more water upon it, but the nail was glowing as if the iron was a living, bleeding body, and the blood was spurting fire. So he threw still more water on it. The water sizzled off, and the nail glowed and glowed.

A wide stretch of the night-darkened desert was illumined by the glow of that nail. Terrified, trembling, the Gypsy packed his tent upon his donkey and fled.

At midnight, between two high waves of sand, tired, harassed, the lone traveller pitched his tent again. But there, at his feet, was the glowing nail, although he had left it at the gates of Jerusalem. Being close to a waterwell, the Gypsy carried water the rest of the night, trying to extinguish the fire of the nail. When the last drop had been drawn out of the well, he threw sand on the hot iron, but it never ceased sizzling and glowing. Crazed with fear, the Gypsy ran farther into the desert.

Arriving at an Arab village, the blacksmith set up his tent the following morning. But the glowing nail had followed him.

And then something happened. An Arab came and asked him to join and patch the iron hoop of a wheel. Quickly the Gypsy took the glowing nail and patched with it the broken joint of the iron hoop. Then he saw with his own eyes how the Arab drove off.

The Arab gone, the Gypsy drove away without daring to look around. After many days, still not daring to look around, afraid to open his eyes when night fell, the Gypsy reached the city of Damascus, where he set up his forge again. Months later, a man brought him the hilt of a sword to repair. The Gypsy lit his forge. The hilt began to glow, from the iron of the nail upon the hilt. The Gypsy packed, and ran away again.

And that nail always appears in the tents of the descendants of the man who forged the nails for the crucifixion of Yeshua ben Miriam. And when the nail appears, the Gypsies run. It is why they move from one place to another. It is why Yeshua ben Miriam was crucified with only three nails, his two feet being drawn together and one nail piercing both of them. The fourth nail wanders about from one end of the earth to the other.

The tale is not, as it at first seems, about the Gypsy as opportunist, for he is merely and unsuspectingly getting on with his work (the finishing of the fourth nail only bespeaks the artisan's pride, for the lancing Romans by then are gone). Whatever justifications for the peripatetic tradition of the Gypsies such a story may offer, it still has the Gypsy busily plying his trade all over the Middle East. It doesn't tell us how he got there, where he came from, or why he left India.

No one can know for sure when or why the ancestors of the European Gypsies left India for Persia. But language is memory, and the presence of the Gypsies' ancestors in Persia is marked by the many Persian words in modern Romani. *Baxt,* Romani for luck, comes from the Persian; *sir* is garlic, *mom* is wax, *zor* is strength, and *zen* is saddle.

Most agree that the exodus began in the tenth century. In 950, however, the Persian historian Hamza wrote (in Arabic) of Bahram Gur, the Shah of Persia between 420 and 438, who, "full of solicitude for his subjects," imported twelve thousand "Zott" musicians for their listening pleasure (although "Zott" is the term that the Arabs then used for all Indians). Sixty years later, in 1011, a similar account appears in the Persian poet Firdausi's epic *Shah Nameh,* or *Book of Kings.* Firdausi expands the story to supply an explanation of the subsequent fate of the "Gypsy" musicians.

> Bahram Gur's local governors each reported to him that discontent was mounting because the rich drank to the accompaniment of music while the poor could not. . . . The wise Shah immediately despatched by dromedary a letter to [his father-in-law] Shengil in India, asking for 10,000 Luris, men and women, expert in playing the lute. When the Luris arrived the Shah received them, and gave each one a donkey and an ox, and to the whole group a thousand donkey loads of corn—all in the hope that they would settle down and farm in his Kingdom. The Luris promptly ate the corn and their oxen, and left the capital. . . . With wan cheeks, they returned at the end of the year and the Shah met them with reproach: "You should not have wasted the seed-corn. Now you have only your donkeys. Prepare your instruments, attach to each a silken cord, and load them upon your donkeys." These Luris even now wander through the world, begging a living, sleeping alongside wolves, living like dogs, always on the road, stealing day and night.

This story, though no doubt apocryphal, has particularly excited Gypsiologists because in Eastern Europe the Roma (as well as others) still play stringed instruments such as the gudulka, which is like the lute though played upright and with a bow. *I* never saw a single one of these pear-shaped instruments, however. Gypsies had all kinds of wind instruments, notably the long, wooden double-reed conical-bore zurla, as well as guitars and violins, on which they puffed and picked and sawed their Lambadas—the Brazilian hit which seemed to have wiped out folk music in the Balkans. (At least one academic was excited by this trend—a ginger Croatian giant called Svanibor Pettan, a doctoral candidate at the University of Maryland. He was writing his dissertation on Kosovan Roma and the Lambada.)

Most scholars believe that the Gypsies left India sometime in the tenth century. A considerably earlier departure date is favored by those who seek a heroic portrait of the early Gypsies: a group of "Zotts" arriving circa 700 in Persia (then part of the Arab Empire). According to this theory, which is based on the work of a nineteenth-century Dutch historian, M. J. de Goeje, the Gypsies came not by land but by sea. And they came by force.

The new Arab rulers, so the account goes, brought tens of thousands of Indian peasants over from the delta of the Indus, across the tip of the Arabian Sea and up the Persian Gulf. They were settled on the marshy banks of the Tigris, along with several thousand buffalo. Although these Zotts came as captives, within a century they were levying taxes of their own on all merchants who passed through their canals and along their roads. This Zott community was clearly regarded as a threat by Baghdad, for in 820 the Caliph sent in troops against them. They resisted for fourteen years: perhaps the only time in history when the Gypsies (or proto-Gypsies) have had their own mini-kingdom or even independent colony. In 834 the next Caliph succeeded in damming their canals and flooding their fields and thereby wiping out "Zottistan." After a gruesome battle in which more than five hundred were beheaded, twenty-seven thousand Zottistanis were captured. They spent three days on display to the jeering crowds of Baghdad; then the entire Zott population was dispatched to the northeast. It was a portion of these who (according to Donald Kenrick) moved north into Armenia and eventually to the Balkans and Europe. Such unskilled, displaced Indians would no doubt have met up with other Indians moving west from Persia with their traditional trades, and, together, they would become the European Romanies. By this account, the earliest Gypsies would have left India at least by 720 A.D.

From the language we can tell that the Gypsies did not stay for very long in the Arabian Empire, which is why the most conservative historians tend not to include the Zotts of Zottistan in their posy of theories. While there are many Persian words in Romani, fewer than ten words

A pair of Rom children playing in the river at Copşa Mică, Romania. In this Transylvanian town all the sheep are black—along with everything and everyone else. The residents drink great quantities of milk in the belief, according to one long-term resident, that it will at least "keep their insides white."

of Arabic origin survive (discounting Turkish words that would have been picked up later, in the Balkans). Only two Romani words are definitely from the Arabic: *kis* (purse) and *berk*, which means breast.

Yet the language is peppered with Armenian: *dudum* is gourd; *bov* is oven; *chovexani* is witch; *grast* is horse; and the Romani for leather is the Armenian *mortsi*. Therefore the Gypsies must have passed through Armenia on their way to Europe. But the most significant influence of Armenian on Romani was a shift in sound. Words pronounced with a "bh"—that is, an aspirated "b"—came to sound like "ph." So that whereas in Middle Eastern or "Asiatic" Romani the word for sister was, and is, *bhen* (as it is in Hindi), in Armenia, and subsequently in Europe, the word is *phen*. It was on the basis of this shift—indeed of this word—that the English linguist and Gypsiologist John Sampson in the 1920s became the first to classify Romani dialects, and thus the Romany migration, into two major groups.

According to the language fossils, however, the invasion of the Seljuk Turks in the eleventh century uprooted the Armenians as well as the Gypsies who lived among them. They moved into the western-Byzantine territories of Constantinople and Thrace—areas still heavily populated by Gypsies—where the first reference to them appears in 1068, in a hagiography written at Mount Athos. From there they spread into the Balkans in the thirteenth century and, soon enough, over the rest of Europe.

The period of Byzantine influence was powerful. Romani contains many Greek elements; and the Greek term for Gypsies, *Atzinganoi*, formed the basis for the Italian *zingari*, the French *tsiganes*, the German *Zigeuner*, the Hungarian *ciganyok*, the Romanian *ţsigani*, the Czech *cikan*, and many other current and generally unfriendly names. The slander was not a late development: the Greek term *Atzinganoi* derives from the name of a heretical sect called Athinganoi (with which the Gypsies were branded for telling fortunes). By the end of the fourteenth century the Gypsies themselves were being listed among the reasons for the decline of the Byzantine Empire.

Ahead of the Ottoman Turks they moved into the Balkans: an order placed by two Gypsies with a goldsmith of the Republic of Ragusa—that is, Dubrovnik—is dated 1378. (There is evidence that they were in the Romanian principalities as early as the twelfth century.) More than any other part of the world, and despite how inhospitable the region has become, since their first appearance there in the Middle Ages the Balkan provinces have been a kind of homeland to the Gypsies. It was from the Balkans that they made their major westward migrations—in the fifteenth century, in the nineteenth century, and now, again, in the postcommunist era. And it was to Eastern and Central Europe that they were repeatedly to return.

Early on in their Balkan existence Gypsies held a curious position in society: they were at once more powerful and, by the nineteenth century, less free than they ever have been since. Both conditions had to do with the structure of rural feudalism. The Gypsies were *wanted*, and detained—not for crimes, but for their talents. Tinsmiths and coppersmiths, locksmiths, blacksmiths especially, as well as the esteemed musicians among them, were valued and even fought over.

With their ability to move between radically segregated classes, between peasant and landowner, and to serve both, they managed to dig out for themselves an economic niche. In social and family life they stuck to their own—by exclusion, to be sure, but also (or eventually) as a matter of choice. Indeed, their preferred lines of work have always enforced separateness and solidarity; as much as the language itself, their professions are a key to their cultural survival (a fact that was appreciated by the communist regimes, who tried, and failed, to convert them into a new and anonymous proletarian force). It must be significant that, even today, Gypsy groups are most often identified by their traditional professions, even if they have not been brickmakers or combmakers or herb-gatherers, and so on, for generations.

Such a group or workforce, typically arriving by migration rather than by conquest, is known in sociological jargon as a "middlemen minority." They are culturally marginal and, as sojourners, they may be ill-at-ease both in their new place of residence and among other equally isolated "relations," off at some other end of the diaspora.

A parallel, at least so far as early Gypsy-peasant relations in the Balkans goes, might be found in the experience of the Central European Jews who migrated to the American South after the Civil War, and made their living selling door-to-door to recently freed slaves. In his book on the Jews of Atlanta, *Strangers Within the Gate City*, Steven Hertzberg speculates:

> . . . commercial intercourse was rooted in the marginality of both vendor and purchaser. The Jew had little capital, spoke broken English, was unfamiliar with regional mores, and in some cases was

perceived as an intruder by native whites. Similarly, the freedman
was disdained and feared by ex-Confederates. Perhaps more impor-
tantly, prior to going South, few of the newcomers had encountered
blacks, and this made them "more willing to respond out of actual
experience of the Negro than out of a twisted history of slavery, guilt
and pathological hate. . . ."

Hertzberg quotes from Eli Evans's *The Provincials: A Personal History of
Jews in the South*: "When the Negro smiled at the Jew . . . the Jew smiled
back." But though many Jews now regard any implied link with commerce as slanderous stereotyping, among most of today's Gypsies this
attitude towards non-Gypsies proudly prevails: dealings with outsiders
are largely confined to business. In hard times, Gypsies, like Jews, have
always been cast as "the enemy within"; they have also, like Jews, been
traders working for themselves, whatever else they also were, and
therefore scorned by people tied to the routine exigencies of agriculture, or by those who worked as employees, for wages.

In both Bulgaria and Romania people described to me the sort of
work Gypsies have done since 1989 as "Jew work" or *biznitsa*. They
meant any work that was not manual; any work in which you made "a
lot" of money without a lot of sweat, and which was therefore, by definition, corrupt. For example, some Bucharest Gypsies sold Carpaţi,
Romania's roughest and cheapest cigarettes, from open suitcases on
the pavement. Their "trick" was to get up very early on the day the limited supply of Carpaţi appeared in the city, buy up the lot, and resell
them at an inflated price. Or they might go to Turkey and bring back a
truckload of distressed blue jeans and sell *them* at a markup. This was
Jew business, Gypsy business—not capitalism, a word that was still
identified here with smart Western imports and American aid. But it
wasn't just the concept of profit that rankled with locals steeped in
communist ideology. It was fear of work itself. The Gypsies, like the
Jews, were guilty of showing initiative: which was strange and suspect
and threatening to people who, under the communists, expressed their
contempt or their despair by doing as little as possible in the jobs that
were their birthright.

In medieval Central and Eastern Europe the Gypsies had work:
they labored on their own in the jobs that no one else would or could
do, and they sold their goods and skills door-to-door. But this for the
moment is where the parallel between Gypsies and Jews as migrant
middlemen ends. Far from the start of a brilliant career, their situation

Jan Marcinkiewicz, the King of the Gypsies on the estates of the Radziwiłł family in Lithuania, pays a visit to Prince Karol Radziwiłł in his palace at Nieśwież. This engraving, from a drawing by Wojciech Gerson, appeared in Jan Jaworski's Kalendarz Polski Ilustrowany za rok 1867 *(Illustrated Polish Calendar for 1867), though the historical event took place in the previous century.*

in the Balkans came more to resemble that of American blacks. Their labor was highly valued—and they paid taxes; but from late in this period until the middle of the nineteenth century they were also enslaved.

Despite their large numbers (some twelve million, as compared with the roughly thirteen million Jews in the world today), the true story of the Gypsies—their origins and diaspora and remarkable internal cohesion—remains an area of almost occult interest. Even the romantic versions of Gypsy life which became fashionable in painting and novels and operas in the nineteenth century did little to arouse serious investigation. And you still won't find an arrow for them among those marking the movement of peoples in the great *Times Atlas of World History.* One must look instead to small-circulation, special-interest publications such as the *Journal of the Gypsy Lore Society*—and, perhaps most interestingly, to linguistics.

In addition to a place of origin and the migratory route, the study of Romani has also yielded a controversial ethnic possibility. This lies in the word the Gypsies widely use to refer to themselves (and literally to mean man or husband): *rom* among European Gypsies; *lom* in Armenian Romani; and *dom* in Persian and Syrian dialects. (And so we see that the term Rom, as in Romany, has nothing whatever to do with Romania, where, confusingly, the Gypsies have lived in great numbers for many centuries. Nor is it, as English Gypsies told the social anthropologist Judith Okely, "cos we always roam.") *Rom*, *dom*, and *lom* are all in phonetic correspondence with the Sanskrit *domba* and the Modern Indian *dom* or *dum*, which refer to a particular group of tribes who may look familiar.

In Sanskrit *domba* means "man of low caste living by singing and music." In Modern Indian tongues, the corresponding words have similar or related meanings: in Lahnda it is "menial"; in Sindhi, "caste of wandering musician"; in Panjabi, "strolling musician"; in West Pahari it means "low-caste black-skinned man." There are references to the Dom as musicians from the sixth century. The Dom still exist in India; they are nomads who do a number of jobs: basketmaking, smithing, metalworking, scavenging, music-making. Not surprisingly, many people have leapt on a Dom theory of origins for the Gypsies.

But not everyone. Judith Okely, with particular reference to British Travelers, deplores all talk of an Indian origin, which she sees as just another way of exoticizing, and marginalizing, this widely traveled and long-resident European people. At the same time, many contemporary Gypsy writers and activists are intrigued, but they argue for a classier genealogy: we hear, for example, that the Gypsies descend from the Kshattriyas, the warrior caste, just below Brahmins. There is something useful about ambiguous origins, after all: you can be whoever you want to be. Among Gypsies, continual self-reinvention has been the primary tool of survival, but the not-knowing has of course also had terribly alienating consequences, as did, for example, the forced name-changing in Bulgaria in the late 1980s. Already, many Bulgarian Gypsies cannot remember their own names. Or at least (and which is worse?) they pretend they cannot. Such experiences have intensified the need to establish a properly Rom identity. For some this has merely meant the ear-bursting clamor of formerly banned Gypsy music, day and night. For others a new identity, which one might call "Hindupen," is growing out of an unprecedented pride in origins.

Geza Kampuš lived at the smart end of Krompachy's Gypsy quarter; roses lined the paved walkway to his door. But just down the road the scene disintegrated into a squalor that, though entirely unremarkable, never failed to shock me. One family, which seemed to consist only of a continually drunk father and three cross-eyed children, lived in an abandoned underground cement bunker. Most of the other families were deficient in menfolk, who were more often in jail than at work (as in Albania, and every place in between, redundancies were soaring in eastern Slovakia, and Gypsies were always the first to go). They seemed to live more or less in the open air. In front of their frayed shacks these Gypsies had yards of mud and rubbish and broken furniture, constantly churned by playing children and the mangy family *rikono*, or dog. Gypsy dogs—ever present, though not quite *pets*—all seem to be lame or one-eyed or stub-tailed, as if their main job wasn't to protect or to appear faithful but to make people feel better about their own shortcomings. And in this region, which according to one published study could claim the highest incidence of inbreeding in Europe, shortcomings were many: cross-eyes, wall-eyes, facial tics—these were trifling defects.

Though the interiors of Gypsy houses in even the poorest quarters of Krompachy were tidy, the outside was invariably a tip (and this, apparently, has always been the Gypsies' preferred arrangement: two British writers, S. G. B. St. Clair and Charles A. Brophy, who in the 1860s lived for three years in Bulgaria, noted the same phenomenon). The squalor was startling in contrast to the lots of the proud, neatly pressed peasants next door, among whom the Gypsies predictably, and in this case understandably, were unpopular. No matter how high the Slovaks tacked that chicken wire, or how assiduously they topped their walls and dividing ledges with broken bottles, they were always planting for the Gypsies as well as for themselves. The Masai of East Africa are said to believe that *all* cattle belong to them; the Roma of eastern Slovakia, it seems, feel the same way about potatoes.

Even where they had not been nomadic for hundreds of years, as in Slovakia, they were not planters. Only in Albania and in pockets of Romania did I meet Gypsies who worked the land—or whose ances-

Roma children playing in their settlement in Krompachy, eastern Slovakia, 1991. In addition to bicycle wheels, the children were keen on tiddlywinks, which they played with bottle caps and tin lids. A group of art students from Prague spent a week painting with the Krompachy kids. The little girls mainly drew fairies and princesses and angels, all with blond hair.

tors had. Gypsies might get work as seasonal pickers, but they didn't grow their own—whether because they thought it beneath them (which they certainly did), or because in their minds or in fact they might be moving on before harvest, or because they had never owned any land. Gypsies worked on cooperative farms under the communists; but they started with nothing and they ended with nothing, pushed off formerly communal land as collectives gradually returned to private hands.

A different explanation was offered by Milena Hübschmannová, a linguist and Gypsiologist from Prague with whom I traveled in eastern Slovakia: no one in their original Indian caste had ever touched a spade. Similarly, as V. S. Naipaul notes, "Land reform does not convince the Brahmin that he can put his hand to the plow without disgrace."

Dr. Hübschmannová had been to India several times and never missed a chance to point out the cultural and social parallels which for her, in addition to language, were the final proof of Indian origin. There was, for example, the *jati* system of economic organization, in which class is linked to and defined by profession (technically, *jat* just means caste, but among nonspecialists castes have been reduced to the four *varna*s—Brahmins, Kshattriyas, Vaishyas, and Shudras, plus Untouchables—when in fact there are about two thousand *jat*s). The system had clearly been replicated among the Roma, and weeding wasn't recognized by them as a job description. The ban on certain kinds of work for the group, or just for their women, was not the only surviving aspect of Indian hierarchy and regulation; equally important was the manner in which a chore was carried out, with elaborate concern for ritual purity.

Milena was so absorbed in her intricate explanation of the *jati* system (counting the numerous castes on a thin finger), that she didn't even notice the middle-aged peasant women who barked us out of the quarter—"Go home, Gypsy-lovers!" and "Why don't you take them back to your institute, you city-scientists, or send them to *Africa*!" We waved goodbye to the pack of Gypsy children who had followed us to Milena's orange Lada and, as we drove away, I asked her about the squalor. Their houses were so clean inside, so lovingly and prettily painted . . . but the yards! The communal space was unusable because of the smell.

I wouldn't quickly forget the slime-covered burial mounds of dead tires; the tangy vegetable pâté of silted-up garbage; the cans and bones and fishheads; the abandoned appliances with their cartoon springs and forlornly obsolescent, detonated look. To my eye, this looked like the ordinary despair and poverty of, say, the inhabited garbage dumps of Bombay. And yet the Gypsy community was full of normally vain teenagers (tattooed, lipsticked, and preening); the adults too were far from resigned, if constant and noisy complaint was any indication; and the children were nothing like inert: a large population of junior mudlarks, so long unwashed that you could hardly make them out, climbed among the ruins, cheerfully playing the games that all children play—pushing wheels with sticks, flipping rusty lids and bottle caps in makeshift tiddlywinks. "It wasn't dirty," Milena impassively explained. "It just *looked* dirty."

Specialists often see what they know to be true rather than what is in front of their eyes. Standing in a stinking slum, Milena could point admiringly to "true Rom culture." She could never see any bad in any Gypsy—a thief was not a thief but, say, someone who, divested of his traditional economic niche, had adapted to a new but still symbiotic relationship with the *gadjo*, from whom he earned his goods in exchange for status in a period of economic and political crisis, status conferred on the *gadjo* by the Rom, who, in the act of unburdening him, offers himself up as a sacrificial scapegoat, etc. . . . She wasn't kidding; nor was she entirely wrong.

According to Milena, Gypsies left their outside space to rot because for them ("as in India"), *other people's* garbage was regarded as especially unclean and contact with it could bring symbolic contamination—to them a greater danger than the disease it would probably also bring about.

For their part, Gypsies can as easily be stunned by examples of *gadjo* squalor that the *gadje* aren't even aware of. For example, keeping dogs as pets in the house, and, worse, tolerating cats, and indeed upholding them as unusually clean animals. Among Gypsies, the cat is widely regarded as *mahrime* because it licks its fur and genitals and so brings dirt inside itself. Just as the Gypsies kept the insides of their houses neat, those who had not totally lost their culture were fiercely on guard against having their own innards polluted through improper cooking and washing; by analogy, as Judith Okely has pointed out, an animal's regard for the crucial distinction between a *zuhho* (pure) inside and a *mahrime* exterior determined whether or not it made an acceptable pet, or meal. And so hedgehogs, whose spines assure cleanliness, are regarded by some Gypsies as a delicacy. And everywhere horses are beloved, partly because they do not foul themselves by licking.

The interior of a typical, tidy Rom household, in Sintesti, Romania, 1994

*Some of the poorest Roma live in the many rural settlements
of eastern Slovakia. Zehra, 1991*

Among British Gypsies some animals, such as snakes and rats (referred to only as "long tails"), could not even be mentioned without risk of pollution. *Saps*, or snakes, were particularly disgusting and dangerously contaminating because of the way they shed their skins, thus converting the inside into the outside, and because they ate other animals whole, devouring *their* dirty skins. These taboos are observed with varying degrees of rigor and range, but nowhere are they absent, neither among the assimilated nor among the most deracinated slumdwellers. So were these customs the trace remains of Oriental caste control, as Milena would insist? Or were they just the superstitious vestiges of hygiene practices that would have been very sensible in nomadic times?

Many customs among the Roma would seem to claim an Indian ancestry, not just in Eastern Europe but wherever they live in diaspora, from Australia to Argentina. Specialists warn against the temptations of theories of cultural monogenesis and stress that sometimes non-Roma also participate in these activities. But the thesis remains an unproven, and for some an irresistible, possibility. The Gypsy activist and historian Ian Hancock points out the use among Roma of the Indian *bhairavi* musical scale, as well as a type of "mouth music" known as *bol*, which consists of rhythmic syllables that imitate the sound of drum strokes. In Hungary a form of stick dancing called in Romani *rovliako khelipen* has Indian parallels (and is also parallel with, for example, British Morris dancing). The Hindu custom of burning the possessions of the dead continues among the Gypsies of Western Europe; British Gypsies still torch the caravan of a dead elder. (And, long ago, in a practice known as "lustering," their widows also went up—which has obvious parallels with Indian *sati*.) The traditional mechanism for solving internal disputes among Gypsies east and west is the tribunal called (by its Greek word) the *kris*, identifiable with the Indian *panchayat*, which takes roughly the same form and serves the same end.

In India, Shiva is known by the trident, or *treshul*, that he carries. Contemporary European Roma use this word to refer to the Christian cross. The worship of the Romany goddess of fate, as she has become, attracts a large pilgrimage to the French Camargue each May, at Les-Saintes-Maries-de-la-Mer. St. Sara, as she is known in Les-Saintes-Maries, was the Egyptian maid of Jesus's two Aunt Marys; she is also identified with the consort of Shiva, the black goddess Kali (also known as Bhadrakali, Uma, Durga, and Syama).

"As in India" (in Milena's fond phrase), only certain groups may eat together without risk of contamination. Because the proper *jati* affiliation of one's acquaintances cannot be assumed, some utensils may be outlawed. Contact between mouth and shared implements is scrupulously avoided in even the poorest households; very often each person has his own knife, which he will carry with him in case he has to eat away from home. In conservative Romany culture (called Romipen or Romanipen), liquids are poured into the mouth through a container held away from the lips, so that they do not touch the rim; and smoke from a shared tobacco pipe is drawn (and in Romani "drunk" rather than "puffed") through a fist made around the pipe's stem. (Anne Sutherland describes a meal with some Rom-American friends in an Illinois diner, during which they preferred to eat with their hands rather than risk the diner's forks and knives.) As in Indian custom, the Roma divide illnesses along ritual lines. There are those which "naturally" (and increasingly) affect the group, such as heart conditions and nervous tension, which may be treated by Gypsy folk doctors, and then there are those which are invasive, in the sense that they spring from unwarranted contact with *gadje* (for these one must consult the relevant physician—i.e., a *gadjo* doctor); these include, of course, all sexually transmitted diseases.

It was only a matter of time before the Roma in their search for a positive identity would recognize and seize on their Indianness.

In May of 1991 I went to Skopje, the capital of Macedonia, in southern Yugoslavia (as it was then), which had been rebuilt after a massive earthquake in 1963. I arrived at the outset of the three-day festival of Erdelez, or St. George's Day, celebrated with verve by Muslims as well as Christians among Europe's largest Gypsy settlement of some forty thousand, who live in what has become a separate town, called Šuto Orizari, or Šutka (pronounced "Shootka") for short.

I was paying a visit to Šaip Jusuf. He was a Djambas Gypsy, which meant that his ancestors had been horse traders or, as he thought, acrobats. Šaip (pronounced "Shipe") had himself been a gymnast, indeed a "Professor of Gymnastics," until he lost a leg. Šaip had also written one of the first Romani grammars and had, in 1953, established the first *pralipe* (brotherhood), or Gypsy club, in Yugoslavia.

The taxi driver from Skopje's Grand Hotel (every East European capital has its Grand) dumped me at the edge of Šutka. He refused to enter the Gypsy quarter. But I was more lost than that. As it turned out Šaip didn't live in Šutka, as I had crassly assumed, but rather—as a friendly young Rom pointed out, looking at my scrap of address— in a mixed neighborhood nearby. This was a run-down suburban sprawl with planted front yards, pebble-paved paths, and rusty gates fronting whitewashed, detached, and modestly curlicued family houses along wide and winding residential streets.

Finally, despite wrong directions gratefully received from a cheerful squad of nine- or ten-year-old barefoot Gypsy boys pushing wheelbarrows of screaming baby sheep, I found the Jusuf household.

Šaip's large, bosomy, giggly wife, Keti, was out in the front yard doing a jig on top of a rolled-up water-soaked carpet. Erdelez was a time of spring cleaning, and everything in the house, from the collection of Indian figurines to the bed frames, would come out for a hosing. The cement yard was slick with water.

Beyond Keti (an Erlije, or Turkish Gypsy) I saw Šaip sitting at a table with two books, a conical polished brass Turkish coffeepot, and matching thimble cup. He didn't see me until I was with him. He was taking off his leg—a pink plastic prosthesis of East European make— to put his shoe on it. When the shoe was on the foot and the leg strapped back onto Šaip he offered me a Sok. The bright-green Macedonian soft drink was produced and we settled in for a delightful one-sided talk of the kind in which Šaip specialized.

"*Aksha, ak, yak; khan, khan, kan. Nak, nak, nak. Jeep, cheep, cheeb . . .*" he began, demanding my repetition after every set of words, complete with comic facial punctuation. I record it phonetically, these words in Sanskrit, Hindi, and Romani for eye, ear, nose, tongue. His excitement was quickly shared, because there were many correspondences, all of them obvious to an amateur. For water there is *paniya*, *pani*, and *pani*; the Sanskrit for hair is *vala*; in Hindi and Romani it is *bal*. "People" is *manusha* in all three languages. The Sanskrit for sun is *gharma*, which became *gham* in Hindi and *kham* in Romani.

"*Me pina pani*," Šaip said, Hindi for "I drink water" (or literally, "I to drink water"). "*Me piav pani*," Romani for the same. "*Me piav Sok*," I offered, doing what I could.

.   .   .

In 1948 Šaip had traveled among the Chergari, nomadic Turkish Gypsies (whose distant relations I would meet in Albania), collecting their stories and their words for his grammar. When he returned to Skopje he began to recite these tales of Romany life to groups of gathered Roma. What must have astonished them most was not the stories themselves, but that he called them out publicly in a strong voice, for in Tito's postwar Yugoslavia, one wasn't *allowed* to be a Gypsy. As under the reign of the Habsburg Empress Maria Theresa, when Gypsies were "elevated" to the status of "New Magyars," Tito's Gypsies would become "Yugoslavs," and, as was equally hoped by other communist regimes, ethnic differences would fade away.

Šaip encouraged people to claim their Rom identity, which for him had become a positive identification only with his own discovery of roots in India. The discovery came from an uncle who as a soldier in the Turkish army had been imprisoned in India in the First World War, and who had found that his Romani gave him Hindi. And Šaip encouraged people to write.

His activism had galvanized his fellows, though he had been displaced by younger and more charismatic—or anyway more militant—leaders by the time I met him. But he was still in there, belt cinched tighter than it wanted to go, the top layer of his white hair dipped in ginger henna; and still he was honored—everyone in Šutka seemed to know him.

Šaip had been very much involved in the organizing of the first World Romany Congress, in 1971 in London, which had been partly financed by the Indian government. It was on the basis of the India connection that the International Romani Union would eventually accede, in 1979, to the United Nations and be recognized as a distinct ethnic group. At the 1978 Congress, in Geneva, the Indian theme was already becoming somewhat theatrical: one of Mrs. Gandhi's ambassadors arrived with pocketfuls of symbolic Indian salt and symbolic Indian earth; and ever since (albeit only from one or two corners), there have been cries for the reunification of "Indian World Citizens" and Amaro Baro Them, Our Big Land, or ancestral homeland.

It was getting dark in Skopje; gathering the rattling brass coffee service, now sludged over with grinds, we moved inside. And there, past the motorcycle which had taken his leg, Šaip's obsession shone.

The Jusuf parlor was a bazaar, or a temple, or both: it was a shrine arcade. There were plaques and figurines and pictures of Ganesha, the

Indian god with an elephant's head. Šaip kept shrines for the mother goddesses Parvati and Durga, and for Kali, the black goddess and, among Roma, the most popular. Kali is the crazy cross-eyed one usually portrayed with her tongue hanging out. Sometimes she has hundreds of breasts.

There, below a satiny Indian flag, above the nailed-up skipper's wheel—representing a wagon wheel and therefore emblematic of the Gypsies—were the Indira shrines: blown-up color snaps of Mrs. Gandhi, Mrs. Gandhi alone, one with Šaip just recognizable behind her right shoulder, another with Šaip beside her in profile. And finally there was a large portrait of Tito, another patron saint of the Jusuf household (Šaip had translated a book about him, which he declined to show me but which he called "a tribute"). On a sofa sat a round young man called Enver, a family friend. He peeled the cellophane off a new packet of Alas cigarettes and delicately stretched it over a wide-toothed comb. This he brought to his mouth and, as a kind of welcome, played on this homemade kazoo a very good "El Condor Pasa": "I'd rather be a hammer than a nail. Yes I would. If I only could I surely would. . . ."

"In 1971," Šaip continued over the entertainment, pausing to rearrange the sorority of plastic Indian costume dolls arrayed across his bookshelves, "24,505 Yugoslavs declared themselves Rom." I imagined 24,505 Gypsies standing up as in a mass AA meeting and "declaring" themselves. "In 1981, 43,125 had."

But the local intelligentsia, the poets of Šutka, had reached beyond describing themselves as Roma. One young man, Ramche Mustapha, a garbage collector by day and a poet by night, showed me his passport: under "citizenship" it said Yugoslav; under "nationality" it said Hindu. *Ramche Mustapha, Hindu!*

They were not trying to disguise that they were Gypsies—as were the many Bulgarian Roma who insisted they were Turkish. Nor were they denying that they were Muslims; they just didn't see any contradiction. Similarly Šaip—originally Muslim but now Hindu—and his Muslim wife thought nothing of going to a Greek Orthodox service at the local church on St. George's Day. When I asked him why they went to Mass, Šaip just said, slowly and clearly, as if he was talking to a very stupid person: "It is St. George's Day." Rather, the poets were embellishing, or simply exposing, their Romipen, or Gypsiness—superficially eclectic, but at bottom something distinct and recognizable—which here they had pinned to the land of origin.

Šaip did not want to hear about how dangerous such claims to a foreign identity had been for Gypsies in the past. For instance, I assured him that the first recorded Gypsies in the British Isles, who in 1505 presented themselves to James IV as pilgrims from Little Egypt, were smartly deported as the foreigners they claimed to be.

In any event, Šaip dismissed events of this kind as "ancient history"—more ancient, apparently, than the exodus from India. And so I mentioned how in 1983 a Rom from Radom, in Poland, had swiftly made an outcast of himself among local Roma with his campaign to "repatriate" all European Gypsies to India. Šaip wasn't suggesting a *permanent* return, he protested—"In that case, we would do better to claim America as our homeland." And to be fair, like most Roma and unlike the rest of mankind, Šaip nurtured no ambition for a homeland, a Romanistan. Certainly such aspirations could be counterproductive: in Germany, for instance, some Gypsy activists' demand for dual citizenship (which Germans are not allowed) plays into the hands of authorities who wish to disown them.

Partly due to other reservations, Šaip's salon of perhaps a dozen young poets was in any case regarded with a certain amount of scorn, especially from the older Roma of Šutka. (The young poets were interested to hear the story of Papusza, who had been so ostracized by conservative Polish Gypsies in the fifties.) That they were writing, and beginning to publish, marked them out from traditional, mainstream Gypsy culture: a culture which emphasizes the collective and eschews the introspective; a culture, above all, that is *live*, as if transcription were the literary equivalent of trading in one's wheels for a trailer.

Poets weren't the only young people in the neighborhood to take up the Indian trend. "Tunes like 'Ramo Ramo' and 'Sapeskiri' (the snake) both inspired by Indian films," the American musicologist Carol Silverman notes, "became instant hits" in Skopje. Many of the young women of Šutka, fed up with the baggy-bottomed Turkish trousers they were supposed to wear (and which used twelve meters of fabric a pair), had begun to wear *saris*. A popular Indian film festival could also explain the new fashion; whatever the Gypsy girls understood of their connection to the actresses, a spontaneous identification had been made.

Of course in a way it was absurd, this India business: imagine making a cult or taking on the costume of the land your own ancestors inhabited over a thousand years ago. To be sure there were customs and values that had been absorbed by the Gypsies in diaspora; but without a religious component and the dynamic of a promised land it seemed altogether anomalous; Šaip's plastic Ganesha collection, all those cute figurines with little-boy bodies and elephant heads, might just have been toy trolls. In the event, it didn't matter: they worked.

One might wish for a Gypsy *hero*, a Gilgamesh or a Gawain or even a Zapata—a warrior or a poet and not this cuddly Dumbo. Yet on closer inspection Ganesha was not a bad mascot for a nascent group of Gypsy bards: Hindu tradition has it that Ganesha was a poetry lover and that he sat at the feet of Vyasa and took down the entire *Mahabharata*. More than that, Ganesha honors the fledgling sense of Rom-Hindu identity, for the elephant god is the patron saint of beginnings.

THREE

Antoinette, Emilia, and Elena

THOUGH I AVOIDED the war in Yugoslavia, all over Eastern Europe I visited battle sites: the burnt-out or torn-down Gypsy settlements. But while following the nationalist torch, from rural Romania to industrial Bohemia, I also became aware of more subtle and covert violences: often they were committed against Gypsies by other Gypsies.

In Bulgaria I found this destructiveness expressed in the stories of two totally dissimilar Gypsy women. Along with Czechoslovakia, Bulgaria is the place where Gypsies have been most comprehensively uprooted from their traditional culture. Many no longer speak Romani. The deep squalor of their settlements—urban and rural, indoors as well as out—is indistinguishable from the worst *favelas* of Brazil, and attests to their loss of Romipen. But there are different kinds of deracination; one also saw it among the privileged. Antoinette was a bright, articulate woman who, as a girl, had been plucked in hope by the Establishment from the usual Gypsy destiny. Emilia, on the other hand, was a victim of the rigorous Gypsy value system which, in the interest of group survival, exists precisely to combat social mobility.

I met Emilia only on the last of several visits to Bulgaria, through her friend Elena Marushiakova—a Bulgarian ethnographer who had herself been punished for challenging the officially designated status of Gypsies. Elena was skinny. She constantly smoked rough BT cigarettes ("Bulgarian Tobacco") and dressed like a student, in a sagging sweater and jeans. With her scraggly, unbrushed hair and freckles, she looked about sixteen—a sixteen-year-old who smoked for show. In fact, she was in her thirties and the mother of children ages ten and four.

We traveled together around Bulgaria, and inevitably we went to Sliven, a town of one hundred thousand, which was widely recognized

Bulgaria's urban Gypsies are among the most deracinated in Eastern Europe. These boys, like most of the street children, are addicted to glue, and they survive by begging and stealing. A few of them, including, in 1991, a nine-year-old girl, are also prostitutes. Not all of them are orphans but they mostly live in train stations, with intermittent periods in children's homes. Sofia, 1993

as "the Gypsy capital" (more than half of its citizens were Gypsies). The night before we set off, another Bulgarian friend said unthinkingly, "Watch out in Sliven. There are a lot of Gypsies." Elena was uncommonly lacking in routine prejudice.

On the long train ride we covered the Balkan Range and crossed almost the length of Bulgaria. The grass crops of different greens and the yellow squares of sunflowers intermittently gave way to strips of orchard: low, closely pruned fruit trees, apricot, plum, and cherry. This bright and busy view was very far from the parched swaths of roadside Albania. The most striking difference, though, was not in the landscape itself but in the revealed determination of its inhabitants. Bulgaria is a quilt, intensively cultivated; and Bulgarians on the train are rewarded with this full-color pastoral picture out of a children's book—between the vast chemical plants with their equally colorful fumes. These excepted, Bulgaria seems like an Eden: rivers and mountains and ancient, painted monasteries; vineyards and soft fruits and seaside resorts, all in a Southern European climate. But to Gypsies such pamphlet-filling variety and resources meant little. They couldn't care less. Truly the sense of place for them had everything to do with the human landscape, and in respect of its large Gypsy population, Bulgaria was barren—a tundra of human intolerance.

Elena described how she had become involved with Gypsies. It started when she was a Pioneer—"you know, one of those very happy little communists with a red bandana." Elena had been in charge of a bunch of Gypsy children on an excursion to the Black Sea. (The groups were segregated, and no one wanted to take the Gypsies, but Elena was the youngest and so she was "volunteered.") Towards the end of the holiday, a bracelet belonging to one of the other Pioneers had gone missing. Elena's group was blamed (it had to be a Gypsy), and would she please, asked the director, produce the culprit? Elena replied that none of her kids could have stolen the bracelet, because they had spent the day in the resort town of Varna. ("None of the Gypsies could swim," Elena said, explaining the day trips away from the waterfront campsite. "The seaside wasn't so much fun for them. It just showed how different they were.")

The director continued to insist. Elena narrowed her eyes in imitation of him as he repeated his demand for a culprit, "or else." "I stuck to the truth," she went on, "because I couldn't think of what else to say. The Gypsy children were afraid because of the bracelet. Or maybe they were always afraid. They had only one set of clothes each, they were very careful of their things, washing their dresses without being told, even the littlest ones. Seven and eight years old. Much tidier than the Bulgarian children."

"So what happened to them?"

"I never knew. Nothing maybe. As for me, I was kicked out of the Komsomol [the Communist Youth club]. This was, in 1975, a serious matter. I understood that now I wouldn't be able to go to university. It hadn't been a problem that neither of my parents were Party members, but now this was being raised by authorities as evidence of our general subversiveness. It was a nervous time. Still, that experience changed me. And you can't imagine—I had been so proud when I got my red bandana!"

Little Emilia had been one of the girls in Elena's group; her parents invited Elena to their house when they heard about the bracelet incident. "Her family lives in one of the oldest, worst Gypsy quarters in Sofia, a place I would *never* have gone before. It was supposed to be so dangerous." But despite the protests of her own family Elena started hanging out there at age seventeen. This *was* dangerous, at the time, not because of the Gypsies so much as the authorities. The family mail started to be monitored (they had no telephone); men in long, gray coats turned up at the house to question Elena and her parents about her activities.

"But it was always slightly comical," she said. With hindsight, I thought. "No, really, it was ridiculous. The police would come and make noises. They would talk about everything except what they were there to find out about. They never asked any direct questions. They couldn't ask about the Gypsies, because, officially speaking, the Gypsies didn't exist!" And this was true: although there was by now a highly visible population of as many as eight hundred thousand Gypsies in the country (nearly 10 percent of all Bulgarians), they had never been mentioned in the census—except in those of the Ministry of the Interior: the police.

Elena gave me the background of what had become her life's obsession. In the 1947 Constitution, Gypsies had the status of a national minority, allowing them at least to use their own language—a status which was scrapped in the revised Constitution of 1971. Now everyone, like it or not, was "made equal." To be equally Bulgarian meant that difference would not be tolerated. At the same time, from 1978 onwards, a law that was unwritten but well understood prohibited interaction between "ethnic Bulgarians" and Gypsies, including even the mention of them in the national press or on television. (Hence euphemisms such as "our dark brothers," still favored by the "liberated" press.) Soon the Gypsies, like the Turks, were all required to Bulgarianize their names; so Ali became Ilia and Timaz became Todor. They were no longer allowed to speak Romani, to play music, to wear "folkloric" clothes. Along with this, Elena the ethnographer repeatedly pointed out, many Gypsies had lost their traditional professions—as basketmakers, spoon- and brush-makers, herb-gatherers, musicians, smiths, and so on. These elements of identity, Elena and I agreed, were obviously more important for a group without land or written records. Now many Bulgarian Gypsies had no idea what kind of work their ancestors had done, and often didn't know what their family name had been only a few generations before.

In Sliven, Elena and I split up (not wanting to overburden any one family), and would meet again in a few days, on the train back to Sofia.

This basket weaver, who lives near Plovdiv, still makes his living by the profession that his family has practiced for centuries. In rural areas, where often there is no work (and no social services), economic crisis has sparked a revival of traditional skills. Bulgaria, 1992

An English friend had introduced me to Antoinette and Gyorgy, and they had invited me to visit.

Antoinette took the rose I had brought her between two fingers and dropped it, still wrapped in its station-kiosk cellophane and bow, into a tall fluted vase. This she arranged on top of the television, making room between two Eiffel Towers: one brass with a thermometer attachment, the other a porcelain *objet*.

"*Eh, oui,*" she sighed, tilting her head and clasping her hands at the bosom. Antoinette collected greeting cards with pictures of women in just such feminine poses. We spoke French, which she had learned at Bulgaria's Frenskata Gimnazia, or French Lycée. She was pleased to have a visitor. She had no one to talk to in French and, it seemed, no one to talk to in Bulgarian. We talked about Paris, which she had visited once and which was, she said, her spiritual home.

"*Georges et moi, nous y sommes allés, il y a cinque ans.*"

"*C'est vrai?*" I dully replied, instigating a full, on-the-rug session with the family photo album: Antoinette in front of the Eiffel Tower, Gyorgy in front of the Eiffel Tower; Antoinette and Gyorgy in front of the Eiffel Tower. . . .

The Gypsies of Sliven were long-settled, and divided between the better-off Christian Gypsies, mostly former ironworkers, and the Xoraxane, the "Turkish" or Muslim Gypsies, never identified with a particular craft; they lived miserably and literally on the other side of the train tracks, behind a high wall erected in the sixties to keep them out of sight, in mini-ghettos with names like "Bangladesh" and "Like-it-or-not." Antoinette and Gyorgy did not live in either settlement; they had a flat in a large cement block which hardly seemed attached to the town and whose tenants were a mix of Gypsy and *gadjo.*

I have tried to avoid stereotyping; and so did Antoinette. Sitting beside me on the patchwork rug, legs daintily tucked under to one side, Antoinette didn't look or move like any Gypsy woman I knew or had seen: she was tall, pale, and blonde, and she was exceptionally—exaggeratedly—prim and girlish. She might have stepped from the pages of a 1950s issue of *Good Housekeeping.* Her red-and-yellow flowered dress fanned about her, the frilly apron tightly fastened in a large bow at the back to emphasize her good waist. She'd teased up her bright hair into meringue-stiff peaks; a yellow pelmet curled over her forehead. She had lovely large sad brown eyes. She wasn't pretty, but no imperfection escaped remedy, and there was something affecting about all the trouble she took, always smiling.

I asked Antoinette why they didn't live in the uptown Christian Gypsy *mahala,* or quarter.

"I don't care to live all crowded in, '*à l'italienne.*' " Whenever possible she employed a continental phrase, distancing herself from the world of Gypsies (who, after all, live more hugger-mugger than do any Italians).

She told me of her early days with "Georges." "Donka, my grandmother, she was against him. She would say: '*Mais ma petite fille, il est*

Gyorgy and Antoinette, Sliven, 1992

un peu paysan' "—to which Antoinette added by way of explanation, "It's true, he is very dark." Antoinette lowered her eyes and placed a light palm over her clavicle. "But oh, how that man can dance!"

That first evening, in a local restaurant, I saw for myself. Gyorgy's three younger brothers had an excellent band, much in demand for weddings. Though he didn't play—he was a European *homme d'affaires*—Gyorgy danced a lot with Antoinette, and they made a spectacular pair on the floor. Occasionally Gyorgy also sang, something from "Engelbert" or Tom Jones. He did an especially good "Release Me." "Pleeeeease release me, let me gooooh. . . . You don't love me anymore. . . ." and Antoinette teared up when he sang it.

"My family was disappointed, you see. I had gone to the Lycée; I was the only *gitane* there, and nobody knew."

The few foreign-language schools in Bulgaria were considered to be the best, and they were generally attended only by the children of high-level apparatchiks. Antoinette was unusual all around. With her brassy hive and modern dress—most Sliven Gypsy women still at least wore long (if not particularly traditional) skirts—she reminded me of an American girl I knew who had been given a new nose for her sweet sixteen: the parts didn't quite match, yet the more dramatic change had been in her expression (always this secret to keep). Some Party connection was necessary to explain the transmogrification of Antoinette; but that she pointlessly denied. It was as if I had asked her if she was a natural blonde.

Denial, self-misrepresentation: this was the significant experience of many Gypsies, particularly in Bulgaria. Here they could pass for members of the even larger Turkish population, which had, especially under Ottoman rule, proved useful. (Identification with Turks among many Bulgarian Roma was not always opportunistic, though; it also represents a rare instance of genuine Gypsy assimilation.) In the former Eastern bloc, however, *everyone* was accustomed to routine and blatant lying, and to ritualized official lying. The Bulgarians, like other whites, were at least frank about their hatred of Gypsies. But this was more predictable than the reaction of Bulgarian Gypsies. At a time when all over the world ethnicity was replacing class or cash as the salient socializing factor, among the Gypsies here the dream was of racial anonymity.

In Sofia, Elena had introduced me to Gospodin Kolev, the only Rom member of the former Central Committee of the Communist Party (Propaganda and Agitation section). Though there were once over three thousand Gypsy members of the Bulgarian Communist Party, they had invariably joined the rank and file. Only later did I learn that the high-ranking Kolev was Antoinette's uncle.

Gospodin (which means "Mister") Kolev was particularly proud of his early advocacy of special boarding schools for Roma, where "they would be taught to be civilized like Bulgarians"—as well as to cook and lay tables. I visited an all-Gypsy "technical" school in Sliven. The kids were supposed to be taught job skills, and so they were, in a

A Muslim Rom baby's first rite, at Stoliponovo, a large, mainly Gypsy housing estate outside Plovdiv, Bulgaria. At six months old, the male child receives his first haircut—for which the entire neighborhood turns out, cheering—and then is dressed up as a sultan and carried at shoulder height around the settlement. A preliminary to circumcision, this custom is called the sunet biaf—*"circumcision wedding," 1992.*

sweatshop setting. (Ten- and eleven-year-olds installed the ballbearings in swivel desk chairs which would eventually be sold mainly, I was told, to Hungarian businesses.) These schools still exist all over Bulgaria; more like orphanages or reformatories, they didn't much resemble the Lycée.

I asked Kolev about the Bulgarian Communist Party's ban, imposed in 1984 and lifted at the fall of Todor Zhivkov in 1989, on Gypsy language and music.

"Bulgarians didn't want Gypsy songs because, at that time, Serbian and Bulgarian music was more popular."

"And the name-changing?"

"As Gypsies in all countries adopt the local religion, so they take local names. They always had Bulgarian names. As for those with Turkish names, they were first changed in 1940, under the *monarchy*. It is true that we took up this campaign in 1962, starting with the Gypsies, so that they might truly become Bulgarians."

Pomacks, or Bulgarian Muslims, were the next group to be renamed, in the 1970s; last, in the 1980s, it was the turn of the Turks. Some three hundred thousand of them were sent on a one-way "excursion" to Turkey—an episode that caused an international outcry which helped to oust the region's longest-running dictator.

"Anyway, the Gypsies did not resist. Why? Because the Turkish names they had were not typically Turkish. A Gypsy Suliman would be called Sulio: they had *already* distanced themselves from the Turks, you see, and so you see they *wanted* to become Bulgarians. All over the world Gypsies avoid showing that they are Gypsies."

He was right about that, although in Bulgaria they mainly did so by claiming to be Turks. . . . Two of the three Gypsies who became MPs after 1989 declined to embrace or even admit to their ethnicity.

In the late 1950s, Antoinette's uncle had joined a Communist Party committee charged with solving "the Gypsy problem." They began, in 1958, with the outlawing of nomadism. Thirty-five years later, Kolev had not changed his views at all. "In a technological industrial society the wandering Gypsy is finished." Here Kolev could be proud: there are no "wandering" Gypsies in Bulgaria. "What is there to preserve?" he went on. "What are the supposed Gypsy professions? Copper has been replaced by plastic. Gypsies were being given the chance to become Bulgarians: differences could not be permitted." Kolev seemed triumphantly unaware that, since the end of his party's rule, those differences had violently deepened. He was sticking with the version of his glory days, and his idiom was Central Committee perfect: "Assimilation is an objective historical process."

But not, apparently, an ineluctable one. "Even now, Gypsies who live among Bulgarians retain their backward habits. They are unclean.

They must learn how to live from their Bulgarian neighbors. The Gypsy ghetto is as black as India."

Good-looking and unsmiling, Antoinette's brother Stefan, a visitor at her apartment one lunchtime, had the steady manner of the doctor he was; and he was as black as an Indian. Skin tone was Antoinette's standard way of describing people, but she hadn't mentioned her brother's. Presently we sat down to a snack of salami rolls stuffed with creamed cucumber cheese. Garnished with colored toothpicks, arranged in a star pattern on a red paper plate, trimmed with paprika-dusted deviled eggs, this pretty, genteel offering was strikingly unlike the plain and plentiful meals I had eaten in many Gypsy households; rather, it looked like another inspiration from *Good Housekeeping*. Antoinette kept a close watch on me. I felt her searching my face for prejudice.

Stefan began to talk about a polio epidemic in Sliven, which had struck especially hard in the poorer Gypsy neighborhood across the tracks. He was one of six Gypsy doctors in Sliven, and the majority of his Bulgarian colleagues, he said, "won't go near the downtown *mahala*. They do the absolute minimum. In that community"—by which he meant the Gypsy community—"the infant mortality rate is twenty-three per thousand. And now this epidemic. Of course it is a problem even for the doctors who are willing. The Gypsies are refusing vaccinations because they have got the idea that the inoculation will sterilize their babies."

I told him a similar story from *The Book of Boswell*, by the English Gypsy Gordon Boswell. "I will not be poisoned," Boswell had told an army nurse attempting to inoculate him. The fear was one of ritual—and perhaps also of physical—pollution incurred by allowing the inner body to make contact with unclean *gadjo* equipment and culture. Antoinette had her own explanation for Sliven's polio epidemic: "The Turkish Gypsies are dirtier than our Christian Gypsies." She was right. Still, it was unclear what kind of dirt she was talking about: grime, or lack of culture.

I wanted to go to the troubled *mahala*, and later I would, but not with Antoinette: neither she nor her doctor brother would go there, at least not with me. Instead, Antoinette offered a tour of the nicer Gypsy neighborhood: "They're not all barbarians, you know!" she said. For Antoinette, the Gypsies were always "they."

Before Stefan went his own way that afternoon, we stopped in a small, family-run café on a corner at the edge of the *mahala*. Antoinette hoped to persuade him to spend the evening with us: she promised music, a wedding feast. It backfired. He was gloomy all right, though not just because of the epidemic and the injustices it revealed. Like his pale sister, Stefan was uncomfortable in his skin.

There are no horses roaming about the cement blocks of Sliven but their image is all over Gypsy households. And they were all over this café, on the wall hangings, on the plates—a wink at a lost life. Like the equine images of horsy English and American girls, these tended to be dark brown. In fact, what is known in the trade as "a Gypsy horse" is piebald: black-and-white, motley. Among Gypsies these creatures, ambiguous if not camouflaged, have always been the most prized.

When Stefan moved to fetch our coffees, another man known to Antoinette came over and, to her immense irritation, sat himself down. Mitko Tonchev had a long, unlined dark face, a wild intensity, and a need to talk. He had come to Sliven because he knew how to weld; there were supposed to be jobs "in industry" here. He was desperate rather than bitter in the knowledge that, as a Gypsy, he would be at the end of the job queue. "It didn't use to be like this. We didn't use to *know* we were Gypsies. Everyone had jobs. Now we are not free in ourselves."

Antoinette was annoyed by this remark and only reluctantly translated it for me, adding that Mitko Tonchev was "neither smart nor intelligent." She showed her contempt for him and his views by peering into her compact the entire time he spoke, and by compulsively opening and shutting the handbag she carried everywhere, with "Paris Elégance" printed in loopy script on the side.

Later, after we'd lost Stefan, Antoinette said she thought it was the wedding party that had put her brother off. "*Pauvre* Stefan, he cannot find a Gypsy wife because he is so intelligent." And he couldn't marry a Bulgarian because he was so black.

The streets of the uptown *mahala*—a Gypsy settlement for more than a hundred years—were packed on this Saturday afternoon in May. A flow of people, mainly young women gyrating in long, hip-hugging skirts, moved towards us down the main street. A few of the girls led a band of zurla players, who pointed the wooden, fluted ends of their instruments straight up, sending a reedy Lambada into the sky. Some of the zurlas were stuffed with money, accounting for the kazoo tone, and possibly for the angle of play. The crowd was not coming from a wedding but from a *čeiz* (pronounced "chayeez"): a girl's dowry and its display in her parents' house for a couple of days before the wedding feast.

Antoinette took my hand and led me into the *čeiz* house. "*Amerikanka, Amerikanka,*" people murmured as we passed. So I had been announced. It seemed that I was a kind of walking Eiffel Tower, a proof of the worldliness of Antoinette.

Inside, it looked like sale day at a discount department store. The walls and floors of all three rooms of the low-ceilinged semidetached house were covered with shiny new "Persian" carpets, towels, bath mats, runners, and rugs, depicting Biblical scenes, peacocks, and

A 1976 invitation to a Bulgarian Gypsy wedding, featuring the betrothed couple

voluptuous odalisques reclining in a harem setting. They were hung like oil paintings—a good space around each and with spotlighting on choice mats. Pinned to these were the feature of any bridal shower: lacy underwear and nighties, tacked at jaunty angles, their corners saucily skewed up as if blown by a sudden wind.

Another room was a crockery shrine: apricot lusterware, gilt-lipped wineglasses, pink tea sets with romantic pastoral scenes, thimble-size demitasse cups—all piled up in a fragile ziggurat on a fuzzy peach-colored altar. There were slippers everywhere: slippers for her, slippers for him, tartan ones, embroidered satiny ones, felt ones, all suggesting low-key domesticity. After marriage, it seemed, shoes were no longer required.

In the next room was the satin-covered bed, strewn with plastic roses and more nighties. On the pillow a large plastic doll sat upright in an all-lace confirmation dress. This doll was an *ex voto*, for the health of (many) children, and it would ride on the hood of a honking car when all the week's worth of marriage ceremonies were through. The couple would never have a church ceremony or registry-office wedding—there would be no official document of any kind. They were already married in Gypsy custom, and the *čeiz* (in place of a bride-price, which was no longer paid among Sliven's long-settled Gypsies) was the proof. There was so much stuff on the bed that the teenage bride and groom, on display along with their booty, were hardly visible. They sat arm-in-arm, in matching ruffled white shirts both buttoned to the throat. She was sweet and shy-looking and seemed embarrassed by the filmy purple bikinis pinned to the wall above her head. The pair held their smiles as if someone was taking their picture, and occasionally someone did.

As we walked home Antoinette described her own *čeiz*. "There were so many gifts that the whole family had to move out and sleep in the car! And mind you, it was a big house. I received important things," she said, reassuring me that a Lycée girl was not going to be fobbed off with a batch of fancy knickers. "For example, my *bibliothèque*," said Antoinette—by which she meant the glass-fronted bookcase where she now kept her own lustrous tea sets and porcelain figurines.

"I didn't want anyone to come, I was mortified of course." The *čeiz* is a Gypsy tradition, and none of her friends from the Lycée would mark their own engagements in this way. "But my parents insisted, and in the end it was okay because many intelligent people turned out." She meant, as she went on to elaborate, that many *gadje* had come to admire her haul.

It was wedding season. The next day we went to another feast, in a subterranean restaurant. Although Antoinette was clearly an honored guest among these festive Gypsies, she immediately regretted having come. On top of our table a pink-sequined, over-made-up wild woman was strutting her stuff; for Antoinette, though, this was not the worst. The bride was hugely pregnant and, worse still, it was a mixed marriage. Antoinette was proud of her Bulgarian friends, but they were not the kind who would marry Gypsies, whom she clearly regarded as white trash. It was all very confusing.

On my last night in Sliven, Antoinette and Gyorgy and friends dined at a restaurant outside of town, in what was once a hunting lodge belonging to Todor Zhivkov. It looked like a rustic ski resort, with little boulders for stools around a rude rock fireplace, and antler chandeliers. I hadn't seen much of Gyorgy this trip. Apparently he was preoccupied with business (the nature of which never emerged). That night he turned up and sat at the head of the table between Antoinette—the lacquered crests of her yellow hair swept up and piled like ribbon candy in a flattened stack of figure-eights—and his secretary, Yuliana.

Yuliana was a young Bulgarian woman who had traded in schoolteaching for a job with Gyorgy—and for a new look: red leather miniskirt and matching stilettos, black leather bustier, and dark lipstick, with thick black liquid-liner drawn around the whole of each eye. To Sliveners this didn't look whorish: it was fashion. And however she looked, as a Bulgarian, Yuliana was a real catch, and not just in her role as girlfriend, which she apparently was, but also as a secretary: hire the *gadji* today, and the business would soon follow. Antoinette seemed to accept the situation.

Near the end of dinner Gyorgy leaned towards me and asked, half-leering, half-hostile, very drunk: "Do you believe in a Gypsy aristocracy?" He didn't mean, one could be sure, the old Noble Savage, but rather a nobility based on character and not on caste. Above all, Gyorgy *"le paysan"* wanted respect. His query was part of an undercurrent of insecurity and accusation which came up, always out of the blue, in questions such as "Would *you* ever marry a Gypsy?"

The next morning, Antoinette and Gyorgy and Yuliana, impressively and incredibly, could not be dissuaded from seeing me off at the station, all three turned out (changed again) in their very smartest evening clothes at 5 a.m. Antoinette waved until I was out of sight, her Paris Elégance bag clutched to her breast.

Back on the train, Elena, who had been at the farewell dinner, was not surprised that I had found this friendly, intelligent woman so unconvincing, so lost-seeming. "They'd be better off in Sofia," she said. Or Paris. In Bulgaria, she said by way of explanation, measures for the "containment," or assimilation, of minorities had been especially severe, and from the mid-1980s increasingly so. And these measures had affected Elena as well.

The Black Sea bracelet scandal had not, in the event, kept Elena out of university. But when she sought to specialize she learned that Gypsies were not considered a suitable subject, even in the Department of Ethnography; Elena had to go to Czechoslovakia for her Ph.D. When she returned to Sofia, she somewhat mysteriously joined the National Ethnographic Institute. "I don't know why they let me in." (Her thesis had been dismissed as romantic fiction.) "Maybe to keep an eye on me. In the beginning, for about two years, things were calm. And then, from 1985, the director started to threaten me. What was different from the past was how openly it was done. There was no sense in which it was wrong to threaten people. He simply told me that a directive had come from the Central Committee which stated that I must cease all agitation in the Gypsy underground"—Elena laughed, not even having to spell out the fact that, by law, there was no Gypsy "overground." "If I failed to cooperate immediately I would be banned from the Institute, and of course from any teaching position. . . . I tried to see it in a good light: if I was made to be a street-sweeper, I would at least, finally, be among the Gypsies." All street-sweepers in the Eastern bloc did indeed seem to be Gypsies.

The train whizzed past a vast and muddy chicken farm. I tried to explain to Elena what chicken batteries in the West were like. She was somewhat baffled by concern for animal rights, especially, for some reason, *chickens'* rights, and even more puzzled that anyone might object to chickens who had been specially fattened-up.

"You have clearly never seen a naked Bulgarian chicken," she said, sleuthing. And then she told me how, during the previous winter's unusually desperate food shortage, she had combed the Gypsy districts of Sofia and bought a chicken from someone she knew and triumphantly brought it home for dinner.

"I had to kill it in the bathtub. Vesselin [her husband] couldn't face all the blood. But I couldn't look either, and I kept missing and it kept not dying. You know it is not that easy to kill a chicken, even a skinny Bulgarian chicken. But as it happened my father dropped by and he finished the job, telling us that we might've flattened it with one of our heavy, unpublished manuscripts. One thing was sure—that I would never be allowed to publish my research. It is funny, isn't it, that what before was merely forbidden is now utterly impossible. . . ." She trailed off, and went to smoke a cigarette in the corridor.

Elena was referring to the usual and inescapable problem, evident all over the former Eastern bloc: economic restrictions had neatly replaced political ones. There was no money for publishing, no paper, and no market for the obscure "scientific" tomes that used to be turned out by every institute and academy. (Everyone under the old regime, whether a literary critic or a gym teacher, was called a "scientist.") Elena reckoned that it would take ten years to get a book published in Bulgaria, *after* it had been accepted by a publisher. An article could wait three years, and if you withdrew the piece temporarily, even for the purpose of updating it, you lost your place in the queue.

The bulk of Elena's research was then still unpublished, though she had managed to get an article into one ethnographic magazine called *Kontakti*. This was a new journal, run by the same people who used to reject her stuff in the old journal. Back then it was called *Rodno-Lyubie*, or *Love for Your Clan*.

I reminded Elena of her promise to introduce me to Emilia, her friend from the Varna excursion nearly twenty years earlier. In the time that it took us to find her, Elena brought me up-to-date on the girl's troubles, which were entirely to do with the hierarchies inside the Gypsy community—structures far sturdier than any government scheme to sweep them aside. After a few tries, we found Emilia at home: a flat in a run-down modern block in Sofia. Unlike Antoinette, she was relaxed and resigned and very frank. Elena told her I wanted to hear her story, and with a shrug she obliged. She spoke in Bulgarian. Elena translated.

"It was the only night I ever spent alone with my husband," Emilia said of her elopement. In 1978, at the age of thirteen, she had run off with Plamen—all the way to his grandmother's house, two kilometers down the road in another Gypsy quarter in Sofia.

"When *my* grandmother eloped, my grandfather came and fetched her on a horse." From Emilia's point of view, things had definitely improved: "Plamen hired a cab. It was a Western car."

Elopement wasn't scandalous in itself. It was a common event among Gypsies, particularly among settled groups such as Emilia's; they had lived for many generations in the same cramped neighborhood of Sofia (which when I saw it still had no running water, only a row of troughs with taps). The old system of bride-buying had become too expensive, and it tended to serve rigid, even dynastic aspirations not much shared by young people. As the only way to avoid an arranged marriage, elopement had never been more popular. In effect it was a euphemism for sexual intercourse, and this in turn was tantamount to marriage. However, the system could work out miserably, at least for the girls. More and more young men were resorting to the simple method of kidnapping; with or without the complicity of the girl, this constituted betrothal—unless something went wrong. At the top of the list of things that could go wrong was the question of virginity. Maybe the girl wasn't a virgin—or maybe she couldn't prove it.

Early in the morning after their night away, Emilia and Plamen returned to their quarter, this time by tram, with the bloody sheet folded into a plastic bag. "The tram was full of half-asleep people going to work. I remember that we were the only people who were really awake. We were so happy." The dawn ride across Sofia was the last moment of calm for the newlyweds: overnight, Emilia and Plamen had entered a thicket of taboos: the potential transgressions that form the landscape of adult Gypsy life—a landscape designed to "contain" women. It wasn't marriage *per se* that did women in: it was the onset of menstruation (though the two usually coincided), from which point on, women had the power to pollute men. But if women were the targets of most taboos and customary laws, they were also (of course) charged with their enforcement.

Once they were back in the neighborhood the first stop was the house of Plamen's parents. The teenagers handed the plastic bag over to his mother, who would perform the necessary forensic tests. Blood alone was not enough to establish young Emilia's virtue; once Plamen and all the other men were shooed out of the house, the bloodstained sheet was laid out on the kitchen table and sprinkled with *rakia*, or plum brandy, the local firewater. The women gathered round and waited.

"It was the most terrifying half-hour of my life," Emilia recalled. For only if the *rakia* moved the blood into the shape of a flower would all be well. "Pig's blood doesn't bloom right," she explained, suggesting how a desperate couple might proceed in trying to cover for lost virginity—or, more likely under such pressure, to cover for the boy's inadmissible failure to perform.

"After the *rakia* test, I went home to my parents, and the next day Plamen came over and asked my mother for my hand. I wasn't allowed to see him until it was sorted out—which was fine with me!" When I met Emilia she was twenty-seven and looked ten years older, except when she laughed.

It fell to *baba*s and *daj*s, grandmothers and mothers, to attempt to arrange all marriages, and so when Plamen came to ask, Emilia's mother refused the boy. Of course it would be all right in the end. They weren't crazy about Plamen, but Emilia had gone off with him, and once she'd passed the test the girl would have to go. "Baba was furious with me."

Though the couple had already eloped, Emilia's family was not going to let such a treasure—with her enormous green eyes, thick black hair, and ample young body—go for nothing. Plamen was made to come back several times and ask again, which was a message to his family to beef up their "appreciation" of Emilia. When Emilia left the table to fetch her photo album, Elena elaborated: "The delay gave his family time 'to go rabbit hunting'—that is, to get together the presents, namely gold, for her *čeiz*."

Like Antoinette, Emilia lit up at talk of her *čeiz*. "I sat there with all my new things for the whole day, right there in the middle of the bed." It was easy to imagine Emilia as a homecoming queen on her float (the bed in her current flat was a draped, four-poster barge of diaphanous lilac fluff). From her wedding album Emilia gave me a picture of herself in all her finery, fronting her game-show haul of brightly colored, alternately furry and lustrous gifts. She wore a white dress and stiff, matching hat that resembled an upended bowl, with flowered tassels hanging down from it like stringed popcorn.

"What is that on your hands?" I asked, doubtful that the leathery, taloned fingers in the photograph could be those of a thirteen-year-old. It was henna—which was used intermittently to "clean" the bride during the week-long ritual of dances and naps and switches of clothes and, finally, an all-girl "baptism" down at the municipal baths.

"The longer the henna stays on your hands the longer your man will love you." Emilia shrugged. "That's what they say." The stained hands were echoes of the bloodstained sheet, which had already been made into a flag and waved through the quarter by a younger sister of Plamen, proud owner of one certified virgin-bride. The bloody flag seemed at odds with Gypsy timidity about sex. I believed the old man from Emilia's neighborhood who told me that he had never once seen

Emilia at age thirteen, in 1978, sitting with her čeiz (dowry)

his wife—and mother of their five children—naked. This same man had a tattoo covering the whole of his paunch: a tattoo of a voluptuous naked female. To the delight of a gathering of neighborhood kids, he could move his chubby torso and activate his tattoo muse, now a true belly dancer.

Looking through the pictures, Emilia was transported. Using Elena and me as stand-ins for bridesmaids, she conducted a demonstration. Led by Emilia, we moved solemnly around the kitchen table, one careful foot after the other, in a procession of the graces (who in the real thing would of course have been three virgins). Emilia had been too tactful to ask me herself, but later she had grilled Elena about my own marital and maternal status. Though infinitely more sophisticated than the women of Albania's Kinostudio, she too, Elena reported, assumed that I was barren.

Returning to the photo album, Emilia pointed to herself on the last day of her wedding week: this time she was turned out as the bride of the Western imagination, in a store-bought, star-bright lace confection. She was carrying her shoes. Seeing my puzzlement, Elena again explained: "After all the dancing, the girls collect." Those dainty slippers—yes, there was a snapshot—would soon be stuffed with new lev notes.

The next picture showed the child bride sitting in a painted wagon crammed with wedding presents and drawn by two horses, with a file of men walking behind. As I pored over the album, Emilia narrated: "We were then driven to Plamen's parents' house, where we would have to live." In the next shot, Emilia is stepping through a doorway— walking over her own threshold, I guessed—but instead of being carried she was herself carrying a small child in her arms, a traditional plea, according to Elena, for fecundity. Later, Elena would add what the photo didn't reveal. Emilia's prayers had already been answered: the perfect bride, she also carried a child in her belly. . . . The last wedding pictures showed Emilia at her final banquet. She is almost completely obscured by money—by the bills that well-wishing guests had pinned to the bride's dress.

There were no more pictures, but Emilia went on with her account of what sounded like one *long* wedding. "The next day my mother-in-law washed me and gave me a small glass of *rakia*." ("To toast her virginity," Elena professionally filled in.) Emilia remembered every detail of her wedding and described the events with fondness and pride—perhaps because, so soon after, things were to go badly wrong.

A week later, sixteen-year-old Plamen entered the army to begin his military service. In those two years they saw each other four times. And then, within six months of returning home in 1980, Plamen was sent away again; caught stealing a record player from a Polish tourist in a department-store cafeteria, he was slung in jail to begin a two-year sentence.

At this point in her story Emilia became animated in a new way (no more shaking laughter). "It was a long wait, and though I had Rumen"—her son by Plamen, who was now fourteen, with chipmunk cheeks, huge eyes, and dimpled chin, just like his mother—"it was not a happy time. Plamen's mother was a witch. I worked day and night, doing all the washing for the whole family, even while I was nursing. Finally I went back to my mother's, which caused a terrible scene. Plamen's father tried to get back the money he had spent on the wedding."

There are few taboos more strongly upheld among Gypsies than that against betraying a man while he is in prison. Plamen had no criminal record when he was sent down for two years; there was no doubt that being Gypsy affected the justice they were dealt, even though theirs were generally the pettiest of crimes. A resigned attitude is reflected in the multitude of Gypsy songs about prison life, and in the numerous prohibitions for those waiting on the outside. At fifteen, Emilia hadn't run off with another man—not yet. But leaving her mother-in-law was unseemly, and if her parents protected her it was partly because they felt that she had married beneath her.

When Plamen came home on parole, about six months into his sentence, he was unrecognizable. "He was blue," Emilia said. "From head to toe: he was *covered* in tattoos. He even had . . ." She could not say the words and so Elena, who knew the whole story, finished for her, "A *rat* tattooed on his penis."

A Gypsy man may ditch his wife, leaving her with only the stigma of having been left—and therefore with her stock drastically devalued. For even if the "divorcée" is still a teenager, she is now likely to land only a divorced man or a widower. Though it was she who would do the leaving, Emilia at fifteen was used goods. And she knew the score. After we had got to the tattoo episode, Emilia understandably lost her enthusiasm for the conversation, and it was left to Elena to tell me how it all turned out. With Emilia we talked about other things for a while, and then went back to Elena's apartment, where I was now staying. She was pleased that I was gripped by this tale, as she had been so many years before.

"There is another, important side to the story," Elena continued, without pause, as we sat on the floor, smoking BTs and eating stewed cherries out of a jar. "You see, Emilia has an older sister, Nadja. I never met her, but she was always referred to as 'the ugly one.' Now *she* was married years before, around the time that Emilia came with me on the trip to Varna. And then Boiko—Nadja's husband—dumped her." Soon it became clear that Elena, always an ethnographer first, was making an interesting point about traditional Gypsy mores. "And why was Nadja pushed out? Because she had failed to produce a child within a year. According to their custom, this was normal—Boiko was acting within his rights as a man." And while Elena talked and I took my notes, Vesselin did the dishes and got the children ready for bed.

"Nadja, kicked out with nowhere to turn, had no choice but to leave Sofia. She took the bus for Varna, and when this became known around the quarter the girls' father forbade even the mention of her name! On pain of pollution, you see." Although there were not so very

Stanka at home in Kostenbrau, 1992

many Gypsy prostitutes, Varna, the resort town of Elena's initiation, was famously the place they went. "But Emilia was not intimidated by her sister's example. As soon as Plamen was back behind bars, she revealed to her parents her love for Branko, a tall nineteen-year-old from Kostenbrau"—a village outside Sofia. And Branko was from another tribe, the Grastari, or Lovara.

Elena was in her element: "The Lovara are [or were] horse-traders. They were the most recently nomadic among our Bulgarian Gypsies, and, at least seasonally, they still are. They keep away from other Gypsies and sell cars and whatever—trade of any kind, gold, and goods for the black market. Some of them are incredibly rich. They regard themselves as the aristocracy and other Gypsy groups seem to agree. Emilia's new connection was a great excitement for her ambitious parents, and even though they knew the dangers, they put baby Rumen into the back room, and pushed Emilia out the front door."

Branko brought Emilia out to Kostenbrau to meet the family. Maybe if they could *see* her, Elena said, reconstructing the boy's reasoning, they would forgive her humble origins ("they weren't *bad*— Emilia's ancestors were brushmakers"; but they weren't great). "She was not received in the main house but instead waited with her flowered suitcase in the dirt drive, outside."

It was not difficult to persuade Elena to escort me to Kostenbrau, where this fancy family still lived. We took the half-hour bus ride out to see Stanka, Branko's grandmother, ostensibly to have my fortune done (Stanka was a famous fortune-teller). Willowy and dark, she had the appealing sallowness of an American Indian and wore her black braids tucked into her apron. I learned little about myself on this visit. But Elena managed to get Stanka to say something of the ill-fated "marriage" of Emilia and Branko. "The girl herself wasn't the problem," the older woman said. "It was how she was raised." Throughout our visit, Stanka's own daughters-in-law or granddaughters-in-law walked up and down the lot, laden with laundry and busily indifferent to us. These were people who used five bowls for washing, two more than the statutory trio, thus dividing not only men's clothes from women's but those worn above the waist from those worn below, and underclothes (in batches of men's and women's, washed separately). This group was strictly against marrying out—excluding not only *gadje,* but all other Gypsies.

"How do you know she will be clean?" Stanka put to us. "What does she know about it? Her people live in the city, in flats. They are settled." Though she didn't seem to recognize it, Stanka's own people were also settled. Travel featured largely in their lore, even if they hadn't budged in ages. This family ran the only restaurant in Kostenbrau—the first privately run place for many miles around. And they kept a large, brightly painted house in the town. It was the biggest on the main street. But they didn't live in it. We found Stanka where they actually stayed, round the back, half out-of-doors, the whole clan of more than a dozen people piled into two small trailer-type structures and surrounded by cars in various states of dissolution: picked over, reassembled, painted up, junked.

This scene, though only suggestive of the peripatetic life, gave a clue to why nomadic Gypsies have irritated governments and sedentary folk everywhere and for all time. Unlike settled Gypsies, whose livelihood depended on a steady relationship with the *gadje* among whom they lived, these took what they needed and moved on. (It was only among transients that swindling was a viable career.) In Kostenbrau, cars were being done up for a quick sale, as Stanka proudly confirmed. In the past, the defects of horses were disguised—oiled or touched up with a tar brush (the equivalent of fiddling with the odometer)—a practice documented not just by Gypsy folklorists but by Rom ethnographers.

We sat cross-legged on a mattress outside, and Stanka fussed with her pipe, finally abandoning it in favor of straight chewing tobacco. I'd come to have my cards read because I wanted to meet Stanka. I knew that Gypsy fortune-telling was pure theater—for sale exclusively to gullible *gadje*. No Gypsy would seek solutions through cartomancy or any other form of street corner or parlor divination. And so I hate to say that Stanka's professional assessment of my situation was eerily accurate. Perhaps, if nothing else, she was a good reader of the human face. But she told me, for instance, in detail, about the illness of someone close to me. When she finished I paid her and she put her cards away. Along with her fee they were stashed under her skirt in the hidden pocket that hung there, loose like a nose bag, beneath the top layer. (The pouch is called a *posoti*. "Designed for stealing," Elena said admiringly.)

Beyond us there was a great flat field. Gazing out over it Stanka looked ever more like an American squaw. She was training her eye on some kind of folly. I asked if I could take a look and she shook her head yes (always confusing in Bulgaria, because their shake for "yes" is ours for "no"). I padded out over the soft ground towards a curious classical apparition. It was a small cement structure, a mini-Parthenon, with pediment, portico, and columns in bas-relief. A great chain lock marked the entrance. This was the tomb of Stanka's husband. In the temple above his grave there was a pair of car seats, a stretch of deep-pile carpet, a selection of imported spirits and liqueurs, and a small TV. It hadn't been touched since he himself had been interred two years before.

Why didn't they live in their town house? Stanka shrugged. "It is for guests." That is, for prestige, like the fitted-out sepulcher which showed that they could afford to throw away furniture and a TV. "What matters is this view," she continued, putting an end to my impertinent questioning. I asked her where she had traveled as a young woman. "Oh, through thousands of fields in every direction: the Carpathian Mountains, the sea, the ocean to the west"—the Adriatic. She never mentioned countries by name.

Did she want to travel like that again, now that it is no longer forbidden? "Nah," Stanka replied, spitting out a great wad of tobacco to make the point. "It is impossible now: the pollution is terrible. It would not be pleasant. Now when I travel I go by car." Without turning her head she pointed her thumb in the direction of an old but still gleaming brown Mercedes in the drive, the most complete-looking motor on the lot.

It was in the brown Mercedes that, only a year after she had arrived in Kostenbrau, Emilia and her flowered suitcase had been returned to the old quarter in Sofia. Stanka had indulged her grandson. She had given Branko permission to marry Emilia—but only in a registry office, which among the Lovara counted for even less than it did among other Gypsies. There was to be no wedding, and certainly no bride-price (which, East or West, is index-linked to the price of a new car).

On the bus back into Sofia, Elena filled in once more. "Emilia became pregnant again, and she and Branko and then baby Rambo lived in the big house." Now I understood: the house was "for guests." "As soon as she had finished nursing, Emilia was sent back. Within six months, Branko of course married again—a big Gypsy wedding. And his family kept Rambo. Emilia tried to get him back. She went with her father and took him, and then, within a few days, the Grastari would come in the brown Mercedes and take him back again."

Emilia had fought for custody in the Bulgarian courts (which alone recognized her marriage to Branko), and won. "And Branko's family would steal Rambo back again." Against these Gypsies, Emilia couldn't win, and she knew it. She still had Rumen, but she had lost Plamen and Branko and Rambo. "Even her parents hadn't protested when she left home for the third time. There was nothing more that they could do for her."

For a while Emilia had stayed with Elena. Then she'd lived in Belgrade and got as far as Slovenia. Now, in the place where I had met her, Emilia and Rumen were living together; she had a *gadjo* boyfriend—a married man, I understood, who paid the rent and came and went. Like her older sister, Nadja, "the ugly one," Emilia was beyond the pale.

Before I left Sofia, I begged Elena to take me to meet Emilia's family, the people who had first taken in the disgraced Pioneer. She hadn't seen them herself for many years. The mother hugged Elena for a long time and burst into tears at the mention of her "little" daughter. "It is impossible at the moment for us to see Emilia. I don't even know where she is living." This wasn't true. Her mother did see her, but these visits were a shameful secret. Had Elena heard the good news, though? Emilia's mother reached into her pocket and pulled out a color photograph, a color photograph of "the ugly one." It was Nadja, Emilia's "barren" and (as it happened) quite pretty older sister, on the Varna boardwalk with her new husband, his trombone, and, in matching bonnets, their brand-new baby twins.

FOUR

The Least Obedient People
in the World

O N   S E P T E M B E R   20, 1993, in the rural Transylvanian village of Hădăreni, two Gypsy brothers, Rupa-Lucian Lacatus and Pardalian Lacatus, got into a fight with a young Romanian, Chetan Craciun, and his father, during which Chetan was fatally stabbed. In retaliation, other Romanians clubbed the Gypsy boys to death with pitchforks and shovels. A third Gypsy, Mircea Zoltan, was "carbonized at home" (as the English-language Romanian reports described it). A group of villagers then went on to torch fourteen Gypsy houses and to damage thirteen others, and that night the total of some 175 Gypsies, whose families had lived there for seventy years, were hounded out of town. Several policemen stood by throughout the evening's events; firemen arrived towards midnight, hours after the blazes began. The fire trucks had been kept away, according to the banished Gypsies, by order of the deputy mayor of Hădăreni, Gheorghe Bucur, who was himself a spectator at the burning. Some Gypsies tried to return to the village in the days that followed, making do in the bits of houses that remained; but within a few weeks they were again forced out. One woman who had tried to go home said she was spat on and jeered at, and was frightened for her life. "They ring the church bells whenever they see one of us," she said, "and we know what that means." A year later, most of the Gypsies were still in hiding, no one had been brought to trial, and the promise of an investigation was a dwindling memory.

The most dramatic change for Central and East European Gypsies since the revolutions of 1989 has been the sharp escalation of hatred and violence directed at them. There have been more than thirty-five serious attacks on settlements in Romania alone, mainly in remote rural areas, and mostly in the form of burnings and beatings, although some Gypsies have been murdered and children have been maimed.

Istvan Varga, for example, a three-year-old boy from Transylvania, was burned to death in a haystack.

Almost immediately after the revolution and the execution of the Ceauşescus, the attacks began, and swiftly gained momentum; settlements fell in a distended domino effect, reaching to the outer edges of Romania. In January 1990, in Reghin, central Transylvania, three houses belonging to Gypsies were set on fire, for no apparent reason, by Hungarians and Romanians acting together. On February 11, 1990, in Lunga, in eastern Transylvania, six houses were destroyed and four Roma died in a fight with local Hungarians. In the same month, near Satu Mare, thirty-five Gypsy houses were destroyed by Hungarian inhabitants of the town of Turulung. In April, in Seica Mare and Cîlnic, Gypsy quarters were devastated; in neither case did the attackers claim a motive, or even a pretext.

Map of Romania showing the locations of violent incidents against Roma

In June, hundreds of coalminers from the Jiu Valley in southwest-ern Romania, armed with clubs, were brought to Bucharest by special train. They were responding to the urgent call of the new president, Ion Iliescu, to end the first major protest against his government. Although the "enemies of the state" (sometimes also called "the ene-mies of democracy") were identified by officials as students, many singled out for attack were Gypsies, picked up miles away from the demonstrations. Roving bands of miners were escorted—by police-men, some victims would later report—directly from their trains into Gypsy neighborhoods. They beat them in the street and in their homes. The belongings of some Gypsies were stolen by the miners, who would claim that they were all stolen goods anyway. One preg-nant Gypsy woman told a Romanian reporter that she had been raped by a miner, or by someone posing as one, in the back of a truck and in the presence of her little niece. An old Gypsy woman had a fatal heart attack after watching her children and grandchildren being dragged from their hiding places under beds and in cupboards and badly beaten. As a final indignity, many of those who had been attacked were then arrested and thrown into Bucharest's Măgurele military barracks, which was being used as a temporary prison.

After the first visit of the miners to Bucharest (they were to return in September of the next year, 1991), a rural Roma camp in Cuza Voda, near the Black Sea resort of Constanţa, was ransacked and destroyed by a mob. The next month a Gypsy quarter was razed in Huedin, Transyl-vania. In October 1990, in Mihail Kogălniceanu, thirty-two Gypsy houses were destroyed by a mob of more than five hundred people: Tartars, Macedonians, and Romanians, groups who see themselves as ethnically distinct but united in their hatred of Gypsies, who here con-stituted a relatively small population that lived apart, in rude shacks on an open field with a dirt road drawn in a ring around it.

In the spring of 1991, fire swept through several towns near Bucharest and farther south, down by the Bulgarian border. In June Transylvania was again ablaze when, in a town called Plăieşii de Sus, twenty-seven houses were razed by a crowd of three hundred people attacking the Romany quarter. Nearby, villagers lynched an innocent man in retaliation for a murder believed to have been committed by another Gypsy. The more attacks there were, the less people seemed to mind—and, worse, the less coverage they attracted, even in the newly freed Romanian press. This wasn't just "compassion fatigue." Arson and murder became an "understandable," and acceptable, trend in a period of painful social transition. Doina Doru, until recently a reporter for *România Liberă*—a newspaper that had been a brave voice in the time of revolution but which had since been subverted by more tenacious nationalist political forces—dismissed the endlessly unfolding "Gypsy story." "How can we worry about the minority," Doina asked me, "when the fate of the majority is so uncertain?" Doina was frustrated about the bowdlerization of her paper, about the shrinking role for people like herself in a Romania that had yet to realize the high hopes, the total belief, of 1989. This was a common riff and plea throughout the former communist bloc. But the cynicism, and the hypocrisy, in Romania seemed acute. While "dissident" journalists balked and whined about the fate of "the majority," the state acted to keep the minority, including the Roma, alive in the public imagination.

Gypsies were a useful distraction from other conflicts. And so the state-owned television explained each attack on settlements as the result of "the provocation of Gypsy thieves," even where the Gypsies played no part in the tensions that cost them their houses, and sometimes their lives. Local authorities took their cue from Bucharest. In Transylvanian Tîrgu Mureş, for example, the fighting between Hungarians and Romanians resulted mainly in the prosecution of Gypsies. The March 1990 attempt by local Hungarians to restore a four-hundred-year-old Magyar high school to its pre-Ceauşescu Hungarian status was met with concerted opposition. Ethnic Romanians were bused into town, where they joined in an attack on the headquarters of the Hungarian Democratic Alliance, besieging some seventy members. When they were finally helped out of the building by the Romanian police, they were severely beaten—by "the entire delirious mob," according to one of the trapped Hungarians, the playwright András Sütő, who was permanently blinded in the attack.

Of the thirty-one people who were investigated in Tîrgu Mureş, five were Hungarians, two were Romanians, and twenty-four were Gypsies. (One of the Gypsies arrested, a man by the name of Arpad Toth, died in captivity. A day after he had spoken to a human-rights monitor from Geneva he was beaten in his cell, though the Romanian authorities claimed that the twenty-four-year-old had died of "natural causes.") In addition, sixteen other Gypsies were convicted of offenses such as possession of weapons and disturbing the peace. They were tried under Decree 153, which does not allow appeal to a higher court, and which, when it was first published in 1970, was directed against "parasites of the socialist order."

The bulibasha, *or traditional local leader, of the Roma of Tîrgu Mureş, Transylvania, with his grandson and probable successor, 1992*

Romania was inducted into the Council of Europe in 1993, a stepping-stone to full membership in the European Community, and one for which a sound human-rights record is supposedly the ticket of admission. The same year a government report stated that the attacks on Roma had "no ethnic connotations"; and a Romanian police report explained the violence as a response to "the horrible situation created by this ethnic minority." There were no prosecutions. Investigations were grudging, and grindingly slow—except when the criminals were Gypsies, or when there was a chance that they might be.

For a while things quietened down in Romania; but the torch moved on to Hungary and Bulgaria and even to Poland, with its tiny postwar Gypsy population. In Czechoslovakia, twenty-eight Gypsies had been killed in racial attacks since the Velvet Revolution which returned that country to democracy. The attitude of the whole region towards the Roma was expressed by Magdalena Babička, a contestant in a 1993 Czech beauty pageant from the industrial city of Ústí nad Labem. Asked what she'd like to be when she grew up, Magdalena won an ovation for sharing her dream of becoming a public prosecutor—"so that I might cleanse our town of all the dark-skinned people."

But the painful transition from life under communism could not account for all the violence. Nor was it always spontaneous or the handiwork of mobs. In Italy in 1995 several Gypsy children were maimed in driveby bomb attacks. And in Oberwart, a town seventy-five miles south of Vienna, four Gypsy men were murdered. A pipe bomb had been concealed behind a sign that said, in Gothic tombstone lettering, "Gypsies go back to India"; the bomb exploded in their faces when they tried to take the sign down. The first response of the Austrian police was to search the victims' own settlement for weapons; "Gypsies killed by own bomb," the papers reported.

Yet these incidents, however brutal, rarely roused the large numbers of eager participants at hand in Romania, where the momentum was soon to be regained. If only it could all be laid at the door of violent, blood-soaked Transylvania. But since the Romanian Revolution it was happening all over the country.

You didn't have to be Romanian to wonder: was there something about the Gypsies themselves that made them so wildly and universally unpopular? Apart from their shared identity as Gypsies, the victims of these attacks had little in common: they were from rich families and from poor ones; they were country folk and city-dwellers, criminals as well as obvious scapegoats; they were children, adults, and old people. None of the victims was a "traditional" nomadic Gypsy; most had been sedentary for centuries, and some were assimilated to the degree that they no longer knew Romani. Was it their reputation as thieves and cheats? But even an ethnic breakdown recently undertaken by the Ministry of the Interior attributed only 11 percent of crime in Romania—all of it petty crime—to the Gypsies, who constitute 11 percent of the population. So what was it about the Gypsies? And what was it about the Romanians?

Romanians have, as the Romanian writer Norman Manea put it, a "sprightly latinity"; Bucharest is "a metropolis glittering with irony and elegance, where misery is disguised as paradox and sarcasm as bantering cordiality." I recognized this among the witty, well-read Romanians I knew. (And "average" Romanians were literate, even literary, at least in the capital. In Bucharest, people routinely bought and sold the books of Emil Cioran, Mircea Eliade, and Eugene Ionesco from the same street tables that traded in the newly available newsprint pornography; it wasn't unusual for one vendor to hawk tube socks, lighter fluid, salami, porn, and the collected works of Jean-Paul Sartre.) In 1946 Ionesco, the Romanian playwright, offered another still apposite description: "In Legionnaire, bourgeois, nationalist Romania I saw the demon of sadism and stubborn stupidity incarnate before me." In 1951 the Polish poet Czesław Miłosz published *The Captive Mind*, a truly seminal work; one critic called it "the most penetrating account of the temptations of total belief." Miłosz tells us what happens to people who attempt to adapt to a totalitarian regime—the corrosions and implosions of forced hypocrisy. He writes about a man of the Eastern bloc—an intellectual, as it happens: "All about him in the city streets he sees the frightening shadows of internal exiles, irreconcilable, non-participating, eroded by hatred." This was the certain fate of the majority. "The Sacred Fire has not gone out," Miłosz wrote. ". . . [It represents] a rebirth of an already once-deceived hope." After visits to village upon riven village, it struck me that the attacks represented, above all, continued life for a stillborn revolution (now referred to by many Romanians as "the coup") in which, with the whole world watching, Bucharest had gone up in flames.

But the frustration began long before 1989. Romanians themselves had been under foreign occupation for sixteen centuries—a fact which has been obscured by the brutality of the Ceauşescus. Such a legacy put me inescapably (if portentously) in mind of a message that Primo Levi, as a prisoner at Auschwitz, hoped would "seep out" to free men: "Take care not to suffer in your own homes what is inflicted on us here." This was the spectacle of the region in the still-early postcommunist days: the violence of violated men.

Emilian of Bolintin Deal

IN APRIL 1991, in Bolintin Deal, an unremarkable rural town about forty miles northwest of Bucharest, a twenty-three-year-old music student was murdered and, in retaliation, eighteen houses were burned to the ground in a single night. Three years later, apart from the murderer, a Gypsy, none of the assailants had been prosecuted. On the contrary, the mayor of this small town had become a local hero: he was *un democrat nou*, eloquent on the principle of majority rule, "the will of the people" and his duty to protect it, and the (ethnic) Romanians' "right to self-determination," by which he meant their right to decide the ethnic composition of their town.

The villagers were unrepentant when I visited Bolintin Deal a few months after the attack. On the contrary, they were proud that their efforts had made the evening news and, better still, that the report had clearly inspired similar events across the country. The only people who were unhappy were the Gypsies, and even they sometimes tried to distance themselves from the Gypsy victims.

Homeless after the event, Emilian Nicholae, an intense young Rom from Bolintin Deal, now stayed in Bucharest, sleeping every night on a different floor. I kept missing him, but I persisted: he alone had been working to revive press interest and to provoke some legal response to the Bolintin purge, which in the glare of fresh and more violent attacks had been more or less forgotten. But he'd heard that an American journalist had been sniffing around his hometown, and he found me. From then on Emilian would appear now and again, without warning, in my borrowed Bucharest apartment; I'd hear his huffing as he thumped up the stairs, hoisting himself along the banister (one of his legs was several inches shorter than the other). If we were lucky, Igor Antip, a common friend, would be there to translate from Romanian, a safer bet than my fledgling Romani. Emilian would come in, so somber that he looked rather menacing, and begin talking where he had left off last time, as I scrabbled for a pen that worked.

Hugging his torso, he would lean against the wall and disgorge the catalogue of injustices that he had been filing away inside himself since his last visit. But he wasn't self-pitying; he was furious. And he was too tense ever to sit or even to unfold his arms, though occasionally he'd pause to recover his breath. Not only lame but vaguely tubercular, Emilian always sounded winded; his voice was muffled by a rasp, and it came over as an expression of persecution rather than respiratory malfunction. His disabilities seemed to leave him no energy for anything but the grave essentials; perhaps they also made him especially sensitive to pain.

He had worked until recently as a junk remover, but what really occupied him was the collecting of memories. Scores of old people had told him their experiences of the war, when some thirty-six thou-

Bolintin Deal, Romania, 1992. These sisters from a wealthy Rom family had been living with cousins in the town for the year since their own house was destroyed by a mob. They didn't go to school because they and their parents were afraid the girls would be attacked.

sand Romanian Gypsies—predominantly nomads—were deported to labor camps in Transdnistria, or over the Dniester River above Odessa in what is now Moldova.

Their stories were as vivid to Emilian as the sight of his family house in flames; and in his intelligent eyes they were firmly related. He had transcribed the accounts in longhand, on loose sheets. But that one night in Bolintin Deal, along with the twenty-six houses, ten years' worth of testimonies had gone up in smoke. Some of these stories had come from members of his own family. They were nomadic Gypsies who had been forced to settle as a condition of their return from the camps—first in another, northern town, and then again in the 1950s in Bolintin Deal.

Under Ceauşescu and Gheorghiu-Dej before him, as under most communist regimes across the region, it was somehow imagined that the very existence of the Gypsy minority could be "solved" by dispersing them among reluctant white communities. From the official point of view, the practice seemed to work tolerably well, at least so long as people were afraid to show their resentment.

Most foreign reporters have described the post-1989 purges of Gypsies as the expression of ancient ethnic hatred between ordinary people which had been temporarily suppressed by the communists. Wrong: in Bolintin, as in most other such villages, the purge may be seen as the inevitable consequence of communist policy. These were fake communities. Like all attempts to assimilate the Gypsies by force, resettlement had backfired.

Emilian despaired at the loss of his files. As far as he knew, no one else had attempted this sort of documentation, and the old people were dying off. Worst of all, he was positive that many of the survivors he had coaxed into recounting painful memories would not again be willing to talk, not even his own grandparents. Some wouldn't speak to him, after the burning of Bolintin, out of fear. Others wouldn't speak to him because these crimes remained unrecognized and unredressed; they were silenced not by fear but by bitterness. It was hardly surprising that most Romanian Gypsies I met mourned Ceauşescu, whom some even called Papa.

Unusually for a Gypsy, and unusually for a Romanian, Emilian believed that even if they might never be heard, amid all the lies that were still common fare here, the testimonies of survivors had an intrinsic value, and that if only they could be preserved their version would prevail. As if he was interviewing himself, he brought an impressive documentary tone to his own account of the murder. And he brought detail: he might have been a crow on a telephone line, watching over the crime.

"April 1991. It was nearly midnight: Mass was held late on Easter. When the service was over, the villagers walked home in the moonless night by lantern light. Some of the young people lingered in the square. Leaning on bikes, a few on the hoods of cars—Dacia sedans and Trabants. They stood around smoking and joking before following their parents home. By one o'clock the small piazza was cleared. Cristian Melinte, the music student, was the last to leave. He had trouble starting his car. When he finally pulled out onto the main road, the Bucharest-to-Bulgaria road, another young man flagged him down.

"In the dark Cristian Melinte could not make out the three figures behind the shaded man. They were two boys and a girl. All but the girl were Gypsies. The young man who had stopped him stuck his head in the passenger window and smiled." Emilian demonstrated. His theatrical power came from being able to talk about "the Gypsy" as a force, an abstraction, and one convincingly mysterious to himself as a storyteller. "The Gypsy greeted Cristian Melinte, who, he reminded him, had been in his brother's class in grade school. Although the music student recognized the Gypsy, he became tense: he could smell the plum brandy on the Gypsy's breath." Emilian paused to raise his hands and elbows and then he lowered his fingers and wrists in a strange three-part modern-dance move that I couldn't read. And then he explained: "The Gypsy held on to the half-open car window—with both hands, all ten fingers on the glass." Of course Emilian cannot have known this; he was inventing a gesture which conveyed both menace and fear of falling down.

"He was drunk. He asked for a ride. Cristian Melinte said no. He said the car wasn't reliable that night, that he didn't have enough gas, that he was already late getting home." Emilian paused again, now speaking and posing meaningly, in the manner of a court lawyer presenting his final summation to the jury.

"The girl, who began by saying she had been elsewhere, changed her story several times during the brief, unjuried trial. The testimony of the other two boys was rejected out of hand: they would, it was understood, defend another Gypsy, one of their own, whatever he might have done. All that was certain was that Cristian Melinte had been murdered, stabbed four times with a long, handmade knife." Emilian carved an arc in the air with his fingers wrapped around an imaginary handle, and then he looked at his hand as if he could see the knife. "The handle and the blade were fashioned from the same piece of iron. One of the Gypsies is now in prison, beginning a sentence as long as he was old: twenty years."

Days after the murder of the music student, twenty-six houses in Bolintin Deal were destroyed or badly damaged, beginning the ripple of retaliation which was to gain momentum, rolling through neighboring villages and eventually to distant parts of the country. A month later in next-door Bolintin Vale, eleven houses were destroyed, and later the same week, just down the road in Ogrezeni, another fourteen. All the houses belonged to Gypsies. In each case, the Romanian attackers were described as having moved through the village in a single swath, a creature soon so familiar as to seem organic: a low life-form, the mob—but one carrying burning sticks, and chanting.

In Bolintin Deal the mob had been methodical: the group had stopped and stood in a cluster like Christmas carolers outside each house, while the town electrician climbed the chimney and neatly clipped the roof cables so that an electrical fire would not catch and spread. Here, the Gypsies singled out were those who lived among the Romanians, as opposed to the greater number who kept to their own quarter, just outside the town line. This was an unspontaneous sort of purge, as if the murder of the music student had been a long-awaited spur.

Three months after the attack, I climbed over the untouched rubble and poked around the ruins of Bolintin Deal, looking for clues about the people who had lived here. Children's debris caught my eye: a doll with one arm off, a strangely pristine pink slipper. I could feel people watching me, usually surreptitiously, but one stood still and directly in my sight path, waiting to be noticed. He had a flat, bespectacled face, a defiant expression under a striped conductor's hat, and he clutched a pitchfork. His gaze, steady, pale, unblinking, told me that as soon as I gave him my full attention he was going to sort me out about what had really happened here.

For the past thirty-three years, Yuri Fucanu had been Bolintin's lone mailman. He had moved here in 1956, the same year as Emilian's parents and most of the other Gypsies who'd lost their houses. This was, I think, a way of saying that as a newcomer himself he had not started with the local prejudices against his neighbors. He elaborated: "We went to each other's weddings." And then, "After the revolution, they became more and more uppity." He meant that the Gypsies had started to make money.

"I have been working for fifty years and still I cannot afford a car. These people are not human. They have four cars. They tore their house down and built a new one, just like that, a big one in the same place in five weeks. You see? They have cars just to play with. They spend all their time taking cars *apart.*"

Most of the Gypsies who had been chased out of Bolintin had indeed made money in car dealing, a natural outgrowth of their traditional horse-trading talents, and one which had become big business since the collapse of the Eastern bloc. As in Bulgaria, it was also the Gypsies who ran the first privately owned cafés in town, two proud and cheerful establishments: neither was much more than a square of poured concrete with a few outside tables and a separate serving shack, but both were lovingly decorated—and in a single color scheme, one lavender, one yellow, right down to the napkins and fake flowers that crowded the small tabletops. The cafés should have been welcomed in this town, with its one gloomy communist-era youth club, but instead they were boycotted. This kind of behavior provided a rich theme for many Romanian jokes about Romanians. In Bolintin, however, envy had been elevated to an inopportune principle; here the stealing that everyone everywhere associated with Gypsies was suddenly and unanimously associated with capitalism. "Property is theft," as Proudhon said; and now, whenever I see a reference to the nineteenth-century French philosopher, I see a chinless Romanian postman with a pitchfork and a striped conductor's hat.

If private property, free enterprise, and café life were new in Bolintin, the concept of theft certainly wasn't. "Under the communists, everyone stole," Mircea Oleandru, the local chief of police, told me. "If we and the Party hadn't permitted it [for the same policemen were still in charge here], there would have been an uprising. But in those days there were limits." Oleandru was a big man with a thin crescent-shaped deputy called Dragusin. They were cartoonishly well matched. "Yes," Deputy Dragusin piped in uncertainly, "when Romanians stole, it was only for food." And so, the pair seemed to be saying, the crime of the local Gypsies was greed, ambition, ostentation.

A Romanian woman whom we found picking plums along the road confirmed that everyone stole before the revolution. "Especially the police. And they stole mainly from the Gypsies. They accepted goods for favors, such as passports. Officials wouldn't accept bribes from a Romanian; they would be too afraid. But from a Gypsy? Who would believe a Gypsy if he reported it? I know this because I had a gold chain that my husband gave me on our wedding day. It was stolen, and I am absolutely sure it was stolen by a Gypsy woman who used to live right there." She waved over her shoulder, down the road. "And sure enough, later I saw it around the neck of the chief of police's wife.

"The Gypsies are clever," she conceded, with equal measures of contempt and admiration. "Even as outcasts they profit. We Romanians don't have their guts. Here I am, picking plums for someone else. They pick these same plums to eat and the rest to sell for themselves. And who can stop them? The fire didn't help. Many of the Gypsies have returned, and they are maybe worse than before." Her hands were stained purple from the plums. As she spoke she rubbed her fingers steadily with a torn bit of rag, but the stain would not come off.

I continued my polling of the citizens of Bolintin. A young woman was leaning on a car in the diamond-shaped town square where the teenagers had loitered that fatal Easter. Twirling a lock of hair around one finger, she stuck with the more popular view: only the Gypsies stole. According to this girl, who wore an ersatz-Chanel T-shirt, they were so keen on stealing that they stole the same things twice. "From right off my clothesline they stole a pair of stolen jeans that I had bought from them."

Before long, the slanders became fantastic. As professional cheats, it was always the Gypsies who supposedly worked to prepare a public appearance or photo opportunity for the Ceauşescus, unfurling rolls of instant lawn over acrid ground and potting flowers in an inch of dirt before yanking them out and bagging them for the next stop on the tour. Of course it is hardly imaginable that Gypsies would have formed any part of the leader's retinue, but Romanians now whispered that Nicolae Ceauşescu himself was a Gypsy—the ultimate defamation.

The despised Gypsies of Bolintin Deal were referred to as Ursari, or bear-trainers, although it is unlikely that their ancestors had ever carried on that traditional Gypsy profession. I met a man from the other, older community, which had been allowed to remain on the outskirts of Bolintin, and asked him how the term Ursari had become an insult applied to the troublemakers. "It's a way of saying that these rich Gypsies were in thick with Ceauşescu. You see, in Romania, all the bears belonged to Ceauşescu." He laughed as he said this; it was a reference to the dictator's legendary pretensions as a great hunter.

In Bolintin, the Gypsies under siege were all relatively rich; stealing was not a consideration here. Those Romanians who despised them now did so because they were themselves unable to adjust to the new world of opportunity and risk. Most people had been too afraid to attempt such innovations during or after the communist period, and they had offered no resistance of any kind—to the Ceauşescus or to the corruption that survived their passing. If the violent attacks now occurred mostly in the remote countryside, it was perhaps in part because those people had had no chance to participate in any of the cathartic (if ultimately thwarted) uprisings in Braşov, Timişoara, or Bucharest. The Sacred Fire had not gone out.

A Social Problem

MIERCUREA-CIUC IS THE capital of Harghita County, Transylvania, the scene in August 1992 of a remote, rural purge and murder. It looks like any socialist-era town: run-down modern, with featureless public buildings and blank squares, and no trace of the fine fifteenth-century Gothic that may still be found in the old Transylvanian capital of Cluj (or, to a Magyar, Kolozsvár). There is no old-world Hotel Excelsior in Miercurea-Ciuc, no Grand or Europa, with a cathedral-size café. And yet here the new seems dated. And you feel that it has *always* seemed dated.

We were early for our meeting with the county's public prosecutor, Andrei Gabriel Burjan. Corin, my young Romanian translator, and I waited in his office: a bare room with a bare desk, a wooden filing cabinet, a large yellowing map of Harghita County, and a calendar with a plump pinup in a denim-theme bikini (red stitching, patch pockets). The same few girlie posters—always blondes—seem to feature in all public offices in Romania.

Maria Rusu, the stout, dark-haired colleague of the public prosecutor, asked why I was interested in Gypsies. "Can't you pick a better subject?" she snorted. "Why don't you write about us—about their victims?" I promised that I would.

Prosecutor Burjan was ruddy and alert and fortyish; he was nearly handsome, and well built, though oddly bottom-heavy. Perched comfortably on his desk, the prosecutor was concerned first of all to assure us that the recent attack on a small Gypsy community in his district had been a "personal conflict, a sort of pub fight that had got out of hand, not an ethnic conflict at all." The incident, he said, had been triggered by a bunch of Gypsies who demanded to be served at the local bar before some "majority Magyars." No one mentioned the more serious attack a year before in nearby Plăieşii de Sus, in which two men died and twenty-seven houses were destroyed. That also had been described as a "personal conflict."

"Such provocations are like pouring benzene on the tensions here," the prosecutor said, undermining his insistence that this "pub fight" had no racial dimension. The publican, a Magyar like most of his customers, had turfed the Gypsies out. And, "instead of behaving," they had responded by entering the plots of the Magyars, formerly collective land, and stealing everything. I interrupted him to inquire if the

Gypsies in Casin, the troubled village in his district, had received any plots of their own since 1989.

"Unfortunately they have not," Burjan conceded. "But this too is their own fault. The law provides that anyone who worked on a cooperative for at least three years is entitled to a share. The Gypsies never apply. They have hundreds of children all the time and none of them, adults either, are ever registered with the town authorities, as they are required to do by law." Casin was home to fewer than five hundred people. The Gypsies there were long-settled, not seasonally hired hands. In such a small town, of course everyone would know exactly who had worked in the local cooperative. But this was not the point. "They never have the documentation," the prosecutor explained. "They have no proofs.

"After the Gypsies filled their carts with Magyar corn and flagrantly drove through the town of Casin, the townspeople were moved to respond. And so you see this was not an ethnic conflict." Around 160 people had become homeless in the ensuing attack. "Do you mean," I asked, "that all the Gypsies whose houses were burned down were stealing corn that day?"

"It doesn't matter," the prosecutor explained. "Every one of them has committed crimes in the past. You see, the Gypsies have a consensus on crime. They live by theft. You may say that this does not justify the attack and I would agree, but I would also say that the villagers had no choice.

"I have evidence that Romanians are the least obedient people in the world," Burjan continued, changing tack. "The Dacian people are fighters, and what happened here was the work of plotters." The conflict at hand had been willfully recast as its opposite: an incidence of the wrongs committed against the beleaguered majority—who, according to some, notably the late dictator Ceauşescu, were descendants of a proud indigenous race called the Dacians. Resurrected by Ceauşescu because they had resisted the invasion of the Emperor Trajan in 101 A.D., the Dacians were nevertheless an odd choice to boost nationalism. For it was precisely their Romanness that for centuries has been a principal source of pride to a people whose language is basically the vernacular Latin of the Roman legion, and who live surrounded by Slavs and Turks.

Corin, though himself a tireless patriot given to expansionist reveries on the theme of Greater Romania, was growing reluctant to translate. "We are promised help and receive only insults," the prosecutor spluttered on, sparked by a fresh jolt of bitterness. In this he was right: both the indifference of the West, which had so recently cheered on these bravely won democracies, and the unbearable self-pity of the Eastern bloc were growing, and they were feeding off each other.

We left as soon as we had extracted from the prosecutor a promise to show us the official files on the Casin case, early the next morning. Falling into the darkening square outside, we walked in a gloomy silence across the plaza. Dead earnest, ever anxious to improve his English, Corin searched (to judge from his profile) for the perfect expression for pomposity: "This prosecutor, he is what you would call a 'puffy ass,' isn't it?"

Back in the hotel, the pleasure of the first cold beer was wrecked by the fact that a subsequent, identical bottle cost twice as much, and the one that I bought for Corin half as much again. It wasn't the seemingly arbitrary price hikes that were galling: it was the shamelessness of the bartender who boredly overcharged us. It could hardly be good business, but cynicism, or fatalism, was stronger here than common sense, and everyone seemed to cheat.

In Sibiu, where Corin came from, the place where Gypsies did their black-market dealing was known as Tsiggy-Diggy Street. (The *ţigani*, or Gypsy, traders of Sibiu specialized in digital watches, hence "Tsiggy-Diggy.") *Ţigan* was used as a verb which meant, among other things, "to rip off," just as its equivalent is used in the American slang "to get gypped."

But in truth swindling was so common in Romania that it was remarkable that the Gypsies, or anyone else, had managed to gain a reputation for dishonesty. The little kerchiefed *bunicuţa*, or granny, who stood in front of the hotel selling green bottles of "kiwi juice" out of a basket, was really and knowingly selling bottles of murky river water, complete with hairy river wildlife. Her Johnnie Walker was tea and corn syrup, and when you went to complain she was gone. But most people didn't feel pressed to cover up or disappear. The woman at the front desk asks for four to six hours to place your long-distance call, and then, when you check up on it four hours later, you watch as she tries for the first time and connects you right away. It's your own fault, though, because you hadn't thought to pay double or in hard currency, because you hadn't established a claim—that is, because you "had no proofs."

It remained a conjecture, but there was, I thought, a subtle difference between Gypsy rip-offs and Romanian ones. As was not the case for the cheating Romanian barman or telephone operator, shortsightedness and dishonesty needn't be a source of moral degeneration for the Rom. Not all Gypsies were engaged in trade. Some still repaired objects or made baskets or brushes or wooden spoons (and sent their wives to sell them in the market). Some were proud specialists who provided particular services, and, like the publican or the telephone operator, the scope of their jobs didn't change. But the job of the Rom traders was to make *money*—not baskets or brushes or copper distillers. And so they made any deal and sold any product. In the past it was horses; now it was cars, or digital watches. On some days, if he had nothing to sell, the trader might have to beg (or rather send his wife and children out to beg). This is not a source of shame; it is just another option, another way to do his job, which is making money.

Upstairs in the hotel, off the long corridor lit by a couple of naked bulbs, I have a room that I know well; it is like many other rooms in the decrepitly modern hotels of Eastern Europe. The narrow single bed is covered with a rectangle of two-inch-high orange fur and one square pillow the size of a linoleum tile. The blanket reaches just to the edge of the bed, so you have to make yourself small underneath it to stay covered. There's the shaky plastic night-table and the incongruous square-dance lamp with its flounced gingham shade. In the lamplight, the toy telephone. (This one is frankly ornamental, without a cord or a jack in sight.) There is a basin in the room and the tap drips. But there is no end of hot water, which makes up for everything. The square sections of false ceilings are so low you can punch them in without even standing on your toes. I kept dreaming that I was sleeping under a blanket of fire, and that as long as I stayed covered I would not get burned.

After the usual hotel breakfast of cucumber, cheese, salami, and boiled coffee, we went back to the public prosecutor's office and found only his stout dark-haired colleague, Maria Rusu. "Domnul Prosecutor has gone on vacation," she informed us impassively. No apology, no explanation, no nothing. "File? He left no instructions about any file. I am not aware of any file."

We had another appointment that morning with the county chief of police, and we went to headquarters to wait. In a thin corridor with facing rows of welded-together chairs, we sat opposite an elderly Gypsy man and two younger men, obviously a father and his sons. The matted look of the younger men suggested a long wait, confirmed by the debris all around them, a dozen cigarette butts on the floor, scraps of food and crumpled wrappings, empty soda cans. A young police officer emerged from a closed door. The father immediately rose to his feet, removed his hat, and smoothed his mustache with a long-nailed thumb. He stood and waited with his feet together and his hands crossed in front of him in the humble position that many people adopt in the presence of officials. The policeman took his time to acknowledge the old man, making his slow way towards him, with a stopover at the receptionist's desk and an ostentatious riffling of a few papers and a pause at the water fountain. It seemed extravagantly off-hand. He did not ask the old Gypsy into his office but spoke to him there in the waiting room. He didn't seem even to see the sons. I couldn't understand what the policeman was saying, but his whole body was rigid with refusal. The old man, still holding his hands in front of him like a sharecropper, nodded and looked down at the shoes of the young policeman and said over and over: "*Da, Dom Capitan, da*"—"Yes, Sir Captain, yes sir . . ."

I had made my appointment with this man's superior the week before, from Bucharest; and he canceled it himself just after the disappointed Gypsy trio had shuffled out (leaving a disgusted bottle-blonde secretary in a tight skirt and spike-heeled evening shoes to pick up their garbage). "I cannot discuss these events with you," he said, even as he fingered my press card, because "a private person does not have a right to know." There was nothing to be done.

Corin said that the false ceilings in the hotels were hung low to make enough room for the lumbering flunkies who recorded conversations. I myself had heard the boys from the Romanian Information Service—a milder reincarnation, everyone supposed, of the dreaded Securitate, or secret police. Through the phone tap they could be heard chatting and unwrapping their sandwiches, lending a train-station din to a call I'd made out of the Bucharest apartment of a journalist friend. Romanians are paranoid, but they are also still having their mail opened for them. The low-tech element made the bugging a bit of a joke, but after several months in Romania I certainly stopped making fun of conspiracy theorists. The whole town seemed to have shut down on us, and it didn't feel like a coincidence.

We could tell we were in an Hungarian district, according to Corin, because there was so much green. Not just the verdant hills but the rounded felt hats; even the houses were painted green, with terra-cotta fish-scale roofs partially hidden behind high, filigreed green wooden gates at the road's edge. It was easy to pick out the Hungarian Gypsies. The men wore their hair to the shoulder, and unbrushed. The older ones wore high black boots and belts four or five inches deep like weightlifters' supports, fastened low over the hip; and their white shirt-sleeves were billowing. In fact, everyone around here seemed to be out of a play about nineteenth-century rural life, and the belled horse-and-carts go clip-tinkle-clop, providing the corny soundtrack. In our lone car, we slowed down for a herd of donkeys in the road, a couple of them shaky-legged foals.

"Ugh!" Corin snorted; an odd reaction to such a sight. "Bulgarian donkeys."

"How do you know they are Bulgarian?" I asked.

"The donkey is a terrible, *Oriental* animal," he explained. "Turkish, Bulgarian. In Romania we have horses."

This was as close as Corin would get to admitting that Transylvania was not altogether Romanian, but the nationality issue was never far away. He judged the status even of animals according to their perceived foreignness. Corin's last name was Trandofir, or "rose" in Turkish, but to him the "foreign" still smelled foul, and, like most otherwise liberal Eastern Europeans, he had a blind spot about Gypsies.

I asked Corin if he had ever been outside Romania (he spoke the weirdly perfect English learned exclusively from books). What, I wondered, could he really understand by the idea of the "foreign"? He said he had traveled abroad once, just after the revolution, to Strasbourg. What had impressed him most on his first foray into the West were the Romanian Gypsies he'd seen there, begging at the train station. Our car swerved under the force of his indignation when he recalled the spectacle: "And can you believe it, they had a little sign saying, 'Please help us, we are *Romanian.*' "

Of course many Gypsies also resent these beggars: they are the only Gypsies that most Europeans see, and are taken as repesentative of all Gypsies, who regard themselves as neither victims nor parasites. Equally, Corin considered it a horrifying notion that to the outside world Romanians were no better than a bunch of Gypsy panhandlers—or indeed than Gypsies of any description: no better, no different. In *Civilization and Its Discontents* Freud famously pointed out that intolerance finds stronger expression in small differences than in fundamental ones. "The narcissism of minor differences": this was Corin's pain, and it was the humiliation of a beggar nation—a nation on the wrong side of Europe. Their revolution was a good show, the best in the region, and now it seemed to many disappointed Romanians that they were just passing around the hat.

I told him that I often encountered Americans abroad whom I found objectionable but could still recognize as Americans. A pointless analogy. Like many Europeans, and like most Eastern Europeans, Corin defined nationality—that is, belonging—by tribe, by blood and culture, not by territory, and certainly not by citizenship. We drove on in silence, and Corin started to sing Romanian folk songs. But again it was his odd and earnest questioning that recovered our buoyant mood. "In your country, Kenny Rogers is considered a peasant, isn't it?"

As if the thickets of ill feeling weren't already hard enough to penetrate, we found that we needed another translator—most people in this region spoke only Magyar. Luckily we soon tracked down Tibor Bodó, the sympathetic journalist who had covered the violence for the local paper, *Harghita Népe* (*Harghita News*). The three of us drove to Casin, along an excruciatingly bumpy and meandering road. But it was bright and clear and fresh, a high-summer day. On either side of us, rising up across open fields, were great golden totem poles, ten or fifteen feet high: Transylvanian haystacks.

"You see it everywhere," he said, referring to the prejudice—"for example in the army. When I was doing my military service, it was always the Gypsies who were pulled out for the worst jobs. They were especially badly treated by the lower-ranking officers. Under Ceauşescu"—Tibor laughed—"only Gypsies and intellectuals were separated out. It was a revelation. Like most people I had never really met Gypsies before the military service. Mostly they were warm and funny, many fantastic musicians."

Tibor lit up, suddenly remembering a Rom metalworker who had been attached to the army. "He would say, 'When I am working the iron, I am dancing—a czardas, or a German march. Copper is more of a French drill.' And when two people were needed to handle a big job—a cauldron, say—it was a waltz. And he would tap the rhythm on metal: you needed a beat to work to. It wasn't just the metal, but the object as well; a horseshoe was always a czardas"—that hysterically jaunty, quintessentially Hungarian rhythm. I knew that metalworkers from many cultures—not just Gypsy Cains—were regarded with suspicion, as hated outsiders. In the car, I told the others that Gypsies had commonly been called not only spies but incendiaries. I told them the story of the glowing, red-hot nail. But whatever their ancient occult connection with fire, it was no longer the Gypsies at the bellows.

Before becoming a journalist, Bodó had taught history and literature to high-school students. The Gypsies, he told us, would only come if free food or clothes were being given out. "There is the real problem. It is nothing to do with ethnicity, it is a matter of education. They don't go to school, and so from the beginning they are outsiders. They never worked in the cooperative, but outside it—for example, trading horses or making metal tools for those who did work the land. . . ." He trailed off. "Everyone was more patient before the revolution."

Tibor was right; but in these parts education itself was an ethnic problem. What language would Gypsies be taught in? Magyar in Transylvania and Romanian everywhere else? What about Romani? Gypsies dropped out of school for the same reason that most people drop out of school. They failed at it. And they failed because the language used in school was not the language most of them spoke at home. No special language provisions were made for them (as they were for the Hungarian and German minorities). So they lost their language, or their chances, or, more usually, they lost both. Although it is slowly changing, this was the case all over Central and Eastern Europe, with the result that in many places (most notably in Bulgaria and in the former Czechoslovakia) Gypsy children from the first grades were automatically stuck into special schools for the mentally handicapped. They weren't retarded, but they were handicapped: they didn't speak the language, and the deficiency had become a widespread excuse for segregation and indeed incarceration—one not likely to be fought by illiterate parents, themselves accustomed to such frank dispossession.

Casin was a row of houses on either side of a dirt road. A general store stocked a few tins of food and coffee beans and tobacco. There was a solid, low-built church; no sign of the famous pub (which was farther along). Five old men in hats sat on the town bench, watching the road. We stopped outside the last house, the home of a woman that Tibor had interviewed for his story in *Harghita Népe*. She had worked in the bar where the fight had ignited on the evening of the attack.

Tibor banged hard on the green wooden gate and soon the lookout window—a doll's-house door in the middle of that solid gate—flew open. Peering down through this junior door I made out the flared socket of a large snout, and then the albino eyes of a very large sow. Mrs. Horváth opened up and, leaning her whole weight against this extraordinary animal to prevent her escaping, invited us in.

Mrs. Horváth settled us around the small kitchen table; she laid out four white porcelain thimbles and set to making some strong coffee to put in them. The ceiling was sweetly stenciled in a geometric pattern of red, white, and green, the colors of the Hungarian flag. In one corner stood a tall white-tiled stove. Painted figurines of minstrels in traditional Magyar costume were on display, evenly spaced along a shelf over a series of red-and-white embroidered linen handkerchiefs that were draped over the ledge like a row of football-team pennants. Mrs. Horváth was a widow, but it was easy enough to imagine that she had always lived alone, so complete did she seem in her cozy parlor, passing out cups of treacly coffee.

"They are vermin," she concluded at the end of a vigorous deconstruction of the Gypsy character. "They cannot live among decent, civilized people. They cannot feed their horses and their huge families, and so they steal. For years we gave them food, regularly, and we accepted this as a kind of tax. In the past, people didn't even report the crimes of Gypsies. They were too scared. But now we have a choice. This is a democracy, and we will not receive them back in our village." Mrs. Horváth had not herself thrown fire on the houses, but she had looked on, along with the rest of the village. "They are far too uppity; it had to be done." She admitted, though, that the problem had not been solved. The Gypsies would return, these or others, and they wouldn't change, but the other townspeople felt better for having acted; there had been catharsis.

Mrs. Horváth described how the church bells had rung out, calling all the villagers together at sundown, as planned. The local priest said a prayer before they all set out to the Gypsy settlement. "It was the obvious meeting place," she pointed out, "because the Gypsies never go to church." We knew that the police had not intervened, and clearly no one worried about reprisals. "The police here walk with their hands deep in their pockets," Mrs. Horváth said, rising to clear our cups. And where did she think the Gypsies should go if they had to leave? To hell. "Where their ancestors are waiting for them."

This vehemence was alarming only because it came from an elderly widow in a red-and-white embroidered apron. Her broad and powerful calves, however, visible as she whipped her sow into its slop garage, also looked like they belonged to another body. "The Gypsies are not human," she remarked with some authority.

. . .

László Gergecy was one of the four policemen responsible for Casin as well as three other hamlets in the valley. "It is a very sad situation," he said, leaning against the wall behind his desk. "But we cannot make them go to school. We fine them and they don't pay; no one has any money. They are isolated and without organization or friends here. But what could we four policemen do?"

He didn't mention the posters, nailed to trees, rallying all villagers to "defend Casin," or the church meetings in which arson attacks were discussed like bake sales. The failure here wasn't so much an absence of manpower as a lack of will and a fatalistic sense that this purge was inevitable.

"Punishment would not be effective here," Officer Gergecy concluded. "You see, we did arrest three people, one suspected of beating to death the young Gypsy [in Casinul Nou]. The whole town camped out here, outside this office, for three days, until they were released." Public Prosecutor Burjan hadn't even mentioned this murder in his rundown of the "pub fight" in his district. The television accounts spoke only of Gypsy thieving, not a word about the death of a young man. And though no one in the town denied that "someone" had died, everyone we spoke to brushed it off, as if he had had his own reasons for getting killed, and it was no concern of theirs.

In Vălea Lăpuşului, or Valley of the Wolves, in the north of the country, another Gypsy community—nineteen houses—had been burned out in retaliation for a horrible crime by one of its occasional members, a man called Oaste Moldovan, who had raped a young woman in her ninth month of pregnancy. Moldovan had a previous conviction, and had been doing time before he returned to the village in 1988. He was released on January 26 of that year on a whim of the late dictator, who had chosen to celebrate his birthday with the randomly magnanimous gesture of pardoning thousands of convicts. The crime of the local Gypsies was to have been slow in turning the rapist over to the family of the raped girl—and, accompanied by the police, they in turn led the mob to the Gypsy quarter. But in Casin, where the crime seemed to be lack of deference to the peasants, as well as extensive small-time pilfering, the punishment was no less severe: the whole group—mainly children—had to go.

Still, you had to feel a little sorry for the slim policeman, alone in his roadside lean-to. He had no car, no telephone, and no partner. In fact, he had nothing except his badge, which in this new era, and in this desolate valley, had no heft.

As we walked down the road to the church, people stopped and stared at us: stout toothless women with crossed arms and kerchiefs knotted at the chin; men with tools plucked from a museum of medieval agriculture.

What is wrong with your Gypsies? we probed, asking for trouble. "Even people who work all day don't have horses like theirs"; "Even the smallest Gypsy children are thieving monkeys"; "They are all millionaires"; "They beat us when we tell them to get off our land"; "They should go back where they come from"; "Why are you foreigners so interested in those worthless Gypsies?"; "They are not human"; "Killing Gypsies is charity, not murder." . . . As we walked away, one woman shouted after us, apparently thinking that last remark a bit rich. "We accept that they are human, but their behavior is not."

"Uncivilized": this was the most common charge against Gypsies. As proof, people would point to the apartments that Gypsies had been assigned and then destroyed. "They kept horses up there," a man in Baia Mare, in the north of the country, had told me, indicating a third-floor flat with scorched windows, recently evacuated by a Gypsy family. I had seen a horse on the upper floors of a modern block in Bulgaria. It seemed incongruous but not unreasonable: where else could a horse be kept? As on council estates in the West, anything left outside would immediately be stolen. "They make their Gypsy fires right on the living-room floor. You see the marks." Although I could think of other plausible reasons for the black streaks, it was true that Gypsy tenants often did break down walls (and rip out windows and window frames and doors . . .)—sometimes to accommodate their larger families, but also certainly because they felt nothing for these appointed places, these alien modern blocks—where they were slotted in among contemptuous neighbors. The flats were as depressing in their way as the cardboard box dwellings of some Gypsies, but they bore no resemblance to the neat and lovingly painted houses of most Gypsies everywhere, however poor.

Gypsies were resented partly because many of their social betters believed that they had been privileged by the communist regimes. But the Gypsies had also been targets of Ceauşescu's program of social engineering, known as "systematization." Romania was to be reorganized on principles of production. Zones (and their inhabitants) were outlined according to their potential for industry, agriculture, or grazing. Systematization called for the leveling of whole districts: the policy was haphazardly carried out, but in the event some seven thousand rural communities were eliminated and their populations removed to cities.

Systematization reinforced earlier attempts to settle all Gypsies, which began almost immediately after the communists gained control in 1947. Most Gypsies were by then already settled; nevertheless, as in the rest of the world, they were *perceived* as wanderers, one and all, and the Romanian government moved to halt the last of the nomads by confiscating their horses and carts. These of course were not only a mode of transportation but a source of livelihood; the ideological mandate of the time, however, held that it was more important that Gypsies be stationary than gainfully and independently employed. Forced settlement failed to achieve assimilation; instead it created a new class of dependents on the state.

Some Gypsies were put into houses vacated by ethnic Germans, who were gradually being "bought" back by the German government, as part of that country's constitutional right of return for all of its ethnic members. The departing Germans were often more prosperous than other groups, and the fact that their houses were allotted to those on the bottom of the social heap added to, and in some places created, the enormous resentment that continues to grow.

It might have looked like favoritism, but this wasn't how the Gypsies saw it. Traditional settlements were destroyed, along with ancient organic networks of families with their mutually sustaining professions. Though the assimilationist policymakers of that era did indeed seek to "normalize" Gypsies by placing them in jobs and accommodations and even political positions that they would not independently have either sought or achieved, at the same time they outlawed all traces of their "backward" culture.

Nicolae Gheorghe, a Romanian Gypsy and a sociologist, recalls his first visit to the new communities. "When I first saw such areas, I was genuinely shocked by the misery there. So many people are concentrated in such a small amount of space. The blocks of flats were built in bad condition. Water is not running. Some Romanians live in these conditions as well, but mostly Gypsies. The result is the deterioration of social life."

And now, in the postcommunist period, Gypsies would not only be the last in the queue for jobs and position and schooling; the burnings seemed to suggest that they shouldn't be allowed houses at all.

.   .   .

"Even God is fed up with the Gypsies," Father Menihert Orban announced, sitting at a table in the cool vicarage of Casin. "They are pagans, heathens." This waxy, frail-looking priest was ethnically Hungarian, like more than 90 percent of the local residents, but he could speak Romanian, and clearly understood the conversation in Romanian between Tibor and Corin. However, the Father refused to speak to Corin directly, in the national language, also their only common language, and this enraged Corin. Here we were talking about "the Gypsy problem" while these two men, a clergyman and a law student, were locked in their own ethnic battle, unable even to look at each other, and speaking only through the fast-tiring Tibor. Father Orban pressed his flat, papery fingertips together, and kept an unblinking watch on our Hungarian.

"Surely," I said experimentally, "the Gypsies present a great challenge to a Christian leader." Corin turned my English into Romanian, and Tibor relayed it in Hungarian.

"They don't come to us," each responded in his turn. "While Hungarians come to church, the Gypsies drink. The entire village was here in my church the morning of the incident. Not one of them a Gypsy. It is not normal for people to live in fear of a minority. They had to be taught humility."

Less than 5 percent of Casin's population was Roma. Why were they so frightening to the rest? Was it because they stole "Magyar corn" and potatoes? Or because they were uninterested in industrious peasant life and, worse, indifferent to its censure? Father Orban gave a clue: "We cannot help them. They are different. They are ineducable." And, it didn't need to be said, in this isolated hamlet, a tug-of-war between Bucharest and Budapest offered nothing like the primitive satisfaction of burning down the settlement of those with no capital at all.

The son of an American Presbyterian minister told me how, in Indiana in the 1940s, his mother would say to him, "We don't hate people, we hate what they *do*." "What about Hitler?" the ten-year-old asked his mother. "Yes, even Hitler," she replied. "We don't hate *him*, we hate what he *does*." Around here, especially in the countryside and in eternally contested Transylvania, what you were—a Hungarian, a Romanian, or a Gypsy—was the most important thing about you. Who you were was identical to what you did: being a Hungarian, being a Gypsy. And the Hungarians and the Romanians hated the Gypsies, whatever they did.

We went last to see the few remaining Roma of Casin, and, after another day of measuring hate, I confess that I had run out of sympa-

A Kalderash girl from Sintesti, Romania, 1994. Her back-tied head scarf and gold coins show that she is married.

thy. The Gypsies were bound to be at least as bad as their accusers, I felt; chances were they deserved each other.

A hundred yards up a climbing dirt path we came upon a small single-room house, a new log cabin, all alone on a gentle hill. Completely isolated, it spoke almost too eloquently for its beleaguered inhabitants. It was pathetic. Then the Gypsies appeared, ducking out from its low door, one at a time. One large family—seventeen people—had returned to Casin and had built this house, fully intending to remain on the site of their old settlement, where only a couple of months earlier sixteen houses had been torched.

It wasn't hard to see why the Czacky family wanted to stay where they were—where, they claimed, their family had lived for many generations. Though they themselves looked poor and ragged, the setting was spectacular. Dotted with ancient trees, the wide-open views of low, terraced hills gave over to golden swaths of sunflowers in the distance. Usefully, in the other direction, there was a lookout over the hostile town. Just below the house on the hill was a dense copse bordered by a bright stream. In the water was an outcrop of some kind. A large rock? No, a small island. Several Gypsy children played there, sitting in the middle and hugging their knees, or standing in the stream holding

The Czacky men, September, 1992, Casin, Transylvania: This was the only family that returned to the settlement, where all sixteen houses belonging to Roma had been torched a few months before. Along with their women—seventeen people in all—they lived in a single-room log cabin which they built themselves.

on to the patch of ground with both hands as the water washed over their legs. Looking down towards them I thought of an entry that I had come across in an archive in Bucharest, from the diary of M. A. Demidoff, a Russian tourist of the Romanian principalities in 1854. He described a sighting of some *aurari*, or gold-washers.

> . . . from the lonely places where such Gypsies lived, the ones that interested us most were the *aurari*, scattered all over isolated islands . . . washing without rest the sands of the Danube, looking for minuscule pieces of gold. We moved closer to look at these poor miseries, with no shelter but their hair, and we learned that they are doing this for all their lives and, our guide told us, that they are paid only 15 centimes a day.

They were unusually tall and thin, the Czackys, and the deep-creased brown skin of the older members gave them a proper connection with the surrounding landscape of old trees. The women wore their black hair long. All the men wore hats, and mustaches as soon as they were able. One shyly smiling boy, with matted cupid locks and only a dirty fuzz on the upper lip, wore a fancy French shirt of dark blue with a flower pattern—a woman's designer shirt, with seventies droopy lapels, but a smart thing all the same. Though only a Westerner could instantly recognize the label status of the blouse, the impact of such finery on the villagers must have been considerable. I had heard that a French Catholic charity had sent duffels of old clothes here just after the attack. Indeed there were still a few French Jesus pamphlets fluttering in the shrubs. This foreign aid was brought expressly for the Gypsies, or for the few who remained, and the smoldering peasants could only look on in disbelief: they were misunderstood; the outside world, it must have seemed, had taken the wrong side. It was hard to believe that anyone could envy or even particularly resent these destitute Gypsies, but there it was, splashed over that flowery French cotton shirt.

Leaning or perching on a wooden cart, rangy figures peered suspiciously out at us as we approached, though they were quick to take in our friendly sign language. They didn't want to talk about the violence. "Before," a thoughtful older man, perhaps the head of the family, told us, "the cooperative belonged to everybody, and there was enough for all. Now they tell us we have nothing. But this is where we live." They belonged to this vast open space; the villagers kept within the confines of their fenced lots, all along the town road.

Our conversation was soon over. Even with two translators, it was extremely difficult to communicate. Tibor struggled to get their meaning. This, it suddenly became clear, was the salient feature of their separateness: they spoke no Romanian, only a poor dialect of Magyar, and no Romani. They were cut off from their Hungarian neighbors, from their countrymen, and from all their fellow Gypsies, whose burgeoning organizations in distant Bucharest were completely unknown to them. Without language they were as other as animals, and that is how people saw them—the pig lady, the priest, the policeman, the peasants in the road.

As we walked away, back down the track to the main road, one of their women came jogging after us, panting and repeating something over and over: *leenda*, she seemed to be saying, *leenda, leenda*. Yes, she wanted to know if I knew "Linda"—I was American, wasn't I? It emerged that, a couple of years before, this young woman had sold her baby to an American woman named Linda—or at least she thought she had. She had been promised a thousand dollars by a man who had come to her when she was pregnant for the sixth time. She was in tears now. What about? About the baby, about the money that never came, about her powerlessness here in this world? The illegal baby market was still going strong in 1990; it was entirely possible that some desperate American couple had paid tens of thousands of dollars in cash for this Czacky baby.

You used to see these trusting twosomes in the lobby of the Intercontinental in Bucharest, just off the plane, waiting to be relieved of their dollars by some smooth-talking baby-dealer. Sometimes they even got their baby, presumably from one of Romania's many orphanages (desperate places, overwhelmingly populated by Gypsy children—a fact that has been ignored by the flock of reporters who have filmed and filed reports of the large population of unwanted children created by Ceauşescu's mandate for population growth). I had never even heard about the mothers; they didn't seem to figure in the story. I hoped there was a grateful American woman named Linda, for suddenly it seemed that no place on earth could be worse than this beautiful valley. *Linda*, she kept insisting in a terrible, rising voice; Linda was supposed to send her a picture of the house where her baby son now lived. Surely I knew her. I told her I was sorry but I didn't, and finally we tore ourselves away.

Slavery

I SPENT MORE THAN a week in Sibiu, a typically Central European, German-founded town in Transylvania, while Corina, my new translator, was being tormented back in Bucharest by armloads of photocopied documents about Gypsies in the Romanian territories over the past five hundred years. Between visits to devastated communities I searched the local library and municipal archive, looking for precedents for these troubling events. Taking time out for lunch, or after closing time, I'd stroll through Sibiu's lively market. One fat Gypsy lady squatted on a small stool that disappeared completely beneath her folds; she was selling elaborately carved wooden spoons, made by her husband out of the palest pine and left unstained and so soft that you could add your own markings with the lightest press of a fingernail. At the other end of the market, a cluster of formidable women—Kalderash Gypsies, to judge by their traditional long, flowered skirts and headscarves—sold packets of contraceptive pills and bought hard currency. You didn't go to their corner for browsing.

Their faces reminded me of another Gypsy—Panch, a boy of seven or eight, whom I had met back in Sofia's main train terminal. Panch's name means five in Romani: he was, simply, his mother's fifth child. But he lived far from home now, together with a dozen other Gypsy children—glue-sniffers and prostitutes—in the dripping subterranean labyrinth of the station's cellarage. Panch was known to all the kiosk keepers on ground level, who regularly gave him cigarettes and buns and candy from their stock. Before showing me the lower quarters he scanned me for detachable parts, returning always to the Swatch fastened to my belt loop. Continually scratching himself and winking with ticks, he seemed incapable of any recognizable emotional response; he was a child but his eyes were divested of innocence. He was other.

The Gypsy women in the Sibiu market were more expressive than Panch—more menacing and more fearful, with their hard mouths and timorous eyes—but *all* their faces, I thought, reflected centuries of unrelieved hate, the expression of the Roma's deep "enemy-memory" (as one historian has called it, in reference to the experience of American blacks). This look is so much the norm that, to most other Central and Eastern Europeans, such a demeanor gives the definition of what it is to be a Gypsy—the black black-marketeer—a stereotype of the

Gypsy "other" no less pervasive here than the flamenco dancer or fancy caravan-dweller is in the West.

On the day I finished photocopying the last rosters of Gypsies owned or exchanged or sold by this or that eighteenth- and nine-teenth-century boyar, or landowner, another attack on Gypsies took place here in Transylvania: the terrible lynching of the two Lacatus brothers, together with the burning to death of another young Rom in the village of Hădăreni.

As usual, the most jarring aspect of the pogrom was the proud candor of the villagers and town officials: "Not human"; "a social problem." One cannot help but think in this context of Nazi dogma—of "lives unworthy of life" (an ideology enthusiastically taken up by the fascist wartime leader Marshal Ion Antonescu). But the systematic, broad-scale dehumanization of the Gypsies in these parts goes back at least to the fifteenth century, to Prince Vlad II—Dracul, father of the Impaler.

In September 1445 Prince Vlad Dracul (Vlad the Devil) captured from Bulgaria some twelve thousand persons "who looked like Egyptians" and took them home to Wallachia, "without luggage or animals"; thus he became the first wholesale importer of Gypsies as slaves. The next recorded batch of Gypsies was the booty of Stefan the Great, dubbed "Athlete of Christ" by Pope Sixtus IV for his crusades against the Turks. In 1471, after a great victory over his Wallachian neighbors, the Prince transported more than seventeen thousand Gypsies back to Moldavia.

Stefan preceded his cousin Dracula in the use of his favorite tor-ture: following this same battle, he had twenty-three hundred of his prisoners impaled through the navel. If Gypsies on the whole were spared this gruesome end, it may have been because they were retained to forge the spears. The time of Dracula (1431–76) preceded full-blown slavery in the Romanian principalities; but the groundwork had been done. There were certainly models for the legions of Gypsy slaves in Bram Stoker's *Dracula* (digging and packing the Transylva-nian soil that will keep the Count "alive" on his travels). Furthermore, the historical Dracula, Vlad Țepeș, seems to have believed that the Gypsies were a particularly fearless (or foolhardy) class of warrior. In the epic poem *Țiganiada*, by Ion Budai-Deleanu (1760–1820), it is recorded that Dracula led an army of Gypsies, distinguishable by their mottled cowhide uniforms, in battle against the ever-encroaching

Kalderash women in the market of Sibiu, Transylvania, 1993

Turks. Here, the Impaler is not at all the archvillain of Germanic and Slavic (and eventually universal) lore, but rather a *national hero*, described in the language of the Romanian peasants, whose image of him this was, and serving the cause of an independent Romanian state. (*Ţiganiada* is acknowledged as the first poem written in Romanian.) Gypsies were in the army all right; in this fantasy, they fought alongside angels.

Sitting in the Sibiu market café, watching the Gypsy women expertly count their money, I found it hard to believe: Gypsies as slaves—the notion goes against every West European and New World stereotype. The Gypsies are catalogued in the imagination as a kind of *definition* of rootlessness and freedom. Had this ignominious episode in Gypsy history become better known, then perhaps that pervasive free-spirit fantasy might have failed to establish itself in the first place.

I had found almost nothing on the subject of chattelage in all the writings about Gypsies published over the past century in the West. There was a polemic of 1837, written in French by the Romanian statesman Mihail Kogălniceanu, with very little in the way of concrete information. And there was a 1939 book by the Romanian historian George Potra, the only full-length account on slavery—written in Romanian, untranslated, and the sole source for every subsequent account. It was out of print but I knew of one copy, at the Nicolae Jorga Institute, on a tree-lined avenue of suburban Bucharest. After two failed visits to the Institute, I appealed to an American friend who'd lived in Bucharest for a decade and who had done research there, and he got me an appointment with the resident historian. This septuagenarian medievalist, who wore thick, round tortoiseshell spectacles, received me in his dark-paneled resident historian's rooms, and questioned me, in French. Halfway through this interview we were served strong black coffee in demitasse cups by the librarian who had twice rebuffed me. Things were definitely improving; nevertheless, I surmised, Gypsies would not be a popular topic here, even from an historian's point of view. Our chat not only severely tested my French but exhausted the complete stock of my knowledge and then my bluff about the fifteenth-century spread of Magyar latifundia and the domination of Saxon *rentiers*, about the miserable Romanian serfs and the rise of Romanian nationalism as even noblemen were reduced to a life of subsistence tilling. . . . But after forty minutes an earlier demand—for a notarized and posted request for the book, written on the letterhead of my own "institute"—was waived. When the still-suspicious librarian finally did produce the book she also gave me one hour and kept my coat as collateral, so that I might have it photocopied in the downtown office of a friend.

The entire book was then translated by Corina. While she struggled to transcribe Potra's antiquated prose, Corina also experienced a (tentative) revelation about the Gypsies, whom she had previously seen only as inexplicably hostile lurkers at her door. Her reaction to the material was evidence of how, astonishingly, the history of Gypsy enslavement, which spanned four centuries, remained unknown even among educated Romanians.

Before 1989, no scholars would have had easy access to documents in the territories. And then, during the revolution, the magnificent library of Bucharest University was badly burned. Apparently too, many important records relating to Gypsies in the Danubian territories were lost. But still, in the archives and other historical institutes of Bucharest, Sibiu, and Braşov, the proofs are there—dusty, faded, and reluctantly served up by doddering librarians or guards who don't even know what they're begrudging you. Lists were what I mainly found—the very sources Potra had given shape to. A picture emerged.

· · ·

For more than four hundred years, until 1856, Gypsies were slaves in Wallachia and Moldavia, the feudal principalities that with Transylvania now make up modern Romania. Some Transylvanians also owned Gypsies, but only in these principalities was slavery an institution, at first guided by the "custom of the land" and eventually enshrined in a complete legal framework.

Standing as the last outpost of Christendom in the midst of the Ottoman offensive—long after the greater part of the Serbian Kingdom, Bulgaria, Albania, and most of the Balkan Peninsula had fallen—Wallachia and Moldavia flourished. Once the Crusades had opened the major trade routes along the Danube that linked Byzantium to the West, the princes of the territories that would become Romania made great fortunes by war, and by supplying food to Constantinople. But from the early sixteenth century, when the sultans finally occupied the Black Sea ports, the strength of the principalities was increasingly maintained by slave labor.

The Latin-speaking Vlachs who lived in Wallachia-Moldavia (and whose descendants inhabit modern Romania) soon recognized the economic value of the Gypsies. Indeed, though an earlier record of Gypsies in the Balkans documents Vlachus and Vitanus, two "Egyptians," as placing an order with a Dubrovnik goldsmith in 1362, the first mention of Gypsies in the Romanian archives looks like a reference to cattle. In 1385, the lord of all Wallachia, Prince Dan I, reaffirmed a gift of forty Gypsy families made fifteen years earlier by his uncle to the monasteries at Vodiţa and Tismana. In 1388, the next Wallachian Prince, Mircea the Old, donated three hundred families to the Cozia monastery. In Moldavia in 1428, Alexandru the Good handed over "31 *ţigani* tents" to the monastery of Bistriţa—the same monastery, with its shaded streams and rising fields, where Kalderash Gypsies today hold their annual festival, robustly ignorant of the taint on this sylvan setting.

It is not really known how the enslavement began. One theory is that the Gypsies came over as chattels of the invading Tartars who made their way along the northern-Crimean route into Moldavia. That is, they were *already* slaves when they appeared in the principalities and, abandoned on the battlefields by the defeated Tartars, they remained to serve their new Hungarian and Romanian masters. (No explanation is offered for the fact that the Tartars left no such impedimenta in the other Central and East European countries they attacked.) Gypsies were always slaves, it was furthermore claimed; they came from a pariah class in India; slavery was in their blood. Such analysis was elaborated on, especially by Romanian historians: slavery was seen to be an improvement on the Gypsies' previous station (about which, even now, nothing has been firmly established), because here at least they were usefully integrated into society. A certain Dr. Wickenhauser, who visited the principalities in the nineteenth century, corroborated the view of earlier and later Romanian historians: Gypsies "wished to become slaves, because this would raise them, if not to the level of human being, at least to a par with good, domestic working animals."

Some Gypsies did manage to remain free, simply by keeping out of sight. Anyone who could not name his or her master when stopped in the road automatically became property of the Crown. Foreign Gypsies who were just passing through—tourists, let us say—were routinely rounded up. The fact was, though, that in legal terms *all* Gypsies were construed as foreigners of a kind: within the principalities, claims on land not only determined social and political privilege but were the basis of citizenship itself. To be "native" (*pamintean*) in the principalities meant literally to be the owner of a piece of land (*pamint*). Peasants could own land but Gypsies could not. As Harghita County's public prosecutor had pointed out, some Gypsies now did qualify to receive land—if they could prove uninterrupted attachment to a cooperative for a minimum period of three years. But the elaborate bureaucratic hurdles erected against them (along with the famous "lost application") persuasively suggest that such provisions were—and are—hollow.

Current attempts to evict them have much to do, as always, with the scramble for land. And so one has to wonder: are the Gypsies really nomadic by "nature," or have they become so because they have never been allowed to stay?

The fate of Romanian Gypsies has been linked to that of Romanian peasants ever since they first shared the same patch of ground six hundred years ago. Together peasants and slaves constituted the lowest stratum of feudal society—creating the impression that there was little to choose from between slavery and serfdom. Indeed, despite the laws against miscegenation, there was a good deal of mingling between them. (Confronted with a particularly racist Romanian, I found that I reached easily for this—to them wildly insulting—explanation of the fact that Romanians on the whole are darker than their Slavic neighbors.)

But only Gypsies were human chattels who could be separated and sold off at whim, like farm animals. At first glance the documents seemed to be medieval shopping lists. To Corina's amazement, and to mine, that is more or less what they were. Shopping lists, or records of exchange rates: one Gypsy for one pig; a team of Gypsies for a team of oxen or horses; a newlywed couple for a few barrels of wine; one man for a garden or for the use of garage space; one Gypsy girl fetched "a pair of copper pots," and another, a defective one perhaps, went for a jar of honey. It was even possible to sell "half a Gypsy," which meant a woman with half of whatever children she would bear: proof that, despite other laws that expressly prohibited it, Gypsy families were systematically sundered.

As their value increased there were fewer and fewer unclaimed Gypsies in the principalities, and so the Crown kept up its stock by importing them. They were brought over in large quantities from south of the Danube specifically to be used as forced labor—a practice that alone explains why Romania is still home to by far the greatest number of Gypsies (some 2.5 million) in any single country.

One hot late summer afternoon in the library of the Nicolae Jorga Institute I sat reading Mihail Kogălniceanu's 1837 treatise on Gypsy slaves. This dark place, with its smell of old straw and its silent, even-handedly unhelpful librarians, did not seem a likely venue for revelations of any kind. But suddenly I realized something, perhaps something obvious. It seemed inescapable that the trade in Gypsies represented a turning point: from the moment that they were imported *en masse*, the prejudice against them was sealed. The term "Gypsy" (and its regional variations) no longer signified a broad ethnic group or race—or even, as it sometimes had, a particular profession, such as musician or metalworker. For the first time it referred collectively to a social class: the slave caste.

> Some masters might even give their Gypsies a bit of land to instill in them a love of agriculture [Kogălniceanu wrote], or—if there was no more field work to be done—allow them to play their music . . . but they lost their liberty . . . so that in the two principalities the name Cigan has become a synonym for slave.

Were the violence and hatred against Gypsies today the legacy of slavery—along, perhaps, with their own difficulty in overcoming low expectations? The idea was certainly widely accepted in relation to others with a similar history, such as African Americans. But then how had the episode of Gypsy slavery been overlooked or dismissed by so many historians?

Later the same day, after the Institute closed, I walked through a long, leafy park and past Bucharest's own replica of the Arc de Triomphe and into the city center—the hotels and tourist offices in Bucharest's smoggy Megheru Boulevard. Here I ran into Nicolae Gheorghe, the Gypsy sociologist and activist who had pointed me towards Potra and the Nicolae Jorga Institute in the first place. As usual he looked exasperated—already wearied by my anxious face, full of questions that only he could answer. But now he opened up. Not only did he agree with this hypothesis; shoulders raised and gesticulating with both hands or pausing to restrain a rogue lock of lank black hair, in the middle of that busy boulevard he offered an interesting proof.

"Take the Rudari," Nicolae said. The Rudari were slave woodworkers (who also did gold-sifting and bear-training), and though they no longer necessarily whittle wooden tools, they still constitute a large Gypsy grouping in Romania. From the time they were first imported from south of the Danube, Nicolae explained, the Rudari, like other bondsmen, were called Gypsies. But they spoke no Romani, and apparently they never had. They shared no customs with the Roma, such as traditional dress or pollution codes. So *were* the Rudari Gypsies? Are their descendants? Absolutely: they were slaves.

The terms "Gypsy" and "slave" were interchangeable; they described a particular social caste. For example, in the eighteenth century, even though they were not legally recognized, marriages between serfs and slaves were on the rise, and it was written into the law that "the Moldavian who would marry a Gypsy woman would become a slave and the Romanian woman who marries a Gypsy man will herself become a Gypsy." And once the Gypsies had become a social group it was only a matter of time before they would become a "social problem"—with all the usual connotations of innate criminality.

Then too, ideas of criminality were also changing. After my first visits to the burnt-out villages I had become increasingly curious about the Ursari—or bear-trainers, as the despised Gypsies of Bolintin Deal were called. With my interest aroused, I found I kept stumbling on related material: a series of advertisements in the *Herald Tribune*, for example, placed by an animal-rights group. One carried a photograph of a bear cub harnessed and with a chain through its nose, and called for donations to help stamp out the practice in Turkey and Greece (the

Poster announcing a slave auction in Wallachia:
"FOR SALE, a prime lot of GYPSY SLAVES, to be sold
at auction at the Monastery of St. Elias, 9 May
1852, consisting of 18 men, 10 boys, 7 women and
3 girls, in fine condition."

campaigners were lobbying for the bears, not against the trainers; there was no mention of Gypsies, their likely keepers).

To the people of Central Europe and the Balkans, these brightly colored, thoroughly mangy troupes of bears and monkeys must have been a wonderful sight in the grueling last years of communism. However pathetic, they were also emblems of a past that would not be modernized or made "productive" in the Stalinist sense. And perhaps they supplied a rare avenue for mockery: for some reason, in Ceau-şescu's Romania people continued to pay money to see clapping monkeys and dancing bears.

I had since met some Balkan Ursari who still lived with and off their bears, and now, in my diggings in rural Romanian archives, I found mention of Ursari slaves. It seems that the ruling princes of Wallachia and Moldavia always possessed a good supply of the families who traveled with their bears and monkeys, collecting for the Crown.

Animal dancing is now dying out from a combination of pressure for animals' rights, war (the bears were big earners in Yugoslavia), and loss of interest among young Ursari. Nevertheless, in some parts of the Balkans you can still see them, loping along roads to the old tune of fiddles, concertinas, and bells. In Jagoda, a small wooded hamlet near Stara Zagora in central Bulgaria, there are a couple of dozen shaggy brown bears, tethered to trees around which they churn mud into moats. But the Ursari and their bears only stopped here in winter, when they'd meet to plan their summer routes and to squabble over the Black Sea resorts of Varna and Burgas; by Easter they were on the road.

Campaigners decry the cruel treatment of dancing bears. But the bears I saw, bought—or rescued—from East European zoos, were clearly loved by their keepers. As the primary bread-winners, and expensive to replace, they were also the best-fed members of the clan. Natasha, one of the Jagoda Ursari, wore a mismatched pair of cheap rubber slippers that had cracked open and had been "darned" with copper wire. That's how careful they were of their possessions; and that's how poor they were. Nevertheless, and though the Ursari in Jagoda indignantly denied it, the Pavlovian training consists of burning the paws of cubs to the sound of music, and offering tidbits of meat. The campaigners also believe that the dancing itself is degrading—the equivalent, say, of forcing men to perform for crowds on all fours.

Indeed, only 150 years ago, Gypsies were themselves dancing bears of a kind. Del Chiaro, the Italian secretary to Prince Constantin Brâncoveanu, wrote in his memoirs about entertainments involving Gypsies:

> In some courts they were painted with soot and with their hands behind their backs, standing before a bowl of flour in which a few coins were hidden, they were obliged to duck for the coins with their teeth. . . . Or else they would be made to catch in their mouths, while running, an egg suspended in the air . . . or to remove from a candle a coin lodged in the wax, without extinguishing the flame. Naturally they burned their lips and hair.

Gypsy slaves were made into clowns, but they were also status symbols, and an essential part of any halfway decent dowry. The haul of

Natasha, a member of one of the many Ursari families who spend their winters in the wooded village of Jagoda, in central Bulgaria, before taking their bears on the road in spring. Behind her is Todor, named for the former dictator. 1992

Mariuta, the niece of the very same Prince Constantin Brâncoveanu, would have been typical for a society wedding: she received from him "Mogosoaia village together with the land; the vineyards, the lake and the mills, and 19 Gypsy families." Without Gypsies even the fairest among well-born maidens might never wed. A letter dated 1785, from Zmaranda Zalariu, the wife of a nobleman, was sent to Prince Alexandru Ioan Mavrocordatos, begging "with tears in her eyes" for a special dispensation of Gypsies so that her only daughter might be "saved" from spinsterhood. The merciful Prince complied, with a deed of four Gypsy families. Similarly, Gypsies were passed from father to son. The will of Prince Brâncoveanu provided that: "The Gypsies . . . from Potlogi village shall go to Constantin [his son], the ones in Mogosoaia village to Stefan; those in Obilesti village to Radu, and the ones in Doicesti village shall be for Matei."

At work in the center of Sofia, Bulgaria, 1992

Though not regarded as quite human, Gypsies nevertheless made good concubines. A pretty girl could fetch a much higher price than a merely hard-working one, or than even a fit and skilled young man. Whereas it was illegal to prostitute one's slaves (the punishment for the *boyar* was incarceration in a salt mine), it was acceptable to give the girls away. In addition to his daughter's dowry, a nobleman might welcome his new son-in-law with a separate gift of "a small Gypsy girl." Nothing of the kind could have befallen a peasant girl, who along with her family was attached to—and in a sense safeguarded by—the land.

Masters always had the power to manumit their slaves, but in special cases the Crown established freedom as a right. If a slave had served as a concubine, and her master had failed to free her before his death, she and her children automatically walked free. This law, which provided such excellent incentive for homicide, was no doubt unknown to the child concubines. It was more likely that, in her capacity as a mistress, the girl would not usefully outlive the needs of her master.

The diary of Erimiten von Gauting, a German tourist who passed through Craiova on his way to Constantinople in 1836, gives a chilling account of such relationships:

> In the evening when the heat went down, I went out into the city, and there I saw a scene that I could not have thought of, not even in my imagination. Along with a bunch of animals, the wife of some boyar had a few gipsies, among them a very beautiful girl of 15, whom she sold to a man for two gold coins.
>
> The girl was to be taken at the very moment that I passed in front of the miserable house where she stood with her family, crying. Her parents, brothers and sisters were all crying, but still she was wrested from the arms of her mother and taken away.
>
> I went up to the barbarian man and told him that I would buy her back, but he was very rich and laughed at my offer of 50 gold coins. He bragged that he had bought her for his pleasure . . . and if she would not obey him he would beat her until she did. He told me that if I wanted to buy gipsies, he had 500, and among them some very beautiful girls. He said he wouldn't mind selling those ones as they had already served him, but with this girl he was really in love and could not part for any price.
>
> I went to the police and have gone and talked everywhere, but they all laugh at my stupidity: "Gipsies are our property and we can do with them what we like."

In Bucharest, von Gauting saw many Gypsy beggars with their hands cut off and heard that their masters were responsible: "One of these told me that his father had killed his master who had wanted to cut off his hands and for that his father was hanged.

"Sometimes the boyars would allow their children some 'fun' by whipping these begging gipsies," von Gauting concludes his Craiova diary, "and they claim that this is part of their daily education. Parents kill and maim as they please; children are taught to take their pleasures from very early on. The gipsies are treated worse than animals."

More than 150 years later, one still sees neatly maimed beggar children (not just Gypsies) in the streets of Bucharest. But now the police and the directors of the main children's shelter in the capital routinely claim that it is the children's parents, always Gypsies, who mutilate them, to improve their earnings (or, as one policeman explained to me, to "give them a profession"). However, a Romanian reporter who was investigating the stump children in 1990 established that these little beggars were organized not by their fathers—in *equipes voleuses*, as the Francophile head of the children's home referred to the Gypsy families—but under professional pimps. These pimps—sometimes Gypsies, sometimes not—also ran the child prostitutes at Bucharest Nord station; and for their trouble they kept them all in candy and glue.

The uniform ignorance among Gypsies, even Romanian Gypsies, about their slave past was striking. Under Ceauşescu, of course, history was deposed by myth. But the Gypsies may also feel that slavery—like their fate under the Nazis—is just another episode in a more or less continuous narrative of persecution. Romanians knew nothing about it either. This is an indication of the status of Gypsies here and in the wider world: an indication of their invisibility.

Near the Black Sea resort of Constanţa lies the town of Mihail Kogălniceanu, the scene, in October 1990, of one of the first of the postrevolutionary purges of the Gypsy population. The residents of Mihail Kogălniceanu do not seem to know who Mihail Kogălniceanu was. He was an eloquent liberal statesman and an ardent and influential abolitionist. More than twenty-five years before emancipation in the principalities, he wrote:

> [Europeans] form philanthropic societies for the abolition of the slavery in America, even while in the bosom of their continent, in Europe, there are 400,000 Gypsies who are slaves and 200,000 others who are buried in the gloom of ignorance and of barbarism!

One hundred and fifty years later, in the town named for the great man, slavery is gone, but the gloom of ignorance and barbarism persists.

No Place to Go

AN OBELISK IN the old center of Constanţa—a four-hour drive from Bucharest—commemorates Ovid's exile and death on the Black Sea. It was from here that the poet sent verses of appeal to Rome, describing the horrors of the land, its barbarity, its chill.

Two thousand years later, Constanţa's oily beachfront gives way to its oily harborfront. Constanţa was and is a major port town, and like all places with boat traffic it attracted not only regional transients and derelicts but an admixture of rank foreigners. The beach retains a seedy seaside charm; everyone was making the best of it—the old men listening to transistor radios on the promenade benches, the picnicking families on the pebbly sand, and the preening teenagers sprawled over the rocks of the jetty.

Twenty miles away, tiny Mihail Kogălniceanu was far from glamorous but it was cosmopolitan in its way: Romanians, Turks, Tartars, nomadic and settled Gypsies, Germans, Macedonians, Moldavians, and Bulgarian-speaking Muslims—called the Gaga'ouz—all lived there. Even the settled Roma community was broken into two distinct groups, one known as the Turks, which meant that they were Muslims (or just that they wore baggy trousers), and the others identifying themselves, mainly by contrast, as Christians. Needless to say in the Balkans, this was no melting pot.

In 1991, nearly a year after the events in which twenty-seven houses were razed and five more destroyed, continuing controversy over the fate of the dispossessed Roma of Kogălniceanu had brought the tension back with a vengeance. My group—Ted Zang, a young American human-rights lawyer; Ina Bardan, a Romanian human-rights worker; and Corin, the translator—entered the village with a trepidation which seemed justified after we stopped to ask directions from a woman (a Tartar, to judge by the squat body and the boxy, notably Oriental face). "What are you doing here?" she barked from behind her garden fence. "Bringing them *aid* I suppose? Why don't you just take them a lit match?" It soon became clear that she spoke for the whole constituency: it was the only thing they had in common. We decided to go to see the Gypsies first.

A dirt road, each blister of rock scoring the belly of our Dacia sedan, eventually led us to a series of crumbling houses—or what used to be houses. Nothing had been touched since the day the buildings were destroyed; it looked like a city gutted by war. Weeds grew high inside the houses, many of which had retained a couple of feet of plastered, handmade brick. One expected to find archeologists sifting and digging around the site. Life for the Roma who had been burned out and who had since returned went on more or less as usual. Dinners simmered on stoves placed here and there around the yard; laundry sagged in the new spaces between walls; children played their toyless games, indifferent to the wreckage.

It seemed extraordinary that people could continue their lives surrounded by the scorched and smashed remnants of the past. But they were defiant rather than stoical. One had to imagine that they were sticking it out and determinedly not moving a single charred brick, as if the only hope of compensation lay in what was so powerfully represented in all that rubble. They were doing what came naturally: carrying on, adjusting, surviving. These Gypsies had neither the money nor the materials nor, most important, the confidence to rebuild. But they weren't timid in telling their story. As in other devastated settlements, I found that the Gypsies, abandoned here after a brief breeze of media interest, would talk, and most often complain, for as long as anyone would listen. It was as if no one had ever asked them *anything*; they had a heaving backlog of documented injuries and denigrations to disgorge, complete with unrelated but nevertheless urgent suggestions, requests, and demands.

Within minutes of leaving the car, the four of us were surrounded. There were perhaps fifty people: dirty, shiny-eyed children and their mothers and aunts and grandmothers, some of them holding babies or great protruding bellies or both, perhaps half of them shouting our way, in tones alternately pleading and hostile. There was just one elderly couple. The man, elegant in his frayed but neat brown waistcoat, kept a fob watch in one pocket as well as three fingers in both. The woman, clearly a life's companion, rested a light hand on his arm, the only silent member of the group, her long, smooth face prettily framed in a faded flower kerchief.

The absence of the elderly here had everything to do with the difficulty of Gypsy life: there just weren't that many old Gypsies anywhere—their life expectancy was twelve or fifteen years below the norm (low enough, hereabouts). And there were very few men of any age. The reasons for *their* absence were more variable. The happiest excuse might be that they were at work, or were looking for work; the more common explanation was that they were in prison. In places as tense as

Kogălniceanu, men sometimes kept out of sight for safety's sake, or so they told us; everyone agreed that women and children, even Gypsy women and children, were less likely to be attacked if they were alone.

"So," Ina Bardan began, "what happened?" In the hours that followed there were many replies and refinements of replies to this absurdly broad question. "In the afternoon of the evening before it happened," a young Rom began, "Macedonians came and warned us." And then, unfurling like a fugue (or indeed like the heterophonous variations of many Rom musical ensembles), every statement of fact was followed on its heels by some denial or abrogation in a different voice: "No, the burning happened in the morning"; "They weren't Macedonians who warned us, they were Turks"; "Nobody warned us"; "They told us it would come the *next* week." . . .

I pressed on, beaming in on the first young man who'd spoken and ruthlessly shutting out the supplications of all others: "The evening before the night it happened, some Macedonians came and warned you. Then what?" The story that emerged contained many common Gypsy themes, contradictions, and complaints.

"But we didn't believe him." "There was no reason to believe." "We've been threatened before." "Before it was better." "We have lived here since 1947 and *nica problema*." "Until this year we had no trouble." "Life was better before the revolution." "When Ceaușescu died the problems began." "This is what democracy means for us." "George Bush should come over and see our democracy." "Why doesn't the U.S.A. help us?"

A young man rolled up a sleeve to reveal a wrist tattoo which read, between commando wings, "U-S-A." "Are there Gypsies in America?"

"Yes," I said, and then, interrupting myself, "but what happened on the night of October 9?"

"There was a fight in the bar." "They gathered in the bar." "They gathered in the German church." "The Germans in the bar told the priest." "The church bells called everyone together." "Drinks were offered." "The priest is a drunk."

Ina Bardan tried to push the conversation forward. "How many people came?"

"Thirty-five." "Three hundred." "They came with benzene." "And tractors and cars." "And steel poles."

"Did you know them? Were they young people?"

"I knew every one of them." "We knew them from school; we asked them why they were doing this." "We weren't doing anything."

"None of us were here, we were in the woods." "We were afraid in the woods." "There are wild animals in the woods." "There were no people here, only animals." "They stole our horses and pigs and chickens." "All this happened in one night." "When we returned the next morning, everything was burned." "We stayed away for three days, and when we came back the houses were still smoking." "There were dead animals in our wells." "And furniture."

Followed by the entire crowd, with the smaller children tugging at our shirts and asking for gum, we walked across a lumpy field to inspect some of the other houses that had been torched, those belonging to the Turkish Gypsies. The town was crumbling but still viable, with hand-carved drains the only remains of disused, grown-over roads. Still, it was not a ghost town. We stopped at a house and a woman emerged, not approaching but standing guard in the frame of her doorway. There was something she wanted to ask us. Could we help, with her daughter? She retreated and re-emerged with a child in her arms—a stiff, folded little girl whose polio-afflicted limbs and paralyzed, expressionless face gave her the look of a wooden doll. Her fingers were frozen into tiny claws and her whole Z-shaped body looked petrified in a moment of action, like the human fossils of Pompeii. Ina took some details from the woman and spoke to her about children's-aid groups and special hospitals in Bucharest, and another mother pushed forward with her own unfortunate child—a different kind of victim.

This little girl had been badly injured when her family returned to inspect their burnt-out house. A still-smoldering beam had fallen on her. Without any apparent concern for the girl's feelings, her mother lifted her dress and yanked down her leggings to show the visitors her shockingly melted vagina and thighs. "She can never marry now," the woman said. The insensitivity of the mother only underscored the fact that here, as in most wars, it was mainly children who were the victims.

We learned that four (or fourteen) policemen eventually did come—after the mob had gone, after the houses had gone—bearing a message for the Gypsies: "You must leave the village, because they will come back and kill you." "But we stay here," one woman explained, "because we have no place to go." "We want to stay here," another added, "because we were born here."

As we walked back to the car, a man came after us. He wanted to give us the names of all the families and all their children. We dutifully wrote them down, some of them common Romanian names—the Mihais and Mirceas and Ioans—but also some beautiful old-fashioned names that seem now mainly to belong to Gypsies. I thought of similar lists I had copied into my notebook from the archives in Bucharest:

> The four Gypsies Harman, Bera, Badu, and Coman, together with their families . . . a few Gypsies: Macicat, Caba, Coste, Babul, Bazdag, Carfin, and Nan, all seven together with their families . . . Luca son of Latco, Alexa, Hertea, Dinga and his brother Manciu, Stefan, Boldor and his brother Gavril . . . Pandrea, Radu, and Butcat . . . Baciul, Coica and his brother Ninga, and Gypsies by the name of Boia, Dadul, Gutinea, and Carfila . . . Talpa together with his children Toderica, Jamba, Molda, Oprea, and Piciman . . .

And how are relations with the other residents of Kogălniceanu now? "Some of them have come to say they are sorry." "They are afraid we will burn their houses." "They brought us some blankets." "They spit on us if we go into town." "We are not allowed in the pub."

The Discobar, a lone gray rhomboid on a corner in town, is the place where the group gathered that night. It looks more like a factory than a pub. Unconvinced, we lingered before entering, gazing up at the tiny yellow half-lit neon "Discobar" sign, high on a side wall. Inside, it was dark and cool: red curtains kept out the afternoon sun. The place was empty. The waiter, a young man with a helmet of black hair and a clip-on bow tie over his white short-sleeved shirt, was leaning on the bar, smoking and talking to the bartender, a fat poached-faced man behind the counter. They were not pleased to see us.

"Why do you want to talk about it after all this time?" the bartender asked.

Ted Zang explained. "Because nothing has happened. There has been no case before the courts, not even a serious investigation. And still these people have no homes."

A shrug. The young waiter looked over at the bartender for guidance. Another shrug, as if to say, You can talk to them if you want to waste your time. The bartender turned away, and tended to the glasses in his sink. The young man dithered, sharpening the head of his cigarette in an ashtray. He picked at the pimples on his chin and glanced at his watch: time to kill. Finally, he turned towards the four of us, standing by in solemn expectation. He looked me over. I watched as a "why the hell not" grin rose over his face. He didn't look at Ted, the only one among us who had spoken. Instead the waiter led me, followed by the others, to a table in the back. I may even enjoy this, I could feel him thinking as he guided me by two upturned fingers at the elbow.

At the table, I shared a corner with the waiter, who was still, and determinedly, holding my elbow, resting the back of his hand on the table like a coaster. No one else was drinking, but I found myself ordering a cold Laziza ("The Famous Lebanese Beer").

Ina was at her most officious: "Where were you on the evening of October 9?"

"I was on my way to visit the Gypsies," the waiter told us cheerfully, tipping back on his chair and clasping his free hand behind the black helmet, impervious to our disapproval. It wasn't that he was confident; he just didn't notice. Clearly he had never encountered anyone who didn't think exactly as he did—except Gypsies.

Mihai, as he was called, didn't need further encouragment. "I am Macedonian," he wanted us to know first off. "What happened here was a war between the Gypsies and everyone else. All the other nationalities were together: Macedonians, Romanians, the Germans, and the rest."

"How did it start?" Ted asked, unfolding his notepad.

"A Turk and a Macedonian were having a fight," Mihai said, the united colors of Kogălniceanu dissolving even as we committed them to paper. Probably mistaking him as one of their own, "the Gypsies intervened on the side of the Turk. A Romanian was caught driving alone through the Gypsy quarter in his truck. He was beaten."

"This," Corin explained, "was the drop that filled the glass."

"Did someone call the police?" I asked, perhaps rhetorically.

"If we had asked the police, they would've done nothing. What can four policemen do?" Mihai had skipped ahead. "There were between three and four hundred of us. On the way to the Gypsy quarter, people joined the crowd. We brought petrol, to finish the job once and for all." Mihai was calm. "There was no killing."

"And what did the policemen do?"

"They watched. And now there are six policemen there."

I wondered if he would be offended if I removed my elbow from his palm. I wondered why I was wondering this. "And the firemen?" I said, smuggling my hands into my lap. "What about them?" We had been told by the Gypsies that the villagers had stopped the firemen from entering their neighborhood. Apparently there was no need to intervene.

"We were there at 12:30 p.m., and the firemen turned up around three. We surrounded the Gypsy houses and set fire to everything. It was planned for two days later, but we thought they might stop us."

"But nobody was arrested afterwards," I pointed out. "Did you really think you might be stopped?"

"This was not a crime," Mihai explained. "It was an uprising." The waiter had earned another cigarette. His two smoking fingers now free, he extracted one from a blue packet—Manhattan 100s.

"And how do you feel about it now?" I asked. Ina curled her lip in anticipation.

"It was a very good idea. We should have done it long before. We have no more problems with them. They don't feel so big and strong now. It was the only way. Everyone used to be afraid of them. Now everyone behaves. They have no more courage. I've seen the people from those houses since, of course. But I don't speak to them. They're more respectful now. They even greet you in the street from time to time."

"If the Gypsies are so well behaved now, why do you keep them out of the bar?" Corin asked.

"They are not civilized. I wouldn't serve a Gypsy."

Seething Ina could not resist (we were all pretty new to the neutral interview): "What does democracy mean to you?"

"To be able to do what I want and nobody should interfere."

The bartender had been listening from his counter. Eventually he joined in, as the people of Kogălniceanu will. And he told us something new: the lone Romanian who was beaten in his truck had been transporting weapons—wooden dowels from the local mill—to a hiding place closer to the Gypsy quarter.

"How did the Gypsies know?"

"Well, they know things, don't they?" he said irritably. His nose sharpened and all of his tiny features were trying to converge on it. "They have no place in this village. If they rebuild their houses we will burn them again. The people here don't trust them. We don't want Gypsies in Kogălniceanu."

There seemed little else to say, and we gathered our things. Mihai gallantly held open the door. Ina offered a proud profile as we filed past. Ted, troubled but naturally polite, managed a somber nod. Corin, not much touched by the deposition, skipped out. Flummoxed or just perverse, I smiled a toothy smile and held out my hand, which Mihai grabbed with both of his, and shaking it like dice, he asked a question that needed no translation: "Can I have your phone number?" I wriggled away and made a dive for the car.

We drove off. I looked out the back window. The waiter was jogging after us. As he slowed and grew smaller, he waved and penned imaginary scribbles on his palm. He looked like a neglected diner signaling to the waiter for the bill. I was speechless, but Ina, at last, was laughing: "So now you see: everything in our country is backwards."

A year later, in 1992, I returned to Kogălniceanu with Nicolae Gheorghe and a busload of Americans, including a reporter from *The New York Times,* some observers from Capitol Hill, and a couple of American Gypsies. Thanks to the vigorous efforts of Gheorghe, a group of Sinti—German Gypsies—based in Heidelberg, had pledged 120,000 deutschemarks (and had given 40,000) for the reconstruction of the houses, on the condition that the Romanian government match the donation. The government had done so, and a criminal investigation had begun—the first and only investigation of an attack on Gypsies in the country. It sounded like a miracle, and at first sight from the bus, it looked like one.

A row of new houses stood on the very site of the wreckage, though some ruins, perhaps deemed still usable, remained. The old couple (the man in the same brown vest, with three fingers in each pocket) stood in front of their new house, shading their eyes to see who was on this unlikely mission. I said hello to them. I didn't think they recognized me from a year before, but I recognized an earlier version of *them:* past their front door, hanging high on the wall, was their wedding photograph—which had somehow survived the blaze—a formal sepia portrait, perhaps fifty years old.

On closer inspection, things didn't look quite so good: the houses were bare, with dirt floors. They were badly made from coarse unpainted cinder blocks. Some walls were stacked without mortar. There was no plumbing and no running water anywhere, just a long ditch filled with swamp water, dug about twelve feet in *front* of the houses and promising some kind of epidemic. The houses at the end of the row were only half built, and except for a few black scorch marks it was hard to distinguish the new houses from those that had been half destroyed in the attack.

The old couple with a pair of great-grandchildren in front of the remains of their house in Mihail Kogălniceanu, which was destroyed by a mob in October 1990. They continued to live in it for three years until new houses for some of the victims finally were built.

To me this reconstruction, however limited, still looked like hope—the only sign of it I had seen in dozens of similarly afflicted villages. To Bill Duna, a Gypsy from Minneapolis, it looked like a slum, and you could watch the emotion as it traversed and variously contorted his face, which resembled that of a distressed child. He was absorbing the degradation in which some of his fellow Gypsies lived. No doubt the site was all the more disappointing for being the great pilot project of cooperation between the Romanian government and the first independent Gypsy groups who were, at last, organizing the fight for their rights.

To the neighbors, the Turkish Gypsies across the lumpy field, these new houses represented an affront of a different kind. Those whose houses had been only partially destroyed got nothing, and so they continued as they were. Far from solving the community's problems, the new buildings had mainly created enormous tension and envy. And some things had not changed. Near the bus the little girl whose lower body had been badly burned was once again being stripped for the visitors; a concerned lady from Washington crouched to take a picture of the wound.

But the building had stopped. Apparently local government had control over the dispersal of the funds, even though the project had been approved by Bucharest. According to Nicolae, who had been negotiating on all sides, the authorities had made it clear that they would continue construction only if the Gypsies abandoned their case in the courts. It was, as Nicolae put it, a choice between peace and justice. To the local Gypsies it was a different choice and a clear one—between justice and new houses. A few individuals or families from the settlement had already dropped their own names from the group led by a local Gypsy leader, Petre Anghel, which had filed charges. Anghel and Nicolae feared that the whole case had been scuppered by their action, and moreover that it was unlikely that those who had negotiated their separate deals would even get their new houses.

By 1994—more than four years after the attack—all activity in the road and in the courts had ceased.

Back in Bucharest I bumped into Emilian, the serious young man and chronicler of the razed village of Bolintin Deal. We had lost touch, and I'd heard that he had got out of Romania. But here he was, waiting for someone in the mirrored lobby of the Art Deco hotel, the Lido, a dark and pleasantly seedy place favored by journalists. It turned out that he was acting as a translator for a reporter from the Philadelphia *Inquirer.* A translator? Emilian had spoken no English when I met him.

He had just returned from nearly a year in the United States, where he had worked in an amusement arcade in Wildwood, New Jersey, owned by an American Gypsy. The experience had changed him. It wasn't just the preppy Oxford-cloth shirt and khakis, or the easy smile and light manner that were so unlike the dour Emilian I had known. It was his gait. Emilian had a new shoe: his legs were the same length now and he no longer lurched from side to side when he walked.

Emilian cheerfully told me that his job at the funfair had been to make "kherndoze," corndogs. He said he was happy to be back and anxious to get on with his recording of Gypsy stories. From his spiffy new blazer pocket he pulled out the tape recorder I had given him for the purpose, two years before. Why did you leave the States? I asked him, bracing myself for a terrible deportation story. And then Emilian hugged me and laughed and laughed. When he finally recovered his raspy voice, he told me that he had lost his job at the amusement park after it was devastated by a fire.

The Other Side

THERE ARE POLES in Poland who spend four hundred dollars on a pair of slacks at stores such as Snobissimo in Warsaw's fashionable Nowy Świat (New World) Boulevard. Not just one or two: there's a whole new class of rich Poles. Their first-time furs and glitzy cars seem garish against the backdrop of grimy, twilit tramways, of sooty early dusk, of unending blue-gray avenues and the standard unmuffled Skodas (a Czech car in the shape of a baby boot whose name in Polish means "pity," as in the French *dommage*).

In Warsaw there is also an abundance of new shops that sell only tarty lingerie, and others exclusively stocking luxury comestibles: whisky and caviar, but no milk. Who goes there? Who lives here? It all looks fake—people and places variously gussied up. But then it *is* fake. Fifty years ago, German soldiers rubbed the city and two-thirds of its inhabitants off the map. Only a few gaunt prewar façades now remain, preserved, perhaps, as a reminder (many of the old buildings are riddled with bullet holes). Poles are obsessed by their history but in the capital they live in a city with no patina. Nothing is old here; and things are often not what they pretend to be.

There is, for a conspicuous start, the Palace of Culture—a neo-Byzantine wedding cake, a gift from Stalin to the Polish people (hard to refuse, and a symbol of how put-upon the Poles have been). Opposite is the Szanghaj, a Chinese restaurant that doesn't serve Chinese food. Nearby, the "Old Town" is a cobblestoned reconstruction of Ye Olde Warsawe, an impeccable Baroque theme park completed in the 1970s. The sense of a stage set, perhaps again to be struck by terrible historical forces: this is the flavor of the unease one feels here, where the names of streets are still changing, and where, in the Ghetto, the foundations of buildings are cracking open. The rubble of the past is actually pressing through, and you stand there staring, as if waiting for a pair of trembling hands to emerge from a crevasse. Perhaps those who rebuilt the area, razed after the Uprising, didn't *want* to bury or sweep away the past. (Though not much fuss is made over survivor sensitivities: for example, Orbis, the state-owned travel agency, chose as its headquarters the very spot where the buses left the Ghetto for Treblinka.)

If places and buildings leave one in doubt about their age or their hidden histories, faces don't lie, in particular those of peasants. (The term "peasant" may sound archaic and condescending, but it is precisely their physical stoicism, many hundreds of years in the making, that mocks the youthful culture of euphemism.) Faces are about the only prewar survivors here—ancient, beet-red flat ones, like that of the bundled womanbulk I saw one subzero morning outside Warszawa Centralna Station, standing guard over a folded blanket which had as its proud centerpiece a single giant root, apparently alone worth the trip in from the provinces—kohlrabi, rutabaga, some dirt-encrusted tuber, a Polish truffle bigger than a human head. Warszawa Centralna, a concrete hangar in the shadow of the Palace of Culture, is the station where you catch trains for the outside world: Koln and Jstanbul and Piotersberg; the place names are written by hand, as printing lags well behind the identity crises of Eastern capitals. The station was also home to the first wave of Gypsies migrating west after the revolutions of 1989, mainly from Romania.

Thousands of Gypsies occupied the station that winter and into the summer of 1990; the waiting room was still a waiting room—one with laundry-festooned radiators. (In recent years, Warsaw has only ever been a stopover on the journey west. You are still likely to see washing in any public toilet—tiny tights and long, graying tube socks: whole families pegged on a movable line.) And still they keep coming in their hundreds. It is usual to have women and children as delicate and dark as Delhians petting your coat and murmuring plaintively as you push your way down a crowded street. They are asking for money.

That, anyway, is what you defensively infer. In fact it isn't at all clear what they want. You could convince yourself that this petting thing has no object, that it is just what they *do*. Whether in Rome or in Warsaw, Gypsies are just not very good at begging. For most, shame wouldn't be the difficulty. Begging, after all, is an ancient profession; alms-giving confirms the virtue and *pietas* of even the poor, and some beggars, such as India's mendicant *sadhu*s, are honored as holy men.

Andrzej Mirga, a Polish Gypsy and an ethnographer, confirmed something of this. "For Roma, the concept of begging, of seeking alms, just does not exist. There is no word in Romani for begging. Instead you might say *te phirav pa-o gav*, 'to go about the village,' and our women went mainly to collect debts for work done by their men, for fixing something, or perhaps playing at a wedding."

The station sleeve-petters, mostly young women of the Balkans roaming cities not their own and found in every East (and many a West) European capital, looked to be suffering from compassion-stimulation fatigue. Though they maintain the plangent tone, in disastrous mimicry of their targets they look through or past the potential donor. People don't want to part with their zlotys. Instead these Gypsies whine at no one in particular and face the coming crowd, boredly scanning for a better class of coat. But then, if they have no debts to collect, they do have reason to feel defeat.

At first, Poles gave generously to the shabby strangers, who were dark and lithe and shiny-eyed—all of which, before it (mysteriously) becomes frightening, is attractive. But Poles today tell you that at first they didn't *know* the station Gypsies were Gypsies. They don't mean that they had never heard of them. Rather they are saying that because the beggars are Gypsies the giving constitutes robbery; and so they see themselves as victims rather than small-time philanthropists. Gypsies lived in these parts before Warsaw was founded in the fourteenth century, but the local postwar population is invisibly small—only some twelve to fifteen thousand Gypsies live here permanently. Like the Polish Jews, Polish Gypsies hardly exist anymore, and those who remain are relatively prosperous and well integrated. Now their identity is being taken over by that of the invasive, threatening, and parasitic refugee.

To many Poles, the strangers were not just poor or parasitic; if they were Gypsies they were dangerously, deceitfully so, and probably diseased to boot. A more lackadaisical kind of beggar would be hard to conceive, and yet the newspapers stayed the charitable impulse of many citizens with assertions that these dark women weighted their skirts with wads of cash, that daily they collected sums five times the average Polish salary, that their suppurating children were spreading meningitis and TB—a campaign which ended in their removal from Warszawa Centralna. Since then they have settled for, and in, the eastern terminal, Wschodnia, out of sight, over the Wisła River.

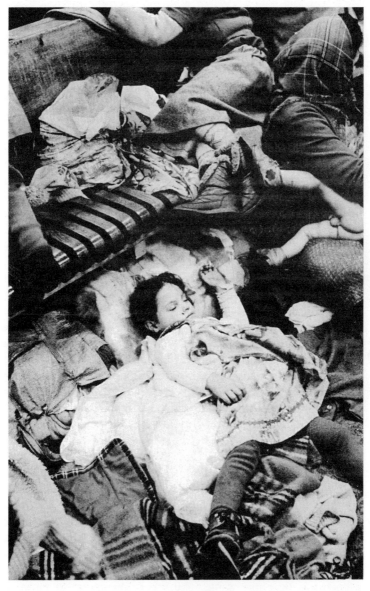

Wschodnia Station, Warsaw, 1990: Hundreds of Roma, mostly from Romania but also from the former Yugoslavia, have camped out here. Some have stayed for years, in the hope of eventual arrival in Germany and the West.

Wschodnia Station is a dank split-level maze of concrete corridors and low-ceilinged waiting rooms with pungent dark patches, the pissed-in corners beyond the low-watt penumbra of Polish bulbs. Here the waiting room has been barricaded and everyone must stand in the halls. Drunks bounce off the dim walls, invisible to bored Soviet soldiers and to the stout, monobreasted Russian matrons in snowboots, waiting for Moskva-bound buses and minding their sacks of Polish loot. These women have sold their Soviet goods in the vast stadium which has become a Russian flea market, and are now returning with bags of zlotys plus plastic kitchen utensils, aluminum pans—items still scarce back home.

The station cafeteria, bright and scented with cigarette smoke and ammonia, is warmed by steaming vats of cabbage, gluey stew, and *golonka*—fried pigs' feet. This is the station's main draw, and men and women at rows of high narrow counters are bent in silence over their bowls, the feet of their stools disappearing in the tide of accumulated butts.

I went inside for a thaw and found two small Gypsy boys near the food counter handing trays to the shufflers in the food queue (they had figured out that begging is not tolerated in cafeterias). Though no one touched him, the littler one squirmed and squealed as if he was being tickled; finally, he pulled his white wool ski cap down over his face, spread his arms, and spun away from us. The older one, taking no notice of his hyperactive colleague, faced me with intent. Without saying a word, he raised his thin black eyebrows in a pity-me teepee and sawed his stomach with a flat upturned palm: hunger. The food was a gift, but seconds later they ran out through the swinging doors as if from a saloon shootout, two dwarf cowboys, a cooked chicken in each armpit.

Later in the day, I saw the boys again. They lived in a shack behind the station, one of thirty or so below the raised tracks, stretching out in a ragtag flotilla of driftwood and rubbish: lean-tos with sitting room only, constructed from cardboard, bits of chicken wire, carpet, and wood—like any shantytown in the world, only here it was wet, and cold enough to see your breath. I smelled the place before I saw it—the weatherproof stench of fear and poverty, human shit. Nobody can be bothered to dig a hole: things are that bad. These were my thoughts, and I was so focused on them, and on not stepping in a latrine, that instead I nearly stepped on a pair of bare-assed middle-aged men, squatting mid-dump. I leapt back, stupidly gasping *eek* like I'd come

The sheltered pedestrian underpass in the center of Warsaw is where many Roma spend their days.

upon a large rat, but they just sat there, chatting quietly to each other, quite unperturbed by exposure to the cold or to me, or to anyone else who might have been watching. Later, when I replayed the scene—of my shock and their indifference, of my stiffness and their loose-limbed ease—I recognized them (again) as children of India. I thought of a description in one of V. S. Naipaul's India books, of people "companionably" shitting along rivers, in streets, beside train tracks. Shitting could be sociable—why not? My association of open defecation with degradation may have been my problem alone. Certainly the shame was all mine (and, indeed, from the Gypsies' point of view, so was the defilement, earned by exposing myself to the act). The two boys from the cafeteria, who *were* hiding, behind some trees, were wetting themselves with glee, and a rare pleasure it must have been, not to be on the receiving end (of some joke, some humiliation).

Sliding down the soggy escarpment, I found in the doorway of one hutch a man on all fours. He was laying a new floor: a flattened cardboard box, former home to a Sanyo TV. One of the main professions of long-settled Gypsies in Poland is carpet dealing. They have big shops, in Kraków especially, chains of them; they sell in the markets; they sell door-to-door. This newcomer clearly wasn't getting any of that, no carpet treatment of any kind. Polish Gypsies, understandably resentful of the bad image of their poor relations from farther east, kept clear of them. But they were not the only ones who distanced themselves from the poorest refugees; so did other foreign Gypsies, such as the score of traders from Bulgaria who also stayed at the station, in the comfort of their own converted school bus.

The Bulgarians were on a business trip. They were buying cheap sweaters—pink and yellow fluffy ones—in Poland and flogging them for a bit more over the Czech border in Bohemia and Moravia. After a few runs, they would return to Bulgaria. These Travelers were doing very well and had no desire to go west. Unlike the Romanian Gypsies along the tracks, the Bulgarian Gypsies in the bus were all fat, with nothing of the victim in their bearing. On the contrary, a chief pleasure among them was the corpulent perusal of the misfortunes of others. One of the paunchiest—some kind of paterfamilias, to judge by the way he interrupted everyone and no one minded, and by the gold rings he had corseting each sausage finger—warned me against speaking to "those dog-eaters," indicating the shack-dwellers. He did the same to a pair of rich Polish ladies who had pulled up in a Mercedes full of old clothes: they'd brought them for the people in the shacks and were now not quite sure how to approach them. After vigorous admonition from the Bulgarian, they gave up and drove away, leaving their bundles in the road. Rich only in numbers, the Romanians had been here for months, regrouping after each bounce back from the German border and in no hurry to return to Romania or the former Yugoslavia.

I am not a train enthusiast. I went to the stations to make new friends. Convoys of westbound would-be refugees from farther east were supposedly being formed by professionals operating out of Warsaw—out of the station toilets, to be precise. (In keeping with the false advertising all over town, the toilets were used for everything but.) These pros—Germans, Poles, Romanians, Turks, and some Gypsies—escort the refugees from Bucharest or from Warsaw to the border, where they show them the safest crossing, or pretend to, and disappear.

German officials, who blame them for the boom in illegal crossings all along their thirteen-hundred-kilometer eastern border, call the guides *Schleppers*, a name that contrasts with the more heroic *Fluchthelfer*, or flight-helper, that was given to those who smuggled Jews out of Germany. Contempt for such dealers isn't new, or unique to Germans: Henry VIII's act of 1530 ruled that anyone conveying Gypsies would be fined forty pounds (and the transported themselves would be hanged). But the German government now doesn't think to look to Romania for clues about the *Schlepper* boom. It does not call the most recent migrants refugees, which would emphasize that they are leaving, indeed fleeing; instead it calls them *Asylanten*, asylum-seekers, emphasizing their arrival at the gates. Some—perhaps not many—of the Romanian Gypsies are fleeing government-approved mob attacks on their settlements. All feel unwelcome in their own country. And yet, the press release says, their arrival *en masse* is due to the efforts of travel agents.

According to border guards, the *Schleppers* are smugglers who have diversified. (And they should know: the guards live on, or off of, the same thin line; as in the children's game, they see *it*, the border, the cracks, while the *Schleppers* eye the pavement, the safe open spaces on either side.) Freer trade has quashed a once-lucrative black market in just about everything, and now the *Schleppers* are reduced to dealing in Gypsies, the blackest market of all. The *Schlepper* elite, however, vies for those few travelers who can really pay. Before being caught on the third consignment, one Polish-Romanian outfit managed to transport twenty-four Pakistanis to Germany in a Ukrainian-army helicopter.

The German public and press, though, have been focusing not on the mercenaries but on their controversial cargo. The term "Gypsies," in its various formulations, is deployed as a buzz word: on the right, it signals the whole impoverished, noxious mess encroaching from the east; in the liberal imagination, "Roma & Sinti" become a synonym for "victim" or "refugee" (ludicrous in the case of the Sinti, as German Gypsies are known, for they have been settled and well integrated for hundreds of years).

In five days of loitering in and around stations I didn't find a single family poised to make the crossing. If anything, the traffic was moving *east*: the returning trickle of people repelled by German authorities. And the *Schleppers* weren't handing out calling cards on street corners.

The track shacks were intended for more permanent use than their appearance suggested. Home for these Gypsies was wherever they wore their hats. For the moment, they weren't going anywhere. The very word "station" suggested as much, and "terminal" even more extremely (as in illness, or boredom); it was the end. Still, the hope of departure was important, and perhaps it was this, as much as the toilets and traffic, that drew once and future Traveler Gypsies to stations all over Eastern Europe. Wschodnia, however, was not even a point of departure but a shelter: trains no longer left from here (the place was used as a bus depot and bus cemetery).

Russian soldiers, Poles, Gypsies—here, all were represented in their most reduced forms: respectively, hated outsiders, humiliatingly costumed for a job that didn't exist; wretched drunks and kooks giving credence to new annual statistics claiming a 30-percent rise in the suicide rate among Polish men; bewildered aliens, maimed or somehow shrunken, whining and begging or just nervously ticking over. Perhaps because I was a token Jew at a Polish train station, to me these diminished people—and the empty tracks, and the human shit, and the mud and cold and atmosphere of detention and destiny about the place—instantly evoked that other last-stop station in Poland, at Auschwitz. In those five days, the eastern terminal came to seem an emblem of the arrested aspirations of the Gypsies, a once gloriously mobile people.

Such weighing impressions could be alleviated by the fantasy that even this bit of Warsaw might one day be rebuilt and memorialized. A well-informed, if nationally biased, tour guide would, for example, conduct busloads of bored Polish schoolchildren through the reconstructed shacks (now labeled "Migrants' Dwellings"), along the restored tracks, and down the uniformly dank station corridors, past a small white ski cap among the children's clothes moldering in a glass display-case. The old cafeteria would now be a new cafeteria.

Somewhere, of course, people were crossing; perhaps operations had moved closer to the border.

Poland is a flat, featureless plain, not improved by its thinning clusters of polluted ever-brown pines. That, anyway, is the view from the Moscow–Berlin express: a blurred tundra marked by pale copses of needleless firs—more spear than tree—and scarecrow birches; a few roofless farmhouses. When you look out the window, it is easy to see why Poland has been continuously overrun, or run through, by its neighbors. There is nothing to stop anyone. There is no place to hide.

Not even behind one's book. Prompted, I suppose, by my copy of Martin Gilbert's *The Holocaust,* the pale, rosy-lipped young Pole in my compartment leaned towards me: "You are a Jewess, isn't it?" Krzysztof Suchocki had never met an "actual" Jew, he confided— almost apologetically, as if this was a character flaw. Furthermore, he confessed, he was no longer sure of his own faith. Catholicism here used to mean opposition to communism, but now it promised only a different loss of freedom. Krzysztof was referring to the abortion debate recently faxed to the motherland from Rome. To him, every- thing had the same value. As he commuted across the entire country, away from his hometown of Suwałki, in the remote northeast near the Lithuanian border, where he lived with his parents and grandparents and wife and small son, and where he would return the next day, everything weighed on him as a threat to personal freedom. Even, obscurely, the Jews, who he imagined were all successful businessmen having a wonderful time elsewhere, now that they didn't live in Poland anymore. Like all Poles, at some level of consciousness he lived uncomfortably among the ghosts of the three million Polish Jews and of all the foreign ones who were brought here to die.

"I *like* Jews," Krzysztof barked, sitting up, buoyant again and searching his pack for his bottle of home-brewed bison-grass vodka, a speciality of his region, the present specimen a speciality of Grampa Suchocki. "Bye-bye, gone is gone, let live and live." He meant to be nice and kept making it worse.

"Here!" He passed the *zubrówka*. "I've seen *Fiddler on the Roof!*"

Though such encounters are routine, it is a cliché to say that Poles are anti-Semitic; and what, anyway, does it mean, to be "anti" some- thing you don't know and cannot very accurately imagine? It means, for example, that in 1995 only 8 percent of Poles (among a few thou- sand surveyed on the fiftieth anniversary of the liberation of Auschwitz) recognized that the vast majority of victims were Jews. To be sure, Poles were pained that their own wartime sufferings had been eclipsed by the Jewish Holocaust. But also it seemed that here paranoia was bound up with nostalgia: less than a century ago, 75 percent of European Jews lived in Polish territory. You don't have to have met an "actual" one to sense that there is something missing here. But there didn't seem much point in asking Krzysztof how he felt about Gypsies.

By contrast, Gypsies, everywhere in sight, are the focus of a more robust hatred—made fresh by the new openness of democracy, which in the Eastern bloc, in comical contrast to the American variety, still means never having to say you're sorry. Walls across Eastern and Central Europe are sprayed with Death-to-Gypsies slogans, too many to be the work or sentiment of a small group. But in Poland, Gypsy-bashing gained local legitimacy because here the strangers really were foreigners—they were refugees. Despite the fact that perhaps half a million of them also perished during the war, including many thousands of Polish Gypsies, Carmen has no place in the Polish imagination.

We didn't speak again, and only nodded when he finally got off at the stop before me. It was as if the rollicking journey in this train coach, mine and Krzysztof's temporary mobile home, was a compressed version of a doomed love affair, played out in fast forward: cozy at dawn, with the tiny cabin lights keeping out the dark sky; mental note of full lips and fine skin (his); a shy introduction; curiosity; offerings of food; jokes; booze; confessions; solemnity; recognition of the other as an alien; contempt; and, finally, indifference.

As you get closer to Germany, you see more and more watchtowers along the tracks, miniature Abe Lincoln log cabins on stilts, from which the Polish border guards, with their binoculars, power torches, and guns, keep a lookout for refugees. But the viewing was poor that day. I joined this train at Warsaw in a blue dawn. Seven hours later, the dim day had barely bothered to begin, and, at 2 p.m., it was darkening fast. As we pulled into Rzepin, the last stop in Poland and the site of prolonged passport control, the only thing I could see looked like two Gypsy men on a bench, across the tracks and lit up in a cone of lamplight under the station portico. They were eating—so fast, so professionally, that they had no talk and no sandwiches, just alternate two-fisted shoveling: salami, bread, salami, bread.

"*Me mangav te jav ando granitza tumensa,*" I rehearsed to the now empty train car in Romani, conscientiously intoning its heavy, Indic, back-of-the-throat aspirates, wondering what the Gypsies would make of it—"I want to go to the border with you." *"Isi ma xarica love; so hramosorav andi gazeta; a-ko isi pomoshinav tumen"*—"I have a little money; I am a journalist; maybe I can help you."

Help? I felt uneasy with my First World guilt. In the former Eastern bloc it is great to be a visiting American. My nation's generosity, or simply its bountiful image, was everywhere repaid to me personally. Here you yourself (as well as what you did or didn't own) were what many people thought they wanted to be. Among Gypsies "USA" tattoos were especially popular. It was only high- and low-minded curiosity that had brought me here in the first place, and now everywhere I felt myself to be a parody of what the Gypsies perhaps all along were only rumored to be: unfreighted, freewheeling. Was I begging or choosing? Who was subsidizing whom?

The Polish controller sat right down and immersed himself in my overqualified navy-blue passport like a boy bent over a stamp collection. He ran a moist finger back and forth over the deep-purple stamp of Malaysia, the oversize invitation to Tanzania, the faint remains of a trip to Mexico, as if trying to unstick some of their national essence. (Uniquely unintriguing to him was the stamp for Albania, or "E Republikes Popullore Socialiste te Shquiperise," with the "Popullore" and "Socialiste" touchingly crossed through by hand.) People believe that Gypsies are dangerous because they have nothing to lose. And here I sat, impatient, even indignant, as this pale guard felt up my passport. Swollen with extra pages, that little accordion and its inky scores of distant anthems was the proof that I was the only one who had nothing to lose. I could just leave.

Hurtling towards the other side—towards Germany, its streets paved with deutschemarks and the attacks on foreigners only a killjoy rumor, as the Gypsies on this side believe—I kept repeating it to myself like a mantra: *"A-ko isi pomoshinav tumen"*—"Maybe I can help you." At Rzepin Station I would be given the chance. I was to tell a story, and then I was to trade it, as a Gypsy would, for another.

Flipping a mental coin, I stood for a time at the streaked train window, peering at the spotlit salami-eaters. Perhaps catching the glint of that coin, one of them paused and looked over to me. He raised his shoulders in a friendly shrug and indicated their stash with an open palm—an invitation to help myself. The border controller's fascination with my documents gave way to welcome disdain; I pulled my rucksack down off the overhead rack and jumped off the train.

Mihai and Ion Bardu were brothers. They were small and slight and dark. They stroked their matching mustaches; each kept the nail of his right little finger long and sharp. Over many other garments which did nothing to obscure their thinness, they wore cheap suits, one brown, one gray, all four flared trouser legs frayed at the floor-grazing, mud-caked cuffs. The Bardu boys were Gypsies from Braşov, the old German town of Kronstadt, in Romania. Lucky for me: I was able to say that I knew the place quite well, and this, along with my much-rehearsed Romani, produced bewildered laughter, together with a private view of many gold teeth and an invitation to meet the rest of their group. The two men had made a trip into town to buy provisions, and were returning with the goods after this sampling session on the station platform—just to make sure that everything was *shukar*, or fine.

The brothers' wives were themselves sisters, and with their seven children, including some younger siblings and two babies, they sat around in their layered skirts and their spent felt slippers, waiting tiredly behind a parking-lot fence by a great heap of rusted rails and scrap metal. They were fairly settled in: a few small flames rouged the ashen bed of an old fire. One rag-doll girl of around five lay crying, limply inconsolable and anyway ignored over an older girl's lap. The rest were amused by my arrival, or maybe just by my accent, and their cheerfully indifferent responses to my *kaj, so, kana, kon, soske*—my where, what, when, who, why—gradually warmed and sharpened. The women, who laughed the hardest, and whose approbation one naturally most sought, never spoke to me directly but always through the men. The Bardus had been camping behind the scrap heap for nearly a week. With two babies they had crossed three borders and more than a thousand miles from Braşov to Rzepin, in slippers. Now they were waiting for a sign—a sign from Vesh.

Vesh was the third brother. Earlier in the week he had taken his family and one of Ion's sons and crossed into Germany. It was no big deal, wading over the silvery Oder, even up here where the water was higher than it was farther down the thirteen-hundred-kilometer border (at the point where the Oder becomes the Neisse). There are low spots everywhere, and there are fewer than a hundred guards for every three hundred kilometers. But there were also deep patches, and currents, and fear among poor swimmers, and poor swimmers with children. Colonel Adamczyk Wiesław, chief of the Polish border patrol, told me how he himself had seen a young Gypsy woman from Romania attempting to cross with two children—holding one in each hand, as he demonstrated with both elbows hoisted to shoulder height. She lost both of them. Officially, fourteen people had drowned; rumor converted the number to 140, or 1,400. There were tales of bodies chewed up by great back-churning diesel trawlers.

The Bardus had come this far on their own, and they were mighty scornful of the many more timorous Gypsies who had forked out five hundred deutschemarks per family to a *Schlepper*. The Bardus got the irony of the professional person-herder telling a Gypsy how to move and travel, and they didn't find it funny. But for this family, as for so many others, when they were thinking of the other side, of the West, pride in traveling know-how gave way to the sensible fear that they would likely be deported or—perhaps preferable to them—jailed. And so the Bardus had booked themselves in for the second stage of a deluxe package *Schlep*, which featured a chaperone component: they were to be met on the western bank and shown which roads, camps, and towns to avoid, and which services could be safely milked and how to do the milking.

Vesh was to telephone his brothers in three days' time, here, at Rzepin Station, where they had paid off a rail employee to take the call. Five days later, no word. Mihai and Ion were convinced that the stationmaster had taken their money and ignored the call. And so they sat by the phone—or rather lurked near it, taking turns blocking the grilled ticket window, peering threateningly at the clerk.

They feared the worst. Had Vesh been nabbed? They didn't know much about their *Schlepper* and, perhaps embarrassed and angry that they'd ever hired one, they were vague about what arrangements—or promises—had been made. Mihai and Ion debated, whinnying with exasperation, over whether to follow Vesh or to hang around, or even (they didn't like to say it in front of the women) to turn back. The day before I arrived it had snowed for the first time. Something had to be decided.

The brothers were skeptical but they didn't have much choice. It was obvious. I would go and try to find out what had happened to Vesh. Flushed with a sense of mission, I overpaid a man with a car to drive me to the point at which he had to turn back, and from there I walked.

It was dark on the bridge over the Oder, except for the lights of the trucks parked all along it. Their Polish and Russian drivers had been waiting for days for permission from German officials to take their Western cargoes east; meanwhile, they had set up camps of their own between the great chrome grilles. Just inside Germany there was a Burger King, with a we're-in-the-West poster promising a "Whopper Orgie!" Russian soldiers, cinched into their padded coats, drank German beer at high counters, untroubled by the amputated wieners and the pools of thin mustard that ran off a limp deck of paper plates.

No sign of a slight, dark, mustachioed man in a cheap flared suit. Onwards, by milk train, to Eisenhüttenstadt, home of Germany's largest refugee reception and sorting camp. If Vesh and family hadn't simply vanished into the fatherland they might just be here, where they would be lodged until the bureaucracy decided their fate.

The camp was easy to find: just follow the refugees—the Africans, the Vietnamese, and the sprinkling of badly dressed white folk, namely the Eastern Europeans (though the Gypsies constitute more than a third of the eight-hundred-plus population at the camp, they keep to themselves and you don't see them on the trains and buses). The camp at Eisenhüttenstadt is enormous: barbed-wire fences (designed more to keep violence out than to keep inmates in), and great three-storied barracks separated by prefab aluminum storage canisters, recently and hastily erected to meet the flow.

Standing in the cold outside the camp office, in a throng of refugees clutching thin pieces of paper etched in a language they couldn't understand, I got a glimpse of the life of the seeker. At the front, with one foot inside the office, Kofi, from Ghana, was jutting chin-to-chin with an irritated camp counselor and insisting that the photograph stapled to his application was a photograph of the wrong African. The counselor insisted that the photograph was a photograph of Kofi. Kofi said no way. This went on for ten long minutes, the upshot being that because he could not recognize himself, Kofi would have to reapply for the same papers and the same picture, which would eventually indicate where among Germany's many refugee camps and halfway housing in cheap hotels he would be processed on to. It would take an additional four to six weeks. Next!

Inside I was given a guided tour. Olaf, my young guide, mumbled that I mustn't speak to the inmates. He seemed embarrassed to have to say it. This, along with the unexpected *intifada* kit—a fringed black-and-white cotton check scarf, army fatigues, and a ponytail halfway down his back—gave hope. Soon I was speaking to a Romany family from Romania. "Do you know Veshengo Bardu?" I asked the man and obvious head of his hovering family. He flinched, I was sure he flinched, but he said nothing. He certainly looked like the Bardus, I thought with some shame, remembering Kofi and his brothers from all-Africa. With nearly three hundred transient Gypsies milling about the place, the identification seemed far-fetched. I spoke to other men in the barracks until Olaf began to paw the ground with one steel-reinforced toecap, indicating that I was pushing my luck.

Inside a staff room, he was happy to tell me how things worked here, and what impact the new agreement between the German and Romanian governments to ease the deportation of Gypsies was likely to make.

"Up until last summer [1992] anyone caught at the border, or more usually anyone who asked for *Asyl* [pronounced "azool"], was brought here, given food and a bed. They filled in a declaration regarding their status, they were given an ID card." He produced a small yellow example. "Eventually they were sent to another camp—sometimes for more than a year—while their case was processed at the *Bundesamt*, at Nuremberg."

"Nuremberg?" The place where fates were decided was the city that saw not only the Nazi war-crimes trials but also the passage of the 1935 race laws—the ones that determined who was a Jew, who was a Gypsy. Then, too, Nuremberg had been the place where fates were decided.

In the previous year alone five hundred thousand people applied for asylum in Germany, favored for its liberal asylum laws and its location.

"In the end, about 4 percent get in," said Olaf. "Among the Gypsies, though, it is only .02 percent."

"What happens to the rest?"

"Deported. The problem in the past was that there was no place to deport them to. Gypsies were often refused re-entry to their own countries—Romania especially. Now their government must accept them."

Romania was paid thirty million deutschemarks to take back its own citizens, in effect from November 1, 1992. Similar deals were in the works between Germany and Bulgaria and Germany and Poland—all of them specifically designed to tackle "the Gypsy problem."

But where was Vesh?

As it turned out, six months later I would go to Bucharest to see what effect the agreement was having. It was immediately clear that none of the deported were to see a single pfennig of the legendary thirty million deutschemarks that had been explicitly linked to their return by

Rudolf Seiters, then the minister of the interior and architect of the deal. In fact the linkage was downright cynical; that money had long since been committed for use in three retraining centers—in Arat, Sibiu, and Timişoara—expressly for the benefit of unemployed ethnic *Germans.*

The agreement stipulated that transport to the "home" country should be paid for by the German government. But before the removals even began, Lufthansa issued a statement saying that they would not transport handcuffed passengers. This snag was not a problem of transport (there was always Tarom, the Romanian airline, which when I first flew it had limited rations of seat belts); this was a problem of credibility. Lufthansa's sensible safety regulation, emerging just when it did, revealed the general assumption that these Romanian asylum-seekers were criminals.

And indeed in handcuffs they went. (Some returnees claim to have been handcuffed to radiators for nights before flying out.) Within the first six months, about twelve thousand had been deported under the agreement. And most of them paid for the trip on their own national airline with what they imagined was their own money. Any cash left over—sometimes as much as two thousand deutschemarks (twelve hundred dollars)—was confiscated. "They took all my money," an incredulous old Rom told me in Bucharest's Otopeni Airport, "and they said it would be given to *charity.*"

It was being assumed by the German officials handling the send-offs that all the money in the Gypsies' pockets was wrongfully acquired—by sponging off the German social services, by working illegally. In fact many Romanian Gypsies who had made the trip had sold up to pay for the trip over, or in any case had brought all their savings with them, as anyone hoping to start a new life would. And so they were returning poorer than when they had left, and many of them homeless as well. It is a common sight at Otopeni to see bewildered returnees, most of them obviously Gypsies, who had flown in at night with no money for even the bus fare home.

Was there any kind of program, I asked an airport immigration official, to help resettle the refuseniks? The place, despite recent renovations, was itself looking a bit like a refugee camp, with people sleeping everywhere. "If they can get all the way to Germany," he replied, with some reason and some of the nostril-flaring contempt that was usual in discussions about the returnees, "I think they can find their way home."

The resettlement problems were compounded by the fact that these confirmed rejects were met with special contempt by Romanians who had stayed behind in the village. Those who could claim even limited success in their trip to Germany (you could make money and keep it if you left before being deported, as those who came back from second or third trips knew) were the object of intense jealousy. The tension was building nicely: that has been the primary result of the Bonn-Bucharest Agreement, which on the Romanian side is baldly known as "the Gypsy Protocol." By joint policy, the Romanian Gypsies had become political rather than economic refugees. But you didn't need to look at international agreements to know that there was nothing "optional" about the travel plans of the Bardus. You just had to look at their slippers. And their eyes. The Rom to whom I had first spoken in the camp, the man I had taken for Vesh, was clearly silenced by fear.

One of the reasons Gypsies wind up with no place to go is that they destroy their passports or identity cards, making it easy for governments to disown them. They know that their identity—self-ascribed or presumed—is not written on those cards. Justifiably enough, they declare themselves homeless, and hope that the German authorities (for it is mainly they) won't be able to return them to a place that doesn't exist. Or they hope, at least, that before they are sorted out and put back on that eastbound bus they will have some months in the "West" (a brand name for cigarettes and jeans, and a catchall word for status, cash, and freedom, which has only gained force since the end of the Cold War).

Before 1989, Eastern-bloc credentials guaranteed asylum for anyone who made it out. The current deal means that even unidentified refuseniks can be deported immediately. But one problem remains: how to tell where they come from? A press release from the minister of the interior outlines the procedure: by language, by confession, and, most ominously, "by the opinion of experts and witnesses." There were already cases, Olaf told me, of zip-lipped asylum-seekers' being sent to Romania willy-nilly. Though they were not registered according to their ethnicity in immigration statistics, they were lumped together in a practice which weirdly acknowledged their homelessness: they were Gypsies, and were therefore to be dispatched to the Black Sea.

Authorities have always nursed fantasies about distant Gypsy reservations—in Madagascar, Somaliland, Guyana, an "island in the South Pacific"—and many places have been seriously proposed. In the sixteenth century, Portugal became the first country to deport Gypsies to its colonies in Africa, and later to Brazil and to India. Though less systematically than Portugal, a hundred years later France was sending Gypsies to Martinique and Louisiana; England and Scotland sent shipments to the West Indies. The historian Angus Fraser points out that this novel method of expulsion was considered acceptable, and useful for the slave labor it provided (cargoes of Gypsies preceded African captives), because the Gypsies were transported only within the empire, and so were not, strictly speaking, deported.

"The problem is," Olaf said softly, "this is not *political* persecution."

I pointed out that there had been serious attacks in the Czech Republic, in Hungary, and in Poland; that only Poland had held a trial over an attack on a Gypsy community (in Mława), and that the case was later dropped. I mentioned that there hadn't been any prosecutions anywhere, and that in Romania the government actively condoned the attacks.

"Condoned is not the same as ordered, or organized, or paid for. Not in our constitution, anyway." We paused to consider the niceties. "You have to understand," he went on, redirecting the conversation to what he saw as the real problem, "many of our neighbors come here just to collect social benefits. By giving them coupons instead of cash, we hope to discourage this kind of visitor."

Some of the Gypsy visitors were indeed imitating their governments: they spoke the imported language of human rights and expected to be paid, or subsidized, for it. Often they were. And though Romania welcomed millions of tons of humanitarian aid in the form of food and clothes (the great majority of which was immediately sold off and never reached the poor and largely Roma settlements and orphanages), *some* enterprising Gypsies took their cue and went to Germany to collect personally their individual aid packages. In Olaf's office, the most culpable seekers these days seemed to be the Eastern Europeans—which was to say, more often than not, the Gypsies. Germans may resent them more than they resent Africans (also arriving in their tens of thousands), because the Europeans are not only poor but are also neighbors, relations by previous marriages of state—and their predicament may thus imply German responsibility.

At Eisenhüttenstadt, itself part of the East until German reunification, such tender consciousness was acute. Here the line between us and them, between West and East, was being demarcated every day.

" 'An element of insecurity,' " I said to Olaf, who tugged on his ponytail, waiting for amplification. " 'Gypsies are an element of inse-curity and thus a danger to society. . . .' "

"Yes!" he said, relieved that I seemed to be catching on. "What we are dealing with here is an *invasion.*"

But it *was* an invasion, and perhaps it was unfair to quote a Nazi document at Olaf. He was himself in a curious kind of costume—part Palestinian, part American GI, part street kid from London or Berlin; and he had mixed-up views to match. Here his combat boots did not look cool; his were just the heavy feet of bureaucracy. Perhaps it is the occupational hazard of the camp-worker, but nevertheless the asylum-seekers had for him become faceless, and when he spoke in his own voice ("you have to understand . . .") he clearly felt they were more degrading than degraded.

"Is it working? What about the antiforeigner attacks, are those stemming the flow?"

"Nothing has made any difference. Nothing except the weather. Germany has a friend in winter."

And Gypsies—in effect stateless—have a friend of a kind in borders. In this part of the world, someone will always remember a different map. The line is rarely fixed (look at maps of bulimic Poland between 1813 and 1945), and the shaded areas on either side are the eternally con-tested no-man's-lands of aspiration and deprivation. Borders are the cordons beyond which the grass starts to get greener. And, so long as visits there are not compulsory, the other side is always a liberation. This is not-home; a no-count zone. Adventure is possible. To Gypsies borders are all these things, but they have also long been the other kind of cordon: a line of police, soldiers, guards; a *cordon sanitaire,* with themselves the supposedly infected minority. Gypsies—unflaggingly borderline people—have no borders cluttering the maps of their own collective imagination. But Gypsies are not spoiled, and these bound-aries are to them also veins of opportunity.

Everywhere the solution to "the Gypsy problem" has at some stage included expulsion. And again the punishment engendered the crime. Kicking them out—for *being* outsiders—confirmed the Gypsies as vagrants and vagabonds. But they adapted, often by living in abandoned and inaccessible forests and wastelands, the countries within countries, and the borderlands. They grew savvy about discrepancies in local jurisdictions and the erratic responsiveness of local authorities to handed-down decrees. They hopscotched along the frontiers, camping. Thus there are and always have been concentrations of Gypsies at the edges of countries and, similarly, within national boundaries, along county lines. Early records find them near the borders between the German states, between France and Spain, in the easternmost parts of the Dutch Repub-lic, in the Scottish Borders. The borderland between Scotland and England, like all unclaimed or locally debated land, has been known in legend for its great populations of brigands and Gypsies. For the stateless inhabitants, such no-man's-lands may be cells without walls, established by mapmaking—what might be called cartographic incarceration.

Patrick Faa was a Border Gypsy, who, in 1715, along with seven oth-ers (six of them women), was deported to a Virginia plantation on a dubious conviction for arson. He left behind him both of his ears (part of his punishment), and his wife, the legendary Jean Gordon. Immor-talized in fiction as Meg Merrilies in Walter Scott's *Guy Mannering*, Gor-don was herself banished from Scotland seventeen years later, on the grounds that she was a vagabond and an Egyptian—though she was already old and ill, and had lost not only her husband but all her nine sons (one murdered, the others hanged). Jean Gordon spent the rest of her days wandering around on the other side, in the English Borders, until she went down (shouting for Prince Charlie), ducked to death by a mob in 1746.

I thanked Olaf and waved to him over my shoulder as he retreated into the warmth of the staff room. On the way out, a man down in the con-tainer barracks we'd visited was waving me over. He was the first Gypsy in the camp I had spoken to. Humming with adrenaline, I moved towards him. And then, in the shelter of one of the prefab bungalows, he spoke: *"Me som Bardu"*—I am Bardu.

The good news was that they hadn't been deported. Yet. On the advice of their *Schlepper* they had ditched their passports. Or rather they had handed them over to him, and now (as I myself had just learned), without these documents, they were slated for immediate and irreversible removal from the asylum process. But the *Schlepper* had promised to return their passports in exchange for a cut of their first social benefits—about four hundred deutschemarks for adults and a little over a hundred for each child. Regrettably, though, he didn't accept coupons.

Vesh looked like his name: both wild and soft, his alert, speedy black eyes boring out through great wrinkly pouches, as rage vied—his next move, only ever the very next thing—with deep longing for sleep. From his vest pocket he produced a pencil about an inch and a half long, and scratched a note on the white side of foil from a cigarette packet.

I rushed to make the last train to the bridge, hoping to reach the Bardus as planned and give them news, along with the German chocolate and net sack of Jaffa oranges I'd picked up at the station. On the German side of the bridge I was stopped by a pair of Soviet soldiers. Perhaps it was only curiosity: I was wearing the same hat as they were—a tall square of fake fur with tied-up ears, the kind pressed on tourists at Berlin's Brandenburg Gate (minus the enameled hammer and sickle). With bruised suspicion they looked hard at me, this rude and female counterfeit; and I looked back, fearless as I realized that they represented no authority, despite their pistols and badges (*their* dinky hammers and sickles). They too were refugees.

Many of the asylum-seekers' camps are the former barracks of Russian soldiers, who have been evicted in favor even of no-hopers like Kofi and Vesh. And now the soldiers themselves, representing no country, were in the process of being returned, if anyone could figure out where to send them.

I made it all the way back to Rzepin Station, panting in the dark. I climbed the rusted rails and looked down at the abandoned fire pit; I scanned the parking lot and rushed back to the station. As I regained my breath, I walked back and forth along the platform, finally stopping to ask the persecuted Polish ticketmaster (in hysterical sign-language) if he had seen those Gypsies. He shrugged, but I already knew they'd gone.

As my train pulled away, I watched the pyramid of oranges until they vanished, my little monument glowing like a traffic cone on the bench where I first saw Ion and Mihai Bardu. Vesh's note was tucked underneath.

SIX

Zigeuner Chips

"THERE IS NO room," said the authorities at the eastern German port city of Rostock, when they were faced with housing two hundred Romanian Gypsy asylum-seekers in the summer of 1992. Thus they echoed the diluvial slogan of a right-wing political party, "The boat is full" (the phrase appears most often as a poster caption under a drawing of a boat, the ark of Germany). Authorities must house asylum-seekers before they are either deported or moved on but in Rostock they simply refused. And so the Gypsies made do outside the hostel, sleeping and eating there and, as the local press put it, "provoking" the people of Rostock into what would become an attack of landmark viciousness. The town cheered when the hostel was firebombed by some 150 skinheads. Room for the refugees was found immediately afterwards.

What Germans had seen on their televisions was a police force with its arms crossed, standing back on a hill, out of the path of whistling homemade Molotov cocktails and stones. In the next month alone, 1,163 "xenophobic" crimes were reported in German cities and towns. Lothar Kupfer, the regional minister of the interior, gave the weekly *Die Zeit* the popular explanation for these events, with a new slant on the boat people:

> When 200 asylum seekers have to live together [with Germans] in a very tight space, this unleashes aggression in the German neighbors. Most of them have long forgotten how they stood in the harbor and looked longingly after the ferry: distant lands, wide oceans, dark-skinned women. When one day [these people] camp in front of an overfilled shelter, take care of personal needs behind the wild rose bushes, and throw their garbage on the rotting playground and then beg on top of it, the longing for foreign lands is over.

Although in many German cities the number of foreigners had radically *decreased*, the most frequently proposed solution to the violence was a tightening of Article 16 of the Constitution: the liberal asylum clause that was installed after the war.

Even as thousands of foreign guest-workers packed their bags, Germans found the issue a welcome distraction from the broader distress of the still-incomplete reunification of the two Germanys. A survey of three thousand people in *Der Spiegel* of October 1992 claimed that 96 percent of Germans were troubled by the "foreigner problem," and endorsed (nonviolent) antiforeigner "measures." . . .

Who were all these foreigners and why were they so worrying? Unusually in a country given to precise taxonomies, *Ausländer*, or "foreigner," is a term which encompasses a catalogue of foreign types; many east and west Germans I met understandably found it hard to say. While even skinheads embraced their international brethren (with their Union Jacks and U.S.-army fatigues), east Germans in particular, so recently refugee material themselves, felt threatened and offended by asylum-seekers. And yet a study by the Central Institute for Youth Research in Leipzig found that in the summer of 1990—that is, before a single asylum-seeker was sent to a temporary camp or assigned housing in east Germany—40 percent of the local youth found them to be "bothersome." The Leipzig deputy chief of police was more precise:

> I won't exclude the possibility that some police are racist. Given the heated discussion about asylum, everyone is surely thinking about all these foreigners who are arriving. It was not smart or reasonable to send them here [to the Eastern states] so soon. Police are not against every foreigner, but only certain ones, like the Sinti and Roma and black Africans.

Foreigners—the more foreign the better—certainly had their uses. The writer Günter Grass also singled out Gypsies among Germany's broad selection of foreigners. In a lecture entitled "Losses," given in November of 1992 (five days after three long-resident Turkish women were burned in their beds at Mölln), he suggested that "half a million and more Sinti and Roma" come live in Germany: "We need them." Both the riot-pressed authorities and Günter Grass were deploying "Sinti and Roma" as a symbol of the stranger. Whether hostile or humanizing, the Gypsies above all were *other*.

In Oberwart, Austria, four Roma were killed by a pipe bomb in February 1995. The bomb went off when the men tried to remove a sign that read "Gypsies Go Back to India." Oberwart is in Austria's Burgenland, where Roma have been settled for more than three hundred years.

.   .   .

In the spring of 1993 the German federal parliament voted to amend Article 16. The message was clear. Days later, at Solingen, a town near Cologne, two Turkish women and three Turkish girls were murdered.

I was in Germany that week. On the walk to the castle from Machern Station you pass wooded glens and enchanted, bramble-buried cottages with low, child-size doorways. It is easy to imagine that the people of this Grimm-like hamlet slept through forty years of communism. Machern, near Leipzig, was an improbable setting for one of the earliest post-unification skinhead rallies. Since then it has been host to what locals see as a never-ending troop of asylum-seekers, though they are housed outside town. (Some three hundred would-be refugees, all of them Roma, were living at Sachsen, a nearby camp.) For a few June days in 1993, Machern also played host to a small group of concerned Germans and Romanian Gypsies who had gathered in the local *Schloss,* or castle, to explore any possible benefits from the migration of Roma in particular. Because they were still filing into Germany in their thousands, while everything conspired to thwart their migration.

I needed no visa to travel to Machern. Participants from the EC were free to come and go. But some of the invited Gypsies were detained by immigration officials and missed all or part of the conference. One of them was a Member of Parliament. What chance, then, did the rest of them stand? These people might be cast out, but they certainly weren't downcast.

One participating refugee expert, whose job it had been to prepare deported Mozambiquans for a difficult re-entry to their country, coached conferees in the "skills" he'd pass on to the disappointed before they were herded onto that homebound plane. On the conference center's visual-aid display board he scribbled:

> *Bescheiden Sein!*
> *Vertrauen Haben!*
> *Fehlschlage Einkalkulieren!*

Be modest; have trust; calculate risks. *Bescheidenheit:* modesty. That is the free advice the nearly departed get for their trouble. A Hungarian specialist involved in job creation for Roma outlined various "development strategies" and "survival strategies," including, in the latter category, collecting bottles for deposits.

At the final session, which everyone was expected to attend, only three Roma remained: two businessmen seeking investors, and Nicolae Gheorghe, the ubiquitous activist. Where had the other three Rom leaders gone? Where was Gheorghe Raducanu, the only Gypsy MP in Romania? And where was Vasile Burtea, the well-spoken representative of the Romanian Ministry of Labor and Social Protection and, according to his business card, "Sociolist [sic] and Economist"? Where was the blue-haired Nicolae Bobu, *Diplomat in drept; avocat* ("degreed in law; lawyer"), president of the General Union of Roma in Romania, and *"ex parlamentar"* (as *his* card boasted)?

While the working groups presented their "findings," the conference organizers looked exasperatedly across the panel to the three empty seats in the front row. These Germans, genuinely interested in seeking workable solutions for Gypsy migrants, were talking among themselves. And then, though I wasn't really looking, I found them.

Stepping out into the eastern German drizzle for some air, from the top of the grandly scalloped steps of the *Schloss* I surveyed the blue puddles dotted over the newly tarmacked parking lot. There they were, the mischievous *crème* of Romanian Gypsies, squealing with delight around a pair of toylike two-door cars—the twin Trabants that they had just picked up for 75 and 150 deutschemarks, or 45 and 90 bucks respectively. The three men looked like boys, all of them small in their even smaller suits, poking around under the hoods of their new wheels like boy teenagers anywhere. They were jubilant—after all, this is what most Gypsy migrants were coming to Germany *for:* to buy cars for resale in the East, at no cost to the German social or welfare system.

I asked the MP how they knew where to buy cars, on such short notice, with little German and a great deal of rain. He shrugged and laughed. Stupid question. No, these were not people who needed to be schooled in survival strategies.

Gypsies like the Machern delegates had been working this route several hundred years before ethnic nationalism was even articulated in Germany; half a millennium ago, many others had made their home in German lands. But still Sinti in Germany do not qualify for *Volksgruppe* status, as do other minority groups, such as the Danes and the Sorbs. So when does a foreigner become a native? The American Constitution originally defined the descendants of African slaves as three-fifths human; and now "native" is still wrongly used in the United States to denote an Indian, rather than merely someone who has claims of birth. The Sinti would never be regarded as natives (except in the sense of "primitives"), let alone as Germans. But could their hosts, who share borders with eight different countries, really entertain the existence of a pure Teuton outside some Frankenstein's laboratory? Of course not. It is the *idea* of the pure-blooded German that is the kernel of German identity, and by extension the cultural values which are deemed to be racially ensured. The Romanian Gypsies would be familiar with this line of thinking, after years of Ceauşescu's rhetoric about the Dacians, the "pure" proto-Romanians. All citizens of the former Eastern bloc shared—or, if they were minorities, suffered from—this dream of a one-race state; Germany was the model.

At work in the German imagining of itself is the sentimental ideal of the *Volk.* Originally a reaction against the French glorification of the individual, the *Volk* myth provided a unifying ideology for a population which was widely dispersed, particularly over the eastern territories. The German Romantic intelligentsia, probably sitting around these very *Schlosses* at the beginning of the nineteenth century, came up with the notion of the *Volk*—epitomized by the archetypal German still found on packaging everywhere: blond, healthy, neat, and busy. To look at any Heidi on a packet of German biscuits is to understand the ideal: inner well-being—as revealed by pink cheeks and lustrous yellow hair—achieved by happy and industrious allegiance (or submission) to the *Volk*.

This *Volk* business provides clues to the special contempt that Gypsies, among many despised foreigners, seem to elicit. First, they appear to be the German *Volk*'s opposite: dirty, dark, devious, idle, and aggressively antisocial. But then, more subtly, these people really do represent a *Volk*. They keep to themselves and they maintain their customs, their language, and their close-knit community, itself always prized above the individual. At least among their own, Gypsies were truly communitarian in a way that Germans could only fantasize about. The Germans offered citizenship to "ethnic" Germans abroad as a reward for supposedly having refused to adopt heathen (Slavic) ways over their centuries-long sojourn in the East; and here, right in their front yards, was a group who really had not—and would not—assimilate.

In the fall of 1992, and again in 1993, I traveled in the new eastern *Länder*, or states, to see how the recent arrivals were fitting in. Posses of Gypsy women—you never see a lone Gypsy—are a common spectacle. Mostly, to guess by their garments, they were of the Kalderash tribe, from Romania. In their bright, reddish, dizzy-patterned yards of skirt, with babies slung in little hammocks over the hip, they appear in an eastern German street like the only color figures in a black-and-white photograph.

A pack of Gypsy women and their children were hovering about the door of the public prosecutor's office in Cottbus, a leafy east German town not far from Berlin and close to the Polish border. According to the guard, they'd been waiting for days for an appointment with anyone and the chance to obtain the release of some of their imprisoned menfolk on the grounds that they were sick of Germany and wanted to—promised to—go away. At the end of the day, still sprawled over the wide front steps of the building, they didn't look like they were going anywhere fast. It seemed brave enough to be hanging around that office at all, given their precarious legal status, but it was easy to imagine how their languid, nothing-to-lose poses and the anti-camouflage clothes might strike east Germans as provocative. They didn't speak to anyone and they weren't *doing* anything, but still their appearance would be read as aggressive. Whatever they did, and despite a long-settled, well-integrated population of about seventy

Ready for new opportunities: Ion Mihai, a Kalderash Rom from Sintesti, Romania, combines his role of bulibasha—*traditional local leader and settler of disputes—with a successful career as a scrap-metal dealer, 1993.*

thousand German Gypsies, by appearance alone these recent arrivals have become emblematic of the unassimilable foreigner.

In contrast to the locals, when they did bestir themselves they moved on with a lightness and skirt-swirling swiftness that made you wonder if what you'd just seen wasn't a handful of confetti flung over the gray cityscape. But something else gave them the air of an apparition, and an anachronism: like the standard-issue Edwardian ghosts of films, they were in period costume. Their men—whom one hardly saw, even though they are traditionally charged with dealings among *gadje*—had kept their mustaches but exchanged their traditional togs for the cheap suits and dumpster-wear of poor people the world over. Yet the women could have been actresses in a film about earlier migrations, playing the "ethnic" counterparts to the new arrivals in frockcoats and top hats at Ellis Island in the crowd scene of Charlie Chaplin's *The Immigrant*. The women sport the same sweeping skirts and back-knotted flowery head scarves that say and always have said: Gypsy.

Wild, untamable, and sexy, Carmen, the original coal-eyed *fatale*, was in her creator Prosper Mérimée's description, "a thoroughbred filly from a Cordova stud." Being a Gypsy, she was also a talented thief. And a murderess. Thus prejudice is complicated by romantic yearnings, which find a sad echo among the Gypsies themselves, always anxious to tell you that they—not the sorners down the road—are the *real* Gypsies. Even the castanet-clacking stereotype is cast as a lesson in danger, and it seems she may be activated at any time, even among the lot of disheveled women behind chicken wire in a German refugee camp. The Gypsy is the quintessential stranger—and strangers are never benevolent.

It starts early, with fear. "Hush ye, hush ye, dinna fret yet / The Black tinkler winna get ye," goes a not very soothing Scottish lullaby. In traditional Bulgarian carnivals—still a feature of peasant life in remote parts of what was once called Thrace—the Plague is represented as an old Gypsy woman; or, more ominously, as a heavy cart pulled along by harnessed Gypsies.

The spy, though, is perhaps the oldest among sinister stereotypes. With their foreign tongue, dark looks, and ambiguous origins; with their expert knowledge of local laws and hedgerows and their tendency to hug the borders; with their disinclination to comply with local custom and their lack of apparent allegiance to anyone—Gypsies were particularly vulnerable to the charge. With no state of their own, and without even the desire for one—a condition both unique and unfathomable, then as now—they *had* to be in the service of some foreign country or sovereign.

The Germans, with their empire at the edge of the Christian world, were especially drawn to the espionage theory, which first crops up in the 1424 diary of one Ratisbon, a Bavarian priest. The earliest imperial edicts anywhere against the Gypsies, issued by Maximilian I in 1497, 1498, and 1500, single them out as spies in the pay of the Turks.

But nowadays they are called fakers of another kind: *Scheinasylanten*—literally, fake-asylum-seekers, or, in the political euphemism, "economic" refugees. *All* migrants move in pursuit of a better life; furthermore, those who uproot themselves are often the most enterprising members of their society (the economic refugee is the hero of the American dream). Still, these Gypsies were not merely ambitious, for "economic" refugees often become so as a result of discriminatory politics. One way was through targeted deportation strategies. But more generally, as Gypsies, they are the least likely to be hired, housed, or schooled anywhere in the former Eastern bloc.

One difficulty in conjuring up genuine—as opposed to economic, or fake—refugees is a legacy of language. No one knows what to call Gypsies. Every language has a term that denotes a strictly social meaning. *Cigan, ţigan, Cygani,* and of course "gypping" Gypsies—these terms are used as adjectives to describe behavior: heretical, rascally, cheating, thieving, hassling. In Eastern Europe, they can also signal flashiness, machismo, and ostentatious sentimentality (all fakery of a kind). And yet many Gypsies *like* the term Gypsy (rather in the way that "queer" is back in fashion among homosexuals), because they are defiant, not ashamed; and also because they don't believe a new name will change the way people see them.

Every country has another, more polite designation: Roma, Romanies, and (in Germany) "Sinti & Roma"; and these terms are often used by non-Gypsies to distinguish between people who are thought to be Gypsies by choice (following a "life-style"), and those who are members of some noble and, above all, vanished tribe.

"Sinti & Roma" has superseded *Zigeuner,* a term which to German ears has begun to sound like "Negro," if not quite like "nigger." The new form is misleading as well (the distinction between the two names cannot be understood by nonspecialists, and so it seems a nervous, or safe, tautology, rather like "gay and lesbian"). In fact, the term Sinti & Roma is just the joining of two distinct Gypsy groups. More confusing still, since the name Roma has emerged as most Gypsies' own favorite to denote *all* of their people, to say "Sinti & Roma" is also something like saying "Sephardim and Jews"—meaning Jews.

While I was in Cottbus a journalist covering the antiforeigner attacks for a local newspaper was brought before the German press council for using the term *Zigeuner.* Nevertheless, these nuances have not yet been fully absorbed: in Bonn I bought a brand of crisps called "Zigeuner Chips" (*"krosser, würziger!"*—"crispier, spicier!"): "Jew Chips" in our analogy, and appropriate considering that Gypsies were murdered in their hundreds of thousands by the Nazis. You can find chocolate creams in Britain called "Gypsies"; but this was Germany, and *Zigeuner* recalled the "Z" tattoo on the arms of early Gypsy arrivals at Auschwitz.

The recent violence was surely in part a bristling against the nervous pacifism that German history has mandated for this nation. Anti-Gypsyism was especially promising as a potential for catharsis. Whereas, by contrast, Germans would never be allowed to stop apologizing to Jews, hardly anyone was seriously troubled by the thought of the Gypsies' feelings or their possible protests. Not even the Gypsies.

The distinction between "genuine" and fake refugees appears in early anti-Gypsy legislation all over Europe, and in England, Scotland, and Germany in particular. In the German lands it was Bismarck who in 1886 first codified the already practiced discrimination between *inländische Zigeuner* and *ausländische Zigeuner*, or native and foreign Gypsies, which in turn became a handy device for ejecting anyone who wasn't a local (while those who were recognized as *inländische* would be counted and monitored by the police). In the eighteenth century, borrowing a Dutch tactic, Germans erected painted signs along the roads, graphically showing the beatings, floggings, and even hangings that apprehended Gypsies might expect. At the same time, it was announced, informers would be rewarded. Bounty hunting had begun. Intensive *Heidenjachten* ("heathen hunts"—but in fact Gypsy hunts) were a feature of the eighteenth-century Dutch Republic. A landowner in the Rhineland tallies among the bagged, that is, captured and killed, in his hunting log of 1835 "Gypsy woman and suckling babe."

Long before this had become popular sport, Denmark decreed capital punishment for Gypsy leaders in 1589, and fifty years later, Sweden specified hanging for all Gypsy males. Between 1471 and 1637, with none of the circumspection that has characterized European union in our time, the consolidating nation-states threw themselves into a cooperative of cruelty. Lucerne, Brandenburg, Spain, Germany, Holland, Portugal, England, Denmark, France, Flanders, Scotland, Bohemia, Poland, Lithuania, and Sweden respectively adopted anti-Gypsy legislation. There was hanging and expulsion in England; branding and the shaving of heads in the France of Louis XIV. Rival provinces distinguished themselves: Moravia severed the left ear of Gypsy women; Bohemia favored the right.

And the Gypsies would not be hard to find. As early as 1686, Frederick William, the Great Elector of Brandenburg and foremost Protestant Prince in Germany, decreed that Gypsies were not to be allowed trade or shelter. As Angus Fraser points out in his thorough account of anti-Gypsy edicts, "in such regulations, the stigmatization which went back to the very earliest imperial legislation was reiterated without further discussion." And so, by 1710, Prince Adolf Frederick of Mecklenburg-Strelitz propounded that even without criminal charges Gypsies could be flogged, branded, or expelled, and executed if they returned, whereas children under ten were to be removed and raised by Christian families. A year later, Elector Frederick Augustus I of Saxony authorized the shooting of Gypsies if they resisted arrest; in 1714 it was declared in the archbishopric of Mainz that all Gypsies were to be executed without trial on the grounds that their way of life had been outlawed. (In 1725, hanging was decreed in Prussia for all Gypsies over eighteen, without trial. By 1734, the age had been lowered to fourteen in some provinces, and a reward thrown in.) Even though Gypsies always traveled in small groups and posed mainly a danger to aesthetic sensibilities, the list goes on and on, with a continuing emphasis on genuine versus false Gypsies, and only minor variations on a violent theme. In 1905, Alfred Dillman wrote in his *Zigeunerbuch* (for use by the Interior Ministry of Security in Munich) that "almost no real Gypsies exist anymore." And the next year, in Prussia, the first "prescription" came in "to combat the Gypsy uncreature"—the *Zigeunerunwesen*.

The difference between native and foreign Gypsies found mutations in the many false distinctions drawn between nomads and settled Gypsies, another index of who was and who was not a "real" Gypsy. Very often, the punishment engendered the crime: just as Gypsies were turned out of the church on the grounds that they were irreligious, the confiscation of their property forced them to become nomadic, or mendicant. Though nomads have sometimes been identified as the pure, noble Gypsies, nomad*ism* has often been invoked as proof of moral degeneration. A Czechoslovak law from the 1950s explains that: "A nomadic life is led by someone who, whether in a group or individually, wanders from place to place and avoids honest work or makes his living in a disreputable way. . . ."

Jerzy Ficowski, the Polish poet, patron of Papusza, and early promoter of Gypsy settlement, gave readers of the *Journal of the Gypsy Lore Society* a progress report from 1950s Poland: "The first great project of the authorities lay in persuading the Gypsies to work on State farms." One hundred and twelve poor Gypsies from the mountainous southern region of Nowy Targ went to the farms at Szczecin in the northwest of the country. Despite a vast improvement in their standard of living, less than half remained. "The second great enterprise was the employment of Gypsies at Nowa Huta." This vast industrial complex was a "community" and steelworks built together from scratch in the 1940s. About 160 Gypsies were "directed there" and more joined them. They resided in special (all-Gypsy) blocks. Ficowski mentions a housing "crisis" among the Gypsy workers; but he is able to point to successes. Children went to school and some illiterate adults also had courses. "The Nowa Huta newspaper *We Are Building Socialism* frequently mentions the Gypsy builders of the socialist city. On July 14, 1952, for example, it published Irene Gabor's photograph." Disappointedly and all too soon, Ficowski tells of the other results of this attempt to create a Gypsy proletariat:

> At times, however, the "anarchical" need for absolute independence provoked Gypsies to flee from the comfort of Nowa Huta and return to a life of misery. . . . Not only the nomads, but even the mountain Gypsies sometimes left. The Gypsies are attracted not so much by the nomadic way of life as by the rejection of authority and the lack of discipline and subordination. "We are leaving for liberty," they would say on quitting Nowa Huta to go back to their old ways. The year 1952 witnessed an event which is inconceivable for non-Gypsy observers. Some families from block 37 betook themselves to a wooded spot in the neighborhood of Nowa Huta, to live there in crude huts made of planks. They said that a house was like a prison to them.

Their departure is perhaps not so baffling to non-Gypsies as Ficowski imagined, at least not to anyone who has ever been to Nowa Huta. This industrialized suburb of Kraków now earns a mention in guidebooks only as a prime example of the ecological disasters that may be the main legacy of those hopeful regimes. Things must have looked different forty years ago, but the "houses" whose rejection so shocked Ficowski are still there: anonymous flats in the monochromatic gloom of an enormous steelworks, whose mills continue to supply more than half of Poland's output and a steady flow of opaque and eye-hurting fumes.

Many Gypsies remain seasonally mobile. Others regularly move, say, every decade or even after thirty years in the same place. Where they have been allowed (rather than forced) to settle, they generally have settled. For example, although travel was soon to be banned, as early as 1893 a census in Slovakia showed that less than 2 percent of the region's thirty-six thousand Gypsies were nomadic. And then, in the two decades preceeding the First World War, nearly a *quarter* of all white Slovaks—more than half a million people—emigrated to the United States.

The fact that public land, including hidden public land, is in our time equally unavailable to Gypsies suggests that the overwrought public response has as much to do with the affront to "normal" values—based on the sanctity of private property—as it has to do with garbage. Officials everywhere have the backing of ordinary people: in an enlightened world, or at least a world lulled by euphemism, it is still okay to hate Gypsies.

In Britain, as in France, Gypsies are no longer simply deported. Regulations vary from province to province (and are often contradictory) but they subtly enforce the same old policy of rejection. East European Gypsies tend to live in ghettos on the outskirts of villages. The reluctance to provide decent and legitimate stopping places means that West European sites are also on the edge of town, typically located at the town dump—so Gypsies become what they are supposed to be: dirty and smelly, and a health hazard. Nor is it surprising that they leave "voluntarily."

In Britain things seemed to brighten with the 1968 Caravan Sites Act, which required local authorities to provide available land. But it emerged that the Act was not intended merely to improve conditions; it aimed to sedentarize ("It is hoped that in the long run the Gypsies will become completely integrated among the settled population"). But British local authorities, like Habsburg noblemen and German princes, were not going to cooperate. As an example from the early 1970s, in the West Midlands alone more than a million pounds was spent on evicting Gypsies from "public" roads, while in the same five-year period only forty-five families were granted legal sites.

Parliament repealed the Caravan Sites Act in 1994—overriding attempts to rescue it in the House of Lords—arguing that Gypsies should pay for their own ground. At the same time, the government tightened planning policy, making it virtually impossible for them to do so. (And once a piece of land is acquired, it is then necessary to make separate applications for permission to live on it, to build a shed, to build a house, to build a stable, etc.; ninety-five percent of the applications fail.) Harking back to the old debate about genuine versus phony Gypsies, Home Secretary Michael Howard confused Members by emphasizing the marginal issue of "raving New Age hippies," and one of his ministers reached for the trusty specter of the nomadic hordes: "We want to repeal this [Act because] . . . the number of those who wish to be nomads has increased," he said, referring to a "leap" from 9,800 in 1968 to all of 13,700 twenty-six years later. No one ever mentions the nearly 4,000 Traveler families—about 18,000 people—who have been on the road because they are still waiting for pitches on official sites, not because they all "wish to be nomads." Repealing the Act instantly relieved authorities of the duty to provide these sites and also gave them powers of closure and eviction (already one local authority, in Sussex, has opted to shut down its site). The inevitable consequence is of course an increase in the number of "nomads." The difficulties faced by people on the road were dramatically compounded by the passing of the 1994 Criminal Justice and Public Order Act that criminalized (among other things) stopping and traveling in any practicable form.

In some parts of the West, the goal of settling Gypsies—though not of integrating them—has been achieved, as it largely has in the former Eastern bloc. And it has been a disaster. Legitimate and traditional work is ruled out, in Britain (for example) by the 1964 Scrap Metal Dealers Act—which introduced a requirement for elaborate invoicing and documentation for every rag-and-bone exchange, insurmountable to most barely literate Travelers (the illiteracy rate is about seventy percent)—or by the simple rule that no work may take place on sites (a van may not even be unloaded). At the same time, Gypsies on official sites are not allowed to leave them for more than brief periods, and so they can no longer do the seasonal farm work that they always have done in England: cherry- and apple-picking, potato-bagging, hop-stringing, and beet-singling. Traditional Gypsy life has mostly disappeared in Britain. But there was, and is, nothing inevitable about that. Mechanization—the machine-made plastic peg—is not really to blame. Rather, it is the work of lawmakers who have pandered to universal but unfounded fears. The legislation of the past few years will likely erode traditional Gypsy life more seriously than the Industrial

Revolution eroded it. Regulations on all sites, public or private, rule out nearly all occupations that guarantee Gypsies some independence. So there goes the trade in Christmas trees, scrap metal, horses, and cars, along with the traveling jobs of tree-lopping, tarmacking, and gate-making. Therefore, inevitably, everyone is on welfare. Very often, those who don't move on become, like American Indians on their reservations, Gypsies *with* problems.

But among Gypsies rich and poor, East or West, the *impression* of nomadism remains, reinforced by a temporary aspect to even their solidly built, long-term lodgings. In Chişinău, capital of the newly independent republic of Moldova, for example, I met a Gypsy who had moved there from Romania and had made a small fortune manufacturing "Chanel" underwear. In his factory he employed over a hundred seamstresses. They were either Romanian or Russian; none of them was a Gypsy, a fact of which the pantymaker was exuberantly proud. He invited me to see his brand-new house—a palace, in fact, with nine turrets, balconies over an inner court, three grand salons whose textured, opalescent walls were elaborately painted with pastoral scenes of romantic-looking Gypsies traveling in caravans. This family was so rich that they feared for their safety, and kept big dogs between themselves and their jealous neighbors. But there were no toilets or bathrooms in this mansion; and though they'd lived there over a year, electrical wires sprouted from holes in most of the walls, as if they had run out of money in mid-decoration. (They hadn't.) The women cooked outside in the courtyard over a fire, and then the whole family ate and slept out there, children all in a heap, as they might in a tent. Jean Cocteau spotted it in the famous Gypsy guitarist, Django Reinhardt: "He lives as one dreams of living, in a caravan. And even when it was no longer a caravan, somehow it still was."

It is a commonplace among nomad-watchers that sedentary people have a fear of travelers not because they are strangers; we fear them because they are *familiar:* supposedly they remind us of who we really are. What Herbert Spencer called our "restlessness inherited from ancestral nomads" (and it was he, not Darwin, who coined the term survival of the fittest) may sound like a wistful fantasy of travel writers—and little use to tired poor people who settle, for a while, when they can. But most Gypsies, like the Caribou Eskimos with their "Great Unrest," have also kept something of their wandering past and reputation; it usefully demarcates them, in their own minds, from the stuck people all around them.

The fear evoked by Gypsies, sometimes aggravated by or coupled with regional underpopulation, has prompted every attempt to assimilate them. Yet the earlier and more central motive behind assimilation was that feudal societies needed them, as craftsmen and laborers. The earliest systematic efforts ("enlightened" compared with the mass killings and brandings of other regimes and eras) must be those of the Habsburg monarchs, the Austrian Empress Maria Theresa (1740–80) and her son Joseph II, who from 1765 shared her throne. Only the communist regimes, using mostly the same tactics, attempted the social transformation of Gypsies on such a grand scale. Under these Habsburgs, Gypsies in Slovakia were inducted as serfs, forbidden to move, to own or trade horses, to speak Romani, to have leaders, or in many cases to raise their own children (who, on the model of the German lands, were taken away to be raised by white Christian families). Maria Theresa insisted that Gypsies be called Ujmagyar, New Hungarians, or Neubauern, New Farmers, and remade in that image. The more positive reform efforts of mother and son—for example, to improve education and housing for Roma—also collapsed because the Hungarian nobility was unwilling to bear the costs. A few weeks before he died Joseph II wrote his own epitaph: "Here lies Joseph II, who failed in all his enterprises."

Sure enough, after his death in 1790, life for Gypsies reverted to normal: one of endless persecution, and general slander (including the charges of cannibalism). On the other hand, no one was interested in their children anymore, and occasionally a philanthropic society came along, such as one started by Slovak doctors in 1929 which brought Gypsy performers to the stage and sponsored a famous all-Gypsy touring football club. Now perhaps worse than persecution was their deepening poverty. "The penalty of imprisonment has no effect on them," a Slovak official noted in 1924, "because imprisonment only improves their living conditions." After the war, and the beating they received from the fascist Slovak Hlinka Guards, thousands of desperate Gypsies migrated west, to Bohemia and Moravia. There was some work for them in these industrial centers, there was room (they often occupied houses abandoned by Sudeten Germans), and there were no other Gypsies—all save six hundred Czech Gypsies had been murdered by the Nazis.

The Communist Party held attractions for Gypsies, as it had for Jews: the Party recruited Rom members, and everywhere the Red Army was—and still is—remembered with affection. However, it wasn't long before this flow to a land of hope was willfully and tragically diverted.

The usual fear of the Gypsy hordes inspired elaborate campaigns of "maximum dispersal"—not expulsion this time but (by 1965) an unconstitutional scheme of "Transfer and Dispersal," which involved demographic planning according to strict quotas. The result was that extended families were separated and forcibly resettled in far-flung parts of the country. Given this background, it is especially depressing that the newly independent, postcommunist Czech government should be manipulating, or enforcing, a migration of Roma, this time eastbound, back to Slovakia.

Since 1993 all Slovaks living on Czech territory have been required to apply for citizenship—even if (following the German model) they were born in the Czech lands. The law looks as if it was designed to disfranchise, and then to evict, Gypsies in particular: nearly all of the three hundred thousand Gypsies in the Czech Republic (or their parents) migrated or were sent over from Slovakia. In order to obtain citizenship now you needed to be fluent in Czech (most Gypsies speak Romani and Slovak), you had to have stable residence for at least two years, and you needed a clean criminal record for the preceding five years. Significantly, the last requirement stretched back into the communist period, when many un- or self-employed Gypsies acquired records for such crimes as "avoiding work" or "neglect," both of which were frequently used as a pretext to remove baby Gypsies to state children's homes. The law has encouraged violence against Roma (even before it came into effect, some Czech residents of Ústí nad Labem got off to an early start by forcing a Czech-born Gypsy to go to Slovakia to have her baby), as well as a surge in asylum-seeking. Several families have been ping-ponged between the two states. Thousands—perhaps hundreds of thousands—are likely to find themselves without citizenship in either the Czech Republic or in Slovakia: that is, stateless.

If Eastern Europeans have just begun to adopt the traditional Western preference for expulsion, there is nothing new about the notion that it is a crime just to be a Gypsy. Equally serious was the offense of *pretending* to be a Gypsy—the traitor, the spy, and the "counterfeit Egyptian"—as if elsewhere there were some nicer, nobler Gypsies, not like our ones.

Evidently the citizens of Elizabethan England really believed that the strangers deliberately darkened themselves with walnut juice, even though this would have been the equivalent of wearing a "kick me" badge. As one English pamphleteer put it in 1610: "They goe alwais never under an hundred men or women, causing their faces to be made blacke, as if they were Egyptians." The stain is a stubborn one. "Gypsies only look black because they don't wash," an Englishman, distressed about his new neighbors, told the *Daily Telegraph* in April of 1969. Their language too was often assumed to be *Rotwelsch*, or thieves' cant, itself proof of delinquency to those who didn't understand it.

The Spanish word *gitano*, like the English "Gypsy," comes from "Egyptian," the most persistent tag, which first turned up in popular Byzantine poetry. The designation was taken up by Gypsies identifying themselves to local authorities, perhaps in the belief that it was better to come from somewhere than from nowhere, and preferably somewhere incontestably exotic (particularly useful for fortune-tellers).

Gypsies have often turned the enigma of their origins to advantage. In the fifteenth century they had already realized that appearance was always at least as important as reality, and that aristocratic credentials, however obscure, were indispensable. Pilgrim status was also good: the Gypsies would have observed, on their way west through Greece and Byzantium, that pilgrims were privileged travelers. And so they came over, the dukes and counts and captains and kings of Little Egypt, along with their colorful flocks of supposed supplicants.

The first Gypsies in the West always traveled with safe-conducts, the ur-passports which were common in the Middle Ages and which, miraculously, were issued to the Gypsies by Sigismund, King of Hungary (1368–1437). It was the official seal that allowed the Gypsies to pass, and, as the story played for fifty years, to pass themselves off as pilgrims (alms-seeking pilgrims, of course) on a seven-year penitential sojourn out of Little Egypt.

They didn't actually dip themselves in tea, but they were performers by vocation and by necessity, and of course the act had continually to be revised and updated. A few decades after their arrival in Western Europe—perhaps the only honeymoon the Gypsies have ever had—pilgrimages went out of fashion. By the late sixteenth century, papal briefs had the wallpaper appeal of deutschemarks in the late 1920s; Luther's "Reformed" church was attracting hordes of Catholics and Greek Orthodox; and (bad luck for beggars) the Franciscan idealization of poverty was now a gilded memory. It was the Protestant and especially the Calvinist churches that lobbied hard, not only against alms-giving but against Gypsies themselves. Martin Luther, in the preface to a 1528 edition of the *Liber Vagatorum*, warned against the knavery of such vagrants and gave the nod to institutionalized repression. For a while in the postpilgrim era, traveling Gypsies were more likely to

A German placard warning off Gypsies, circa 1715. The inscription reads: "Punishment for . . . rogues and Gypsies . . ."

appear as themselves, as itinerant performers, craftsmen, and traders. This did not endear them to local people, and especially not to local craftsmen and traders, whose guilds, or unions, were more effective than any police in moving the competition along.

The more exotic Gypsies appear to be, the more "genuine" they are considered and, paradoxically, the more acceptable they become (in the local imagination, if not in the local pub). Whoever best fits the stereotype wins. Gypsies wearing their traditional clothes—or costumes—are "safely" in the realm of folklore, and it is the business of folklore to domesticate, or defang, the strange. Gypsies who have abandoned their traditional dress are no longer so good to look at; accordingly, they are not recognized as a tribe but as a nuisance. At the same time, fashion has prettily appropriated the stereotypes: from the grand nineteenth-century costume balls of England and France, where ladies turned out as Italian contadinas, Turkish concubines, and Gypsies, to "the Gypsy look" as introduced by Yves Saint Laurent in the sixties. Once you can *wear* them, the strangers at the edge of town cease to seem so scary.

From the Gypsy point of view, exoticism has had its uses. At least until the age of mass travel, people paid more for performances by strangely dressed people from some faraway place. And it was their Indian origin which formed the basis of their successful demand for special ethnic status within the United Nations. Above all, foreignness keeps people at an acceptable distance. Even John Nickels, the American and relatively rich Gypsy who runs the amusement arcade in Wildwood, New Jersey, kept his sons out of school for this reason: he was afraid they'd mix with what he called "American girls," maybe even marry out, a threat, over time, to the survival of Gypsies.

Foreignness has of course more often boded expulsion, though authorities have not always felt that they needed such a pretext. When it became clear in sixteenth-century England that many of these Egyptians were in fact native born, a new order "for avoiding all Doubts and Ambiguities" was introduced; and the death penalty (which remained in place from 1562 until 1783) was extended not only to those "in any company or Fellowship of Vagabonds, commonly called or calling themselves Egyptians" but now also to those "counterfeiting, transforming or disguising themselves by their Apparel, Speech or other Behaviour." The lucky ones were counted among the rogues and "Sturdy Beggars," who were "to be grievously whipped, burnt through the gristle of the right Ear with a hot Iron of the compass of an Inch about." And soon the death penalty expanded again, to cover "those who are or *shall become* of the fellowship or company of Egyptians" (my emphasis).

The conundrum is that their survival has always required adaptation (inconveniently for their advocates, this does involve deception) and the continuous rejigging of their "ethnic" identity. Most Roma will have several, and often simultaneous, professions in the course of their lives; from the Gypsy point of view, it is neither odd nor inconsistent to be both an MP and a used-car dealer. If they have been partly responsible for their ambiguous and sometimes frightening image, it is because they have not wished to be merely the victims of that image. I think it was with admiration (albeit with regrettable timing—the year was 1943) that the Gypsiologist R. A. S. Macfie wrote in the *Journal of the Gypsy Lore Society:* "Ready as Gypsies are to change their religion and folklore and add new words to their vocabulary, the tricks by which they live have never altered."

Since the war, in the former Eastern bloc, the forced assimilation of Gypsies has been more insidious, such as the practice (particularly prevalent in eastern Slovakia) of sterilizing women during hospital births and very often without their knowledge. Less underhand measures also continued, including the confiscation of Travelers' children by Christian charities; this was common in Switzerland until 1973.

And, always, there is no mercy for those Roma who protest. As recently as the 1980s in Poland, for example, Gypsies who had failed to capitulate to the settlement laws instigated in 1964 were finally expelled from the country and stripped of their citizenship. A similar demotion befell Gypsies who were deported from Germany in the late 1970s and then rejected by their native Yugoslavia. Busloads of such people have zigzagged around Europe for a decade. The postwar designation of "stateless person" (given to displaced Gypsies who had survived the camps) was at the time a convenient way of disowning them; they were shunted from office to office and from country to country. Nowadays, statelessness brings guaranteed protection under the Geneva Convention. And Gypsies no longer qualify: they are called Romanians, Bulgarians, etc., even though they are not recognized as such in those countries.

Every state in Europe has engaged in grandiloquent crusades against the Gypsies. But in sheer volume of anti-Gypsy legislation, the Holy Roman Empire—the complex of European territories founded by Charlemagne but always symbolized by and identified with the German crown—matched the rest of Europe taken together. Germany has always been in the van.

SEVEN

The Devouring

E VERY PERSON IS part Judas, part Christ," a tall, bearded Rom from Estonia told a Polish television crew, glowing in their bright flare lights. "Only luck decides him." He was answering a question about why he thought the Nazis had attempted to annihilate the Gypsies.

It was past midnight, and the crew was filming inside the death camp of Birkenau, fifty years to the night after the last of some twenty-one thousand Gypsies at Auschwitz were murdered. For the first time ever, Gypsies had gathered from all over Europe—dozens of busloads mainly from the Eastern bloc countries—to commemorate their murdered kin. Hundreds of people were staying up in an all-night vigil inside the camp, and apart from a few impromptu, single-voiced dirges they neither sang nor played music; they just sat unceremoniously together, comfortable in tracksuits and shorts and casual print shirts.

The next day, in 110-degree heat, there were hours of formal tributes; these were also unprecedented. The Polish prime minister, Waldemar Pawlak, spoke, as did the Israeli and German ambassadors. Letters from Václav Havel and Lech Wałęsa and the Pope were read out. Rajko Djurić, the Rom poet and president of the International Romani Union, made a passionate call for recognition. The Shero Rom, or head Gypsy of the Polish Roma, gave a lyrical speech in a typically Rom ululation. One can state unironically that his appearance alone attested to the significance of the occasion: he was decked out in a shiny black shirt, purple leather shoes, straw Stetson, and, resting on his enormous belly like the glistening catch of the day, a fat tie of woven pearls. Later, in the modern cathedral of the town of Auschwitz (which inescapably resembles a vast brick-and-concrete crematorium), the red-robed cardinal of Kraków conducted a full incense-swinging, three-hour Mass in honor of the Gypsy victims. A Rom

priest read the liturgy in Romani and an angelic choir of Roma children sang down from the gallery. Amazingly for a scorching Wednes-
day afternoon, and for a Mass with a Gypsy theme, the place was
packed, mainly with Poles.

At around two in the morning on the night of the camp vigil, I
began the long trek into Oświęcim, or Auschwitz town, to the hotel. I
walked and walked along the seemingly endless perimeter of the camp
towards the main road. Coming up at fifteen-foot intervals, the concrete stanchions marked the boundaries; they were still joined by
barbed wire, their crooked tips like periscopes turned on the camp.
Suddenly I was beyond the light of the candles, the torches, and television crews. But it probably wasn't the dark that sent me jogging back
to the Gypsies and their buses. It was the barking dogs; it was
Auschwitz—Auschwitz by night. Back at the scene of the vigil, I found
a friend in Karpio, a large and somber Polish Rom who gave me a lift
to my hotel. He told me that his grandmother and grandfather were
killed in the camp and shrugged in convincing indifference when I
asked him how he felt about such a commemoration. Karpio's vehemence was reserved for the Sinti—the German Gypsies—who had
refused to join the others in the camp and had haughtily arranged for
their own mini-ceremony, by invitation only, inside the German con-
sulate in Kraków. "Fascists," Karpio called them.

That night I held my own involuntary vigil. The Hotel Glob was
built over the main train station and all through the night the building
shook to the rattled screams and vibrating honks of the night trains.
Even the timetable never lets you forget that you are in Auschwitz. I lay
on top of the scratchy narrow bed in my *wagon-lit*, wondering about
the Estonian Rom's words: "Only luck decides."

Baxt, or luck, could also be translated as destiny, or fate. By chance,
two days later, I flew across Poland with the Rom poet Rajko Djurić,
who was living in Berlin, in exile from his native Belgrade. As the LOT
stewardess passed out chocolate bars at six in the morning, we talked
about the Old Testament and the Jewish sense of history, and I asked
him about Romany *baxt*.

"*Baxt*," Rajko said, raising his eyebrows and lowering his eyes, "is
the occupying idea among Roma on this earth."

It means more than *devel*, or God, and more than *beng*, the devil.
The idea of *baxt* among Roma could be low—literally gambling in casi-
nos. Or it could be a woman. Certainly one's children could "be" one's
baxt, Rajko said; indeed, it was influenced by many things: how well

one kept traditions such as respecting the *mule*, or spirits of the dead, and avoided uncleanness of all kinds. ("If I am unclean I have no possibility for *baxt*.") *Baxt* was against social cohesion, Rajko thought, for it wasn't measured collectively. In its lowest form *baxt* was no different from fatalism, and encouraged passivity among the Roma.

Rajko had been an eloquent speaker at the Gypsy Holocaust memorial. While he spoke, people waved little banners bearing the slogan (the words above a broken wheel, the numbers below) *na bister / 500,000*, "Don't forget the 500,000"—the 500,000 murdered Gypsies. Now, as we landed in Warsaw, he said, "Above all, *baxt* is concerned with the present and the near future."

Gypsies have no myths about the beginning of the world, or about their own origins; they have no sense of a great historical past. Very often their memories do not extend beyond three or four generations—that is, to those experiences and ancestors who are remembered by the oldest living person among them. The rest, as it were, is not history. Such a feeling is perhaps a legacy from the days of travel, when the dead were literally left behind; but it continues to serve a people who even when settled are hard-pressed to survive.

The Second World War and its traumas are certainly within memory; but there is no tradition of commemoration, or even of discussion. Some thought that such talk might actually be dangerous: "Why give them ideas?" a young Hungarian Rom asked, fifty years after the event. Under the Nazis, the Gypsies were the only group apart from the Jews who were slated for extermination on grounds of race. It is a story that remains almost unknown—even to many Gypsies who survived it.

In Balteni, about forty kilometers northwest of Bucharest, I met a survivor of the deportations of Gypsies to Transdnistria, the area of the Ukraine occupied by Romania during the war. Here, according to the Romanian War Crimes Commission, between 1942 and 1944 thirty-six thousand Gypsies lost their lives.

"There were many, many people," Drina said, her eyes narrowing as if she was trying to see back through fifty years to the winter when her family was packed with hundreds of others onto trains that dumped them somewhere north of Odessa and east of the Bug River. I knew about the long trips in cattle cars. It could take weeks to get from Bucharest to camps located in the occupied territories; and when Drina's thin frame shivered in the hot sun I learned it had been very cold. She seemed eager to tell me something. She paused for a while—hand on brow, looking at the ground—as if she hadn't visited these particular memories in a very long time and was trying to find them. It seemed that no one had ever asked her this question. And then she spoke, clearly and without emotion, in the voice of a courtroom testimonial. When she told of the perilous crossing of the Dniester River, over which lay the occupied territory and, somewhere, the field that would be her home for two years, her children and grandchildren all gathered to listen, as if they also had never heard this fascinating story. Some of the assembled women shooed the children away.

"Everyone rushed to go in the first trip." I glanced up at Igor, my Romanian friend who was translating. "Yes, yes," Drina said, seeing my doubt: "You see, the boats were made of paper." She paused to look for a sample, and picked up a scrap of cardboard lying in the dust at our feet. "Yes, the boats were like this. They'd go down after three or four trips. You tried to go in the first crossing." I guessed that Drina—about ten years old at the time—had seen a boat sink, probably one over-loaded with deportees.

Not long before I met Drina, the Romanian Parliament stood for a minute in silence, honoring Marshal Ion Antonescu, the fascist wartime leader who was responsible for the death of 270,000 Jews and the deportation of the Gypsies (it was the forty-fifth anniversary of his execution for war crimes). The deportations to Transdnistria are now being explained as an effort by the marshal to "save" the Gypsies from the death camps in Poland. (At his trial, Antonescu himself offered a different justification: "Thefts and murders that occurred in Bucharest and other cities were being covered up [and] the public appealed to me to protect them.") The Romanian King Michael, with his own hopes of rehabilitation, gave another, more convincing version in 1991: "The Roma people were singled out for particular repression mainly because they had no defense or protectors outside Romania. The nomads who were persecuted were especially easy targets due to their lack of papers and documentation."

Drina did not speak in any detail about the family of her child-hood, but she let us understand that many of them had died in Transdnistria. It seemed that in her family death was never far away. Four days before she spoke to me, Luciano, her seven-year-old grand-son, had died. That was how we met: because I could drive, and because my friend Igor had a car that would serve as the hearse.

These still mainly nomadic Kalderash Gypsies kept close to the old way of life. The men banged out copper *kazans*—small domestic distillers—and the women moved purposefully around the camp carrying wood and buckets of water, with long, flowery skirts and two long braids tied together at the bottom and woven with "coins" (having lost their gold, they used numbered industrial aluminum tags to the same effect). There were a few dogs with pruned tails, and horses scrounging for sustenance in the dry grass. The children looked shy and wild; the women, clearly wary of prying eyes, seldom dropped their fierce expressions, even though we were their invited guests. It was hard to believe that they lived so near the capital, and not in some dense far-away forest, or in some modern Gypsy's memory.

One night a month or so later Igor and I paid another visit to the camp of Drina's family. It was about half a mile from the highway and easy to miss: there was no road, only a lumpy field you had to bounce over. The Radus had a half-built brick house near the entrance to the camp, but in the summer they abandoned it in favor of a tent, constructed with three poles and great swaths of thick smoke-streaked canvas, and taller than two men at the apex. Inside it smelled of burning wood.

The men lounged against the bales of hay that comprised the tent's furniture, or lay on their sides propped on an elbow; the women knelt or crouched. Igor and I sat cross-legged and shared their scorched dinner of roasted corn on the cob and tomatoes and onions with rosemary, all of us picking with our fingers from a couple of dented tin trays. The fire brought out the flavor of the food—or the flavor of the fire: everything tasted the same and very good.

During this period of mourning there was a ban on alcohol and all the talk seemed to be about lost or missing things, but the mood was almost festive. Florică, one of the fierce-faced women, gave me her favorite recipe. "The best chicken cannot be bought," she said. "It is not the same. You have to find one, see it move, the fastest are the best." After "finding" a racing chicken, you wrapped it, feathers and all, in clay and roasted it—*slowly*, she emphasized rather severely—"inside" a fire: flame on top and flame underneath, until all the wood has burned. Next, you let it sit for a long time in the embers, until they're nearly gone too. And then the clay comes off, she demonstrated, sitting regally upright and gesturing as if she was opening an enormous atlas. The feathers are stuck in the clay, and you have your chicken, smooth and tender "as an egg." During the mourning for Drina's grandson, meats were also forbidden, and in Florică's mime show the chicken had grown to the size of a sheep.

We heard how, around twenty years before, Ceaușescu's police, the Securitate, had come and searched these tents and the daughters and stolen all the gold from their necks and hair—an experience shared by many Romanian Kalderash, who keep all their valuables in (wearable) gold form. Gold was the dowry that ensured prestige for the family and decent marriages for their daughters. The bright coins—with their mottoes and dates and bearded monarchs—reflected the presence of an ancestor, alive, prosperous, and at large in those realms. They didn't store them in velvet boxes or in binders of clear plastic sheets; no, they were drilled through and showily displayed on the throat or the hair as proof of membership of this high-class Gypsy tribe (deracinated, settled, and other despised Gypsies had no gold). Many proud Kalderash had let me inspect the coins they wore: thin and thick yellow gold, often a hundred years old.

In the tent, I mentioned the self-proclaimed "King of the Romanian Gypsies," Ion Cioaba, a rich Kalderash from Transylvania, who

Members of Luciano's family listen to the Orthodox priest's words for the dead boy. Afterwards he was buried, outside the graveyard, at Balteni, Romania, 1992.

had talked a lot to the press about the restitution of Kalderash gold. They seemed amused at the idea of it; no one could convince them that they would ever see their Franz Josef coins again. It seemed pointless to mention war reparations.

Lina, another of the fierce women, "remembered" the days before the war (she couldn't have been forty), when they still traveled all the time, how they'd have to "dig the children out of the snow," and how even through those long winters in camp none of them ever got sick. "Our children could not make it now," she said, perhaps remembering Luciano. It was such simply uttered truths—suggesting the unrelenting hail of occurrence, most of it sad—that made me understand their lack of apparent interest in their eventful and tragic past.

The dead boy's father was still quietly inconsolable, but his mother and aunts spoke of Luciano with passion, particularly about their long search for medical treatment. They had traveled from hospital to hospital in Bucharest, and, though the child was never properly examined, each time they were sent away with a different horror diagnosis—first meningitis, then AIDS (which in Romania is mainly a children's disease)—and an ever-sicker little boy. The Radus would have been more convinced if doctors just came out with it and called their disease "roma": a degenerative condition and, to judge by the way people reacted, a disfiguring and contagious one as well. Igor confirmed the prejudice among the "white coats" (as the Radus referred to all medicos). He'd first met the family when they flagged him down for a lift; they were trying to get Luciano to the hospital, for the fifth time. ("Can you imagine having to hitchhike to a hospital with a frail child?" Igor said. And with all your relatives?) He offered to accompany them, hoping to shame his complacent countrymen. A doctor did finally see the boy. Guessing that he was suffering from malnutrition and other consequences of neglect, he returned him to Igor with a shrug and the comment that "these people are ineducable."

At the next stop, Bucharest's Hospital #9, the staff insisted that Luciano be kept in the hospital, against the family's wishes. Among Gypsies a stay in the hospital for any reason other than giving birth could only mean death. But somehow Igor persuaded the Radus that it was necessary, and they reluctantly installed themselves in the waiting room, and then outside on the hospital grounds, for the next three days. Later, Igor gleefully described to me the multiplying numbers of relatives and friends who gathered in this vigil, and the growing alarm of the hospital staff, who were palpably relieved to return the boy and end this unscheduled *hadj*. A few months earlier, some two thousand Gypsies from all over Britain, Europe, and the U.S. had flocked to England's Derbyshire Royal Infirmary to pay their last respects to Patrick Connor, a much-respected figure in the British Traveler community. Like the Radus they occupied the cafeteria and the toilets until they were evicted, and then for two weeks they camped outside. People gathered to say goodbye, but also to make amends and to appease the departing spirit, who could cause serious trouble from the other side. All of this had to be done *before* the death.

With a seven-year-old boy, there was no question of amends to be made, yet Luciano's family may well have expected that his spirit would be as miserable as they were—aggrieved that he was not to get his full share of life. And one could guess that for Gypsies, as for everyone, the death of a child is especially hard to bear, and perhaps understandable only as the work of evil forces.

Gypsies everywhere went to unusual extremes to prevent death. Not just the death of loved ones, but of any known ones. It went beyond compassion into the more exigent realm of the superstitious. The vigilant would attempt to scare death away, perhaps literally by screaming at it, or by raising their skirts and flashing at it. They might try to trick death by changing the name of a sick person to that of someone they hated—a known thief, or a policeman—with the idea that no one, not even death, could want to inhabit *that* soul. Others would try to fob the bad luck off onto some other creature. In Britain in the 1940s, Brian Vesey-FitzGerald recorded how Gypsies suffering from pulmonary disease attempted a symbolic transference by breathing three times into the mouth of a live fish, and then throwing it back into the stream from which it had been fetched. The hope was that, confused, death would go for the fish.

Finally, the last doctor told Igor—not the parents—that Luciano was suffering from a massive brain tumor. Whatever he had, it was clear to everyone but his family that he was going to die soon. As Igor stood for a moment, trying to think how to deliver this news to the crowd outside, the nurse asked him why he had bothered to get involved. For their part, the Radus were unwilling to accept the diagnosis. The child was frail, fading, in pain—but for his family, long after the battle had been lost, this was war. Observing the Radus' rage against death, even after it had come, offered an insight, I thought, into the general reluctance of Gypsies to face squarely an episode in their history of sustained and violent death on a massive scale.

The Radus' difficulties did not end with Luciano's death. When I first turned up behind the wheel of Igor's Dacia station wagon, he had been dead for four days. The customary three days was pushing it in the summer heat, and he really had to go now. The coffin was placed in the entrance of a specially erected boy-size tent, in front of which a circle of wailing women sat on the ground, their skirts spread around them like saucers. Farther removed, the men enumerated to Igor their difficulties in securing a priest and a proper church service for Luciano. I stood before the little pine box, framed by the open flaps of the tent, looking down at a very small dead boy in a panama hat.

Luciano was wearing a clean brown sweater and a pair of brand-new jeans. His pockets were stuffed: blue wads of lei notes in one, and a comb, a small mirror, and a sewing kit in the other—provisions for the road. On his feet he had factory-fresh plastic slippers, dark brown and molded to look like tie-up shoes, including the stitching and laces, two neat bows in lacquered relief. He had one hand over his heart, and though the nails were very long, as if they were still growing, the stiff claw formation of his fingers was unmistakable. His hat hung at a gangster's jaunty angle and obscured most of his face; only his small mouth, with cracked lips slightly open, was clearly visible. Deep in the coffin beside his head rested a plywood model boat.

At noon we were sent back to Bucharest, with four members of Luciano's family, to buy food for his *pomana*, or funeral feast. Washing, or brushing one's hair, was also forbidden during the first period of mourning; our disheveled group made quite an impression. They never once stopped shouting in the battle to get served before other people and to get a lower price. This was what people did in busy markets, it's what markets were *for*. But the glass-fronted bakery seemed to require another etiquette. There, tired Romanians queued quietly, pushing their heavy bundles forward bit by bit, like long-distance passengers at an airport waiting for passport control. Wild with heat and grief and pressed for time, our friends marched to the head of the line and threw their money at the terrified girl in her paper bonnet, demanding bread, all of it. They didn't get everything they asked for, but while a few women in the queue hissed and cursed them, and even spat at them, they did get served. It was the quickest way of getting them out of there.

Chattering away on the ride back to Balteni, they had already forgotten these routine humiliations, and they were oblivious of Igor and me in the front seat. They looked up only when someone tapped at the

window. We were stuck in a traffic jam at Bucharest Nord train terminal when a middle-aged woman with one tooth and blood running
down the insides of her legs made her unsteady way over to greet us.
She'd been dancing a drunken jig for the idling drivers, and was naked
except for a sarong made from a Romanian flag, with a hole in the
middle where the hammer and sickle had been cut out. Her eyes were
half closed and she was laughing a terrible laugh. Even unshockable
Igor was expressionless and still. But our passengers were chortling:
they seemed really to find it funny—or maybe, after the bakery, their
pleasure derived from the spectacle of someone so incontestably more
damned and crowd-confounding than themselves.

Any relief at our safe—and well-stocked—return was extremely
short-lived. It next fell to me and Igor to secure the services of the
local Orthodox priest, a bearded old fraud who, having already
refused to don his robes for a dead Gypsy boy, posed with elaborate
benignity for a photograph he begged me to take. They never came to
church, he complained, they didn't even marry in the church. It was
true: Gypsies didn't marry in churches *or* in registry offices; they had
their own ceremonies and parties and then they got on with having
their families, and when people died, *that* was when they needed, or
wanted, the church. Death was a uniquely fearful business for them,
and the use of the church and its *gadjo* keeper was an extra precaution.
The priest warmed a bit when he learned that I was American, and he
was ours when I pressed a wad of near-worthless blue lei notes into
his dry palm.

Luciano's funeral was under way, and the Radus and their friends
moved barefoot over rocky dirt roads to the church. There were two
cars. I drove the first one (a multicolored, vaguely souped-up Yugo
belonging to one of the young men), with the priest at my side. Igor
followed in his Dacia station wagon, with Luciano wedged in the back.
I had the musical horn, which the proud owner kept urging me to
honk continuously, despite the already deafening accompaniment of
shrieking zurlas and clanging lids on stewpots on either side of the car,
and the wailing women bringing up the rear. I doubt if I could have
made that car go fast, but neither could I keep it rolling at the mourners' pace, and it stalled every few minutes. In between, I was signaled to
stop so that children could scatter corn kernels against evil spirits at
intersections (all cross formations inspired such preventive measures);
and I was stopped whenever Igor stalled, with the usual result that his
back door would fly open and the coffin would slide halfway out.

The Radu family—some of Luciano's sisters and brothers and his uncle—in their camp at Balteni, Romania, 1992

Above the banging of pots and blowing of all horns, the priest shrieked chat: he'd never been to America but he had traveled in an airplane; had I seen much of their Romanian countryside?

Inside the small whitewashed church, it was cool and dark, and quiet at last. Luciano's many sisters and cousins stood all around him holding slim, lit candles, along with his father, whose great gut heaved with quiet sobbing. Not one minute of their mourning was free from hassle, though; this moving scene was soon ruined by the crashing around of some drunken churchwarden up by the altar.

Back out in the hot day, the wailing expanded to include violent breast-beating and the tearing out of hair. One woman fell against me and collapsed in a fit with jerking convulsions and eyes rolled to white, after which the others, not to be outdone, stormed the gravesite, just beyond the church graveyard. They were not allowed to bury their dead within its boundaries, alongside the non-Gypsy residents of Balteni. And perhaps this suited them, for they were fearful of cemeteries. After the priest had sprinkled red wine, from a regular labeled bottle, over the boy's body and the lid had been nailed down, Luciano's coffin was slid into a front-loading sepulcher. It looked like a large doghouse. Some of the mourners, still in their fancy suits, then sealed him in with shovelfuls of wet cement. It was at the *pomana* afterwards that I met Drina, Luciano's grandmother, who had survived the wartime deportations. It was there, fifty yards from Luciano's grave, that she told me about paper boats on the Dniester.

In the 1960s, Bert Lloyd, the British musicologist, wrote that many Gypsies he met in the course of collecting their songs "could not distinguish the war period." He referred to those who had remained comparatively free in wartime Romania as well as to those who had experienced the deportations. Drina was among the latter. And perhaps her vagueness or lack of engagement was not so very surprising. These were people who, fifty years on, could not get a doctor or a priest and who could barely do their shopping without starting a riot.

At fifteen, Karoly Lendvai lost everyone. From his town of Szengai, seventy-five miles southwest of Budapest, he and his family were rounded up by Hungarian police and forced to walk forty miles north to Komárom, to the notorious Csillag internment camp which was run by the Arrow Cross, the Hungarian fascists. Fifty years on, Karoly Lendvai's memory was undimmed.

"As we were marched through, others joined our group, more Gypsies and more gendarmes," he told a Reuters reporter in the summer of '94. "Some babies died along the way, and some would-be escapees were shot, left by the roadside. No one knows who they were. . . . We were in the camp about two weeks with hardly any food. . . . More people died as typhus broke out, and others were killed. The dead were thrown into a huge pit, covered with quicklime. There were layers upon layers of dead. I do not know when the pit was finally filled because one day we were herded into cattle cars to be taken who knows where."

Lendvai was saved by an air raid. In the confusion of sirens and bombings he escaped into the woods "for about a year . . . [and] I never saw the others again." Lendvai hadn't heard of the word Holocaust and, at sixty-five, he still could not quite believe that all of this happened simply because Gypsies were Gypsies; but he knew that his family had all been murdered. Prisoners of the Csillag internment camp were transported to Auschwitz.

"Rot you Jew-Gypsy!" Lendvai remembered an Arrow Guard screaming at him as he was being pushed onto a train. The curse still troubled him: "Why," he interrupted himself to ask the journalist, "why did he call me a Jew?"

Estimates of the number of wartime deaths of Gypsies range in Hungary alone from eighty thousand down to ten thousand, and most recently the vagueness has allowed "revisionist historians" such as László Karsai to claim, absurdly, that no more than a few hundred Gypsies "vanished." The fate of many Czech Gypsies is still mysterious, though in 1994 Paul Polansky, an amateur historian from Spillville, Iowa, discovered documentation of the murder of at least eight thousand Gypsies, half of them killed on Czech soil. Poland had a much smaller prewar Roma population; out of around fifty thousand, more than one in five died. But even there, in the land where most of the killing took place, amnesia is endemic. Writing not long after the war, Jerzy Ficowski noted:

> With the exception of two songs from Auschwitz, sung very rarely, I have not noticed any trace of the War years in the present life of the Polish Gypsies. They rarely mention their martyrdom and do not like to dwell on that subject. . . . Their way of life has not changed at all. The ovens of the extermination camps have been forgotten. Their fertility is very great and the natural increase of population very high. The vitality of the Gypsies has conquered death.

The Romani word for the (Gypsy) Holocaust is *porraimos,* the devouring. In addition to a haunting evocation of the events themselves, "the devouring" usefully describes the continuing suppression or denial of the Gypsy case. (Appropriately, *porraimos* is a term even less well known among Gypsies than "Holocausto.")

Visits to the famous scenes of the Nazi crimes do little to evoke the experience of those who lived and died there. Some groups of victims are invisible—for instance, homosexuals—because they have been actively excluded. But even where atrocities are fully and graphically illustrated, the unspeakable tends also to be unimaginable. Writers have begun to say what most visitors to death camps have kept as a guilty secret: that they felt very little here, in Auschwitz, for example; that their strongest feeling may be ambivalence about their own visit to such a terrible and sacred site now somehow a museum and a tourist destination, littered with children and Coke cans. In Kraków, bright posters and brochures offer day trips to holidaymakers: to the Tatra mountains, to a salt mine, to Auschwitz. On my last trip to the camp, the postmodern "Auschwitz experience" was complete when the taxi driver, Szczepan Kękuś, boasted that he had been Steven Spielberg's driver during the filming of *Schindler's List*, and pressed the photographic evidence into my hand. There was Szczepan and Liam; there was Steven and Szczepan. "You can call me Steve," Szczepan said, as I stepped out at the main camp gate.

Compared with the vivid photo library of Nazi imagery that we helplessly house in our heads, the live tour mainly obfuscates (*inside* the camp there is a tourist hostel and a cafeteria, racked with ham-and-cheese sandwiches). In the case of the Gypsies, this sense of distance has a further dimension: one could easily imagine that these particular people had not been here at all. The Polish guide, whose batch of Swedish tourists I tagged along with, never once mentioned the Gypsies (and in her version the story of the Jews at Auschwitz emerged only after a stoic account of the Polish victims). When, following the tour, the Swedes had repaired to the cafeteria, I asked her about the Gypsies. "Even here in Oświęcim the Gypsies didn't work." That was all she had to say about the twenty-one thousand Gypsies murdered at Auschwitz-Birkenau.

The site of the *Zigeunerlager*, or Gypsy camp, is marked on the wall map in the arched entrance to the vast pitch of Birkenau. It was in the row of barracks farthest from the main gates, which meant that the Gypsies had a good view of both the gas chambers and the crematoria. Apart from a few crumbling brick chimneys, there is nothing left of the thirty-eight-barrack Gypsy camp.

Three and a half kilometers down the road, at the main camp of Auschwitz, prison blocks have been converted into national pavilions, each describing the particular losses of one or two countries: U.S.S.R.; Poland; Czechoslovakia; Yugoslavia and Austria; Hungary; France and Belgium; Italy and Holland. A separate exhibit called "The Suffering and Struggle of the Jews" is housed in Block 27. Other blocks (4, 5, and 6) contain, along with photographs and documents and technical explanations of the killing machinery, the things that the murdered left behind. Here in a glass case was some of the seven tons of women's hair found on liberation, packed in parcels of twenty-five kilos apiece and ready to be sold, at fifty pfennigs a kilo, for suit linings. (I asked the Polish docent why the hair was all one color—mousy brown. The gas, she said. Zyklon B made all hair and skin tone the same.) And here was a wall of mainly wire-rimmed eyeglasses; another of toothbrushes and hairbrushes; of portrait photographs of loved ones; of children's shoes with straps and buttons; of little dresses and coats.

Standing in front of the display of brown leather suitcases, I tilted my head to read the familiar Jewish names, each one carefully painted, with an address, in large thickish white letters. Confronted by all these possessions—the ordinary appurtenances of bourgeois life in civilized, settled prewar Europe—it struck me that one reason the Gypsies do not have a presence here at Auschwitz, or in our private, mental archives of the Holocaust, is that none of these things was theirs. They seem to have disappeared, without a trace.

It takes no work of the imagination to be struck by the absence of the Gypsies from the even more obvious places: the vast literature of the Holocaust. The Gypsies' oral and itinerant traditions, along with widespread illiteracy, have not thrown up great numbers of Gypsy scholars. And there are few in-depth histories of the *porraimos* by non-Gypsies; the Roma are equally absent from both the popular and the general scholarly histories. Even in the primary sources—the legal enactments that the Reich contrived to control and, eventually, to kill them—the Gypsies are obscured.

Under the name "social deviants" they were included in laws designed primarily for the institutionalized handicapped (the first victims of mass killings). In July of 1933 there was the Law for the Prevention of Hereditarily Diseased Offspring, in November of the same year, the Regulations for the Security and Reform of Habitual Criminals and Social Deviants. Under these "measures," Sinti and Roma were involuntarily sterilized. Two laws of 1935 banned marriage and sex between Germans and non-Europeans, including Gypsies. Although again they were not mentioned by name, semiofficial commentary on the Nuremberg Laws stated that: "In Europe generally only Jews and Gypsies are carriers of alien blood."

Nazi policy towards Gypsies was continually sharpening and, as it did so, it redefined them. So whereas in the 1937 Laws Against Crime they are counted among "those who by antisocial behavior even if they have committed no crime have shown that they do not wish to fit into society: beggars, tramps (Gypsies), prostitutes, persons with infectious diseases who do not follow treatment, etc.," in later legislation they appear in a new troupe: "Jews, Gypsies, and Poles." As with the Jews, debate about whether they should be defined culturally or racially has always dogged the Gypsies. The Nazis used both categories; and even-

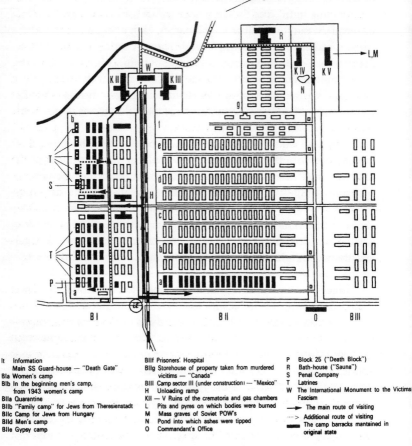

PLAN OF THE FORMER CONCENTRATION CAMP
KL AUSCHWITZ II — BIRKENAU (BRZEZINKA)

It	Information	
	Main SS Guard-house — "Death Gate"	
BIa	Women's camp	
BIb	In the beginning men's camp, from 1943 women's camp	
BIIa	Quarantine	
BIIb	"Family camp" for Jews from Theresienstadt	
BIIc	Camp for Jews from Hungary	
BIId	Men's camp	
BIIe	Gypsy camp	

BIIf	Prisoners' Hospital	
BIIg	Storehouse of property taken from murdered victims — "Canada"	
BIII	Camp sector III (under construction) — "Mexico"	
H	Unloading ramp	
KII — V	Ruins of the crematoria and gas chambers	
L	Pits and pyres on which bodies were burned	
M	Mass graves of Soviet POW's	
N	Pond into which ashes were tipped	
O	Commandant's Office	

P	Block 25 ("Death Block")	
R	Bath-house ("Sauna")	
S	Penal Company	
T	Latrines	
W	The International Monument to the Victims of Fascism	
→	The main route of visiting	
···>	Additional route of visiting	
▬	The camp barracks mantained in original state	

The Zigeunerlager occupied the two rows of barracks identified as BIIe, beyond which lay the prisoners' hospital, the crematoria, and the gas chambers. Between February 1943 and August 1944, twenty-one thousand Gypsies were killed at Auschwitz.

tually, as biological explanations were supplied for every aspect of culture and behavior (criminality among Gypsies and, along with other attributes, sexual deviance, venality, and power hunger among Jews), the two categories became one. When the deportations of German Gypsies began, shortly after the outbreak of the war in 1939, the rules governing inclusions and exemptions paralleled the later regulations used in the transports of Jews to the East.

From the start, crime prevention was the main pretext for the incarceration of Gypsies—and later for their extermination. The German police confined them to *Zigeunerlager* as early as 1934—that is, before the regime had even decided who was a Gypsy. In June of 1936, the chief of police of Berlin was authorized by a circular (i.e., not by a law) to arrest all Gypsies in Prussia, and immediately six hundred Sinti and Roma, with their wagons, were corralled under police guard into a sewage dump next to a cemetery at Marzahn, a suburb of Berlin. The location of this *Zigeunerlager,* the largest created so far, was doubly punitive for the Gypsies, with their elaborate codes of hygiene and their superstition about graveyards. But the goal of the city authorities was accomplished: to clear the streets of Berlin before the start of the Olympic Games. (Gypsies were also sent to Dachau from 1936—that is, three years before the outbreak of war.) With only three water pumps and two toilets, the six hundred Gypsies on the sewage dump quickly succumbed to disease; the official response was: "Massive loss of life in the restricted area only interests us insofar as it represents a threat to the non-Gypsy population." Inmates were assigned to forced labor, and those who survived until 1943 were then sent to Auschwitz.

The experience of the Gypsies had some striking peculiarities. Long before the rise of the Nazis to power, there were Citizens' Committees which successfully lobbied for the clearing and internment of Gypsies in proto-ghettos which eventually became streamlined and regularized as the municipally administered *Zigeunerlager,* such as the one created at Marzahn. Indeed, when the Nazis came to power they did not need to invent the legislation used to "Combat the Gypsy Plague." Despite Article 104 of the Weimar Constitution, which guaranteed equality before the law, from 1899 the security police kept a central *Zigeuner* register. By 1911 these files included fingerprints and photo IDs, not just for criminals but for all Gypsies over six (clearly regarded as the same thing), and in 1926 the Bavarian Law for the Combating of Gypsies, Travelers, and the Work-shy empowered the Bavarian police to send Roma and Sinti to workhouses for two years. They were thus already punished simply for being *Zigeuner.* The Bavarian law was adopted everywhere and expanded to meet the local needs of other states. Those registered in the twenties automatically became subject to the racial legislation of the thirties. The fact that they were already widely recognized as "a problem"—to be dealt with, significantly, by local police and not just by the SS—made it easier to disown them later, in scholarship, in trials, in calculations about compensation.

The Holocaust historian Lucy Davidowicz states a view shared by many of her colleagues when she writes that "only in the last year of the war did the Nazi ideologues begin to regard the Gypsies not only as an undesirable social element, but also as an undesirable racial element." Nazi policy towards Gypsies was indeed full of contradictions, but this is plainly untrue. The deportations to Auschwitz were not the beginning of a racial assessment of Gypsies (though in most cases they represented its conclusion).

During their time in Marzahn, and soon in many other camps, inmates were forced to submit to detailed examination by the anthropologists, psychiatrists, and other "scientists" employed by the Office for Research on Race Hygiene and Population Biology in the Reich Department of Health. In 1937, health officers could produce "a table several meters in length on which in tiny, millimeter size letters and numbers the genealogical tree of all Gypsies living in Germany for the last ten generations had been charted"; it would, they said, be used to research "the future development of all peoples, especially the German." Nazi interest in the racial characteristics of Gypsies may be documented from the year they were elected to power, and it grew and grew—even though Gypsies represented a tiny fraction of the population. These "special camps" became the prewar laboratories for the research team headed by the child psychologist, and now "race hygienist," Dr. Robert Ritter, who ultimately gathered thirty thousand genealogies. His aim was to establish the hereditary character of criminal and asocial behavior.

Ritter and his team, including his assistant Eva Justin, made their rounds, equipped with syringes, calipers, eye-color charts, and pots of wax to take masks of Gypsy faces, which, in photographs taken by the team, are invariably terrified and bewildered. (To ensure efficient work, the doctors had the police at their disposal.) When the personal histories that the Gypsy subjects spluttered out failed to add up, the team completed classification according to such categories as "appearance" and "way of life."

Eva Justin originally gained access to Gypsies still living free by posing as a missionary. In her influential reports she recommended that full and part-Gypsies, including the educated and assimilated, be sterilized; education of Gypsies was fruitless and should be stopped. Often after one of her visits, the interviewee and sometimes the entire family would be removed to a camp. Such experiences—however mutated within the collective imagination—offer an explanation for the universal wariness, indeed the hostility, that Gypsies still evince about being interviewed, particularly on questions of kinship.

The racial classifications of these pseudo-scientists determined lives. For some reason—for example, romantic fantasies about noble savages—"pure" Gypsies were deemed less dangerous (and of course a great deal rarer) than those with some German blood: the opposite of the Jewish case.

Such findings in a Gypsy's chart could result in loss of citizenship, in sterilization, and in eventual deportation. Among the victims of the new classification were highly decorated army officers who had no inkling about distant Gypsy relatives before being plucked from service to the Reich. According to the memoirs of Rudolf Hoess, the commandant of Auschwitz (not to be confused with Deputy Party Leader Rudolf Hess), one such casualty was "one of the earliest members of the Party, a part-Gypsy who had a large business concern in Leipzig and who had participated in the war and had been decorated many times"; another was the leader of the Organization of German Girls in Berlin. The fact that some Gypsies joined the Nazi Party has troubled a number of Jewish historians, who see it as proof that Gypsies were not and cannot have been seen as the "mortal enemy." But it would seem more likely that, as with Jewish collaborators, these were mainly individuals making cynical calculations for their immediate survival.

Ritter's definition of a part-Gypsy was more inclusive than that of a part-Jew. If two out of sixteen of a person's great-great-grandparents were Gypsies, that person was classified as part Gypsy, and so later would qualify for admission to Auschwitz. (By contrast, a person with one Jewish grandparent—four great-great-grandparents—was not usually affected by Nazi anti-Jewish legislation.) Ritter was de-Nazified in 1950. In February of 1964, Dr. Justin was acquitted of any wrongdoing by a Frankfurt magistrate.

In an extreme example of a common view (and one which echoes those very classifications), the Holocaust historian Yehuda Bauer asserts that, for Nazis, the killing of a Gypsy was qualitatively different from the killing of a Jew: "Roma were not Jews, therefore there was no need to murder all of them." Certainly there was talk of saving some Gypsies. Himmler—who famously remarked that "everyone has his special Jew" (that is, one he would argue should be saved)—had fantasies of maintaining a kind of live diorama of "pure" Gypsies, a living museum in which each of the major tribes would be represented. However, it is probably safer to look at what the Nazis did than at what

Dr. Robert Ritter draws blood while a colleague and the woman's husband look on. In the course of trying to establish a racial basis for Gypsy deviance, Ritter's team collected blood and hair samples, face masks, body measurements of all kinds, and more than thirty thousand Gypsy genealogies.

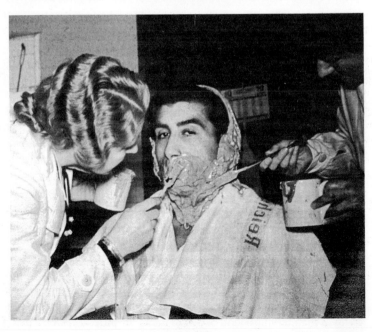

Dr. Sophie Ehrhardt, a member of Ritter's team, and an assistant making a mask with soft wax

they said. Local authorities routinely ignored instructions to exempt "pure" Gypsies, which in any case they would have been hard-pressed to find.

Although Gypsies were not mentioned by name in any of the regime's major racial laws, the policy towards them was clear enough, and increasingly it was spelled out. Measures adopted in 1939 on Himmler's orders explicitly state:

> Experiences gained in the struggle against the Gypsy plague and knowledge derived from race-biological research have shown that ... the final solution of the Gypsy question ... must be approached with the basic nature of this race in mind.

Contrary to the provision for exempting "pure" Gypsies, but in line with the general radicalization of racial policies, the fate of Gypsies became linked with that of Poles and Jews after the Nazi conquest of Poland. Adolf Eichmann, like several other high-ranking Nazis, including Reinhard Heydrich, subsequently made the recommendation that the "Gypsy Question" be "solved" simultaneously with the "Jewish Question"—for example, by appending "three or four trucks" of Sinti and Roma to the trains transporting Viennese Jews in 1940 to the *Generalgouvernement* (of German-occupied central and southern Poland).

The invasion of the Soviet Union in June of 1941 marked the transition from persecution to mass extermination for both Jews and Gypsies. Units of the regular army and the police, but particularly of the SS *Einsatzgruppen*, began the mass shootings of Gypsies (and Jews and Russians and hospital patients) in Russia, Poland, and the Balkans. The killings were justified by the old claim that the Gypsies were spies—numbering perhaps as many as 250,000. No one knows with any certainty how many were killed by the roving murder squads. These still-unresearched episodes—along with great gaps in knowledge concerning the occupied territories—make it impossible to give a precise figure for Gypsy victims.

German soldiers were said to have been demoralized by these killings, and methods described as "more humane" were sought. In early 1940 the first large-scale experiments in *Sonderbehandlung* (special treatment—that is, death by gas) included those first judged to have "lives unworthy of life": the chronically ill, the mentally and physically handicapped, and Gypsies. The use of gas as a method of mass murder, and thus the beginning of the Final Solution, began at the death camp near the remote Polish village of Chełmno, on the Ner River, on December 7, 1941: the same day that the Japanese attacked Pearl Harbor.

It was the ghetto at Łódź, home to 160,000 Jews and only fifty miles down the Ner, that soon became the main source of lives unworthy of life for the death machinery at Chełmno. Gypsies were incarcerated with Jews in the ghettos of Białystok, Kraków, Łódź, L'viv, Radom, and Warsaw. Detailed accounts of Gypsy life in the ghettos are hardly ever included in chronicles of these places, where many more Jews lived and died. It may therefore be useful to give some details here (taken largely from Ficowski's *Ciganie na polskich drogach*, "Gypsies on Polish Roads").

In October 1941 a section of the Jewish ghetto was hemmed in with twelve thousand meters of barbed wire especially ordered from Poznań, and wrapped around the area twice. This double fence, along with a water-filled ditch and a series of security posts, separated off the future Gypsy ghetto. We are familiar with the Nazi love of categories and subgroupings, however meaningless; it remains unclear why in each ghetto (and in the death camps) the Gypsies, who invariably formed a relatively small contingent, were isolated from the Jews and from other prisoners.

Although German Gypsies had been put into German concentration camps as early as 1934, in November of 1941 Łódź became the first place in Poland where Gypsies were gathered for extermination in a camp setting. Here they were completely sealed off, and were out of sight: only the few Jewish doctors who treated a typhus epidemic, and then Jewish gravediggers, witnessed their end.

At Łódź, Nazis took a broad view of who qualified as a Gypsy. The inmates—within four days they numbered five thousand—included circus workers and vagabonds, "people roving like Gypsies" (*nach Zigeunerart umherziehende Personen*), German Sinti, Romanian Kalderash in their flowing flowery skirts, many Hungarian Gypsies, as well as some rich Viennese ones—for example, a family by the name of Weinrich. A list of their confiscated belongings includes gold watches, gold brooches, diamond earrings, amber earrings, earrings made of Hungarian gold coins and gold francs, coral and emerald rings, gold chains, and so on. Why bother to copy out that inventory? Perhaps because it seems a way of placing them, via their heirlooms and baubles, among the rest of the victims, with their relics in glass cases.

Between November 5 and November 9, according to the personal and precise instructions of Adolf Eichmann, five transports were sent to Łódź from transit camps in occupied Austria. If in some places Gypsies were picked off, shot at, or lynched haphazardly and their deaths not even recorded, at Łódź there was elaborate and meticulous preparation. Each transport carried exactly one thousand prisoners (the last held 1,007, though the surplus did not compensate for the number that died in transit). And all trains were supposed to arrive in Łódź at 11 a.m. Any deviation from this schedule was duly noted, and an attempt was made to recover the timetable on the following day. So, for example, in the second transport, from a camp in Furstenfeld, 186 men, 218 women, and 596 children arrived at 5:50 p.m., or nearly seven hours late. They were therefore made to spend the night in their sealed trains, in a siding; the unloading (accomplished in the prescribed thirty minutes) took place the next day. The total number of Gypsies brought into the ghetto was eleven dead and 4,996 living. Of those, 2,686 were children.

"Dr. Vogl from Prague"—a prisoner doctor (and survivor) from the Łódź ghetto—was made to sign death certificates with the cause of *Herzschwächenheit*, or heart trouble, for scores of Gypsies who were hanged or suffocated. Kalman Wolkowicz, who worked as a prisoner orderly at the Jewish hospital (Gypsies were not treated there or anywhere else), remembers a moment when the music coming from the Gypsy camp stopped. After playing was declared *verboten*, the silence was interrupted only by yells and screams of the SS and of their victims. Wolkowicz also noted extreme malnutrition in the Gypsy ghetto, and that the job of doctors sent in there was only to separate out the sick.

Abram Rozenberg, who worked as a gravedigger in the ghetto, had the job of bringing dead Gypsies to the Jewish cemetery.

> There were 3–4 such transports daily. There were eight to ten corpses each time, with old people and children among them. . . . I noticed that most of the corpses were battered, some having bruises on the neck which indicated that they were hung. . . . Many corpses were massacred . . . with broken arms and legs. They probably resisted. I don't know for sure, but having seen the corpses I arrived at this

conclusion. . . . I found out that the Kripo [the Reich's Krimi-
nalpolizei] came every day ordering Gypsies to hang their kin. The
hanging took place in a blacksmith's shop at 84/6 Brzezinska St. . . .

Gypsies—like the Jewish inmates—were also made to act as policemen and guards over their own people: "Behind the double barbed
wire fence . . . there were three Gypsies standing guard. They were
camp policemen, wearing armbands and carrying billyclubs. Upon
seeing the approaching SS *Scharführer*, or officer, they ran towards
some Gypsies standing nearby and beat them severely." Forcing the
victims to take part in their own extermination made them into the
asocials and criminals they were cast as in Nazi ideology; somehow it
had to be—or had to be made to be—their fault.

Long before the creation of a camp for the Gypsies at Auschwitz,
the ruthlessly genocidal character of their murder was clear enough.
Once in the ghetto, and later in the death camp, the pretext of criminality was no longer necessary. The alleviation of this especially labo-
rious hypocrisy must have eased the killing, particularly the killing of
very small "criminals."

Abram Rozenberg remembered the murder of a child:

It was in the Fall, I don't remember exactly what year [1941], when
at nine, ten in the morning a wagon arrived and I together with my
co-workers removed a box with corpses in it. At that point we heard
a child's wailing. Impulsively we jumped aside, but within a second
I approached the box and opened the lid. A small Gypsy child fell
out. It had convulsions. I cut the rope which was still on its neck,
with a pen knife. The child convulsed for a while, but soon regained
consciousness. We could not understand what the child was saying.
We deliberated how to hide the child, but just then Sztajnberg, the
cemetery chief, came with Hercberg, the prison boss, and they told
us to take the child back to the ghetto hospital. They soon contacted the Kripo, who took the child out of the hospital. The next
day the child, dead, was brought to the cemetery. It was savagely
murdered. It was a girl, 3, 4 years old.

Six hundred and thirteen Gypsies died inside the Łódź ghetto; the
rest were sent to Chełmno, the experimental extermination camp
where 350,000 people were murdered. "The experience with the Gypsy
prisoners in Łódź," Ficowski argues, "was to serve the Nazis in orga-

nizing a huge center of annihilation of the Gypsies in Auschwitz [a year later]." Jan Dernowski, a Pole who witnessed these transports on his way to work, remembered a daily column

> of about ten three-ton trucks, bearing SS licence [plates]. These trucks, tightly covered by tarpaulins, were escorted on either end by armed Gestapo men carrying machine guns and traveling by car. . . . Looking on with horror at this procession of death—since I well knew the purpose of this voyage—I heard cries and moans of the transported from beneath the slightly lifted tarpaulins. They were cries not only of women and children, but also of men, handsome, genuine Gypsies.

One of the few prisoners who escaped from Chełmno, Michal Pod-klebnik, remembered that "after the liquidation of Jews from many small towns, transports from the Łódź ghetto started arriving. First came the Gypsies, about five thousand of them, and after them the Jews." The immediate motivation for the removal of the Gypsies to Chełmno was not ideological: it was fear of the typhus epidemic that was ravaging their horribly crowded section of the ghetto. Generally it was Jews who went first to the gas chambers. This too was mostly prompted by pragmatism: the houses of Jews were needed to accommodate returning Germans.

Chełmno was a death camp, not a concentration camp, and prisoners were usually killed on arrival. But before they were allowed to die, the Gypsies, like the Jews, were subjected to the usual grotesque deceptions. They were promised "good food and a transfer for work in the East." But first, a shower. It was January. They undressed in a heated room and passed through a door marked "To the Bath." They were told that they would be taking a shuttle van to the bathhouses, but in fact the charade fell apart here. Gendarmes beat the prisoners into the trucks. These were mobile gassing units which then transported the dead to a dumping ground in a wood—and a grave shared with Jews—before returning for the next load of "bathers."

There were no survivors of the Łódź Gypsy ghetto, which existed for only two months. The *Biuletyn Kroniki Codiennej* (the *Daily Chronicle* of the ghetto) for April 29 and 30, 1942, reported:

> In the buildings left by the Gypsies relatively large quantities of provisions were found, such as vegetables, sugar and bread hard as

rock. All provisions were disinfected with chloride. Some other things, such as clothing, musical instruments, knives etc were also found there. After clean-up is completed the buildings will be turned into factories for the manufacture of straw shoes.

A year later, in February of 1943, the first transports of German Gypsies arrived in the new camp at Auschwitz-Birkenau. The inmates were mainly German and Czech Gypsies, but they also came from Austria, Poland, Russia, Croatia, Slovenia, Hungary, Holland, Lithuania, Norway, Belgium, and France.

Mieczysław Janka, a Polish survivor, remembers the Gypsy family camp next to the hospital at Birkenau. "The Gypsy men would accompany our singing while their women danced. For this we would throw them bits of onion and cigarettes. One night the Gypsies were taken away and burned." Outsiders' recollections of the *Zigeunerlager*, cut off as always from other inmates, were often of sounds—we heard them (they would say), their singing, their playing, their crying, their moans and screams, and then, "one night," their silence. That night was August 2, 1944.

The *Zigeunerlager* differed from the rest of Auschwitz-Birkenau in several ways. Gypsy men, women, and their many children were allowed to stay together, as families. (There was also a Czech *Familienlager*.) Until near the end, they also kept their hair—and their possessions and their money, which made it possible, in the beginning, to buy and barter for food. They wore their own clothes, with black triangles sewn on—black for asocial (or sometimes green, for criminal); and with a "Z" for *Zigeuner* tattooed on the left arm. And at first, as my Polish guide disdainfully pointed out, they were not sent out on work duty; they were not listed in the *Arbeitseinsatz*, the register of working people. Gypsies therefore were not subjected to the regular selections, in which doctors the year round sent naked prisoners trotting either to the right or to the left—to work or to their deaths. Towards the end, uniformed young Gypsies were sent to work in the main camp, and a group of two hundred women was sent outside the camp to level the ground and to gather stones in their skirts. Otherwise the Gypsies were only "selected" once: when the entire camp was liquidated under high-level orders from Berlin. By then only around four thousand out of twenty-three thousand Gypsies remained alive.

Josef Mengele, the notorious Nazi doctor, was particularly interested in the Gypsies. When the orders came for their mass murder, he was devastated; he had become passionately involved in his research. Nevertheless, according to one witness, he was "all over the camp" that day, tracking down every last hidden child. Those who had escaped the previous night's transports he put in his own car and drove to the gas chambers himself. And the Gypsy children went willingly, for this was a man who had long shown them affection and given them candy; they adored and trusted Mengele, and would run after him calling, "Uncle Pepi! Uncle Pepi!"

Mengele maintained what one of its passengers called "a very macabre sort of ship of fools": a special block of dwarves, giants, people with one blue and one brown eye, and—of overriding interest to the doctor—twins. According to one prisoner doctor who was made to work with Mengele, "In the Gypsy camp [he] kept samples of hair, eyes [of twins], equipment to take fingerprints, handprints, footprints." And once he'd finished he would send their body parts—eyes especially but sometimes the whole head—to his old institute in Berlin before sending the remains to the crematorium (autopsies on twins were performed separately, in a special lab near the crematorium). Many of the twins were Gypsies. And some of his Gypsy twins were not twins: seeing the preferential treatment (better food, clean bunks, no beatings) some women presented two children of the same size as twins. Twins had their own block in the men's camp, the women's camp, and in the Gypsy camp. They were especially valuable subjects for the study of "identical inherited dispositions"—towards criminality, in the case of Gypsies. Though it was true that most twins had a better chance of surviving than regular prisoners, this was not the case for all. In one night Mengele personally injected fourteen healthy Gypsy twin children in the heart with chloroform, in order to get on with the dissection of their corpses.

No reason is given for the bundling of Gypsies into their own camp, behind their own electrical fence, where conditions were atrocious even by Auschwitz standards. Perhaps they were separated out in the interests of unrestrained research. If the early urban Gypsy camps were ideal sites for initial genealogical work, Auschwitz-Birkenau was a perfect death lab. Mengele was perhaps unusually appreciative of such opportunities; he was also the head doctor at Birkenau, and, it seems, was given free run of the Gypsy camp. In this segregated zoo of captive subjects, rare diseases could be cultivated and observed, and "cures" tried out. In Dachau and Buchenwald Gypsies were injected with sea-water to discover, on behalf of the German navy, how long humans could survive on saltwater. At Auschwitz disease and hereditary conditions were the main interest (though tests of acid on skin or injections in the eyes to change their color also took place here, among other exotic experiments). Thus an outbreak of scabies was the occasion for a treatment which involved moving the lacerated patient at set intervals from cement tub to cement tub, each containing a different salt-and-acid solution. And when treatment failed, autopsies could be performed immediately.

Indeed, if there was disagreement between doctors over which among competing ailments was most badly ravaging a particular prisoner, he or she could be dissected without delay. Mengele shot, or, as he would say, "sacrificed," his favorite pair of twins, a "splendid set" of seven-year-old Gypsy boys, to settle just such a "dispute" (tuberculosis was suspected). "It must be there," Mengele had insisted to one of the prisoner doctors, and then he returned an hour later, "now speaking calmly." He said: "You are right. There was nothing." In that time he had killed both boys and examined their lungs and other organs.

The menu of epidemics in the *Zigeunerlager* included typhus fever, typhoid, scurvy, dysentery, and scabies, along with lice and boils. There was a makeshift hospital—sick Gypsies were not sent to the main hospital which was just next to their camp—but the only medicine was a small amount of camphor. Women gave birth on top of the stovepipes which ran horizontally along the length of the barracks. And some of them didn't: in advanced stages of pregnancy women might be injected with typhus fever to see the effect on the fetus. A witness counted eighty-six such cases.

The most exotic ailment to develop in the camp was noma—a normally rare form of gangrene affecting the face and mouth. In his memoir, Commandant Hoess evinces a distinct *frisson* as he reports on the outbreak. The "children [were] sick from noma, which always terrified me because it looked like leprosy; these emaciated children with big holes in their cheeks, this slow decomposition of the human body!"

It is well known that noma is caused by malnutrition and extreme debility; nevertheless, Mengele found a racial explanation for the disease. Observing a "little bundle of bones"—a Gypsy boy with advanced noma—Mengele asked another prisoner, "Would you believe this kid is

A Nazi photograph of a Gypsy in the Bełżec concentration camp, marked for reduction by the photographer, 1940

ten years old?" He attributed the child's decrepitude to membership of "this kind of race," rather than to a fatal iatrogenic condition—that is to say, one nurtured by doctors.

Similarly, a colleague and friend of Mengele's, referred to by Robert Jay Lifton in *The Nazi Doctors* only as Ernst B., spoke of the conditions in the *Zigeunerlager* at Auschwitz: they "were atrocious . . . worse than in all other camps," and constituted "a very great problem." Dr. B.

added, "Since I survived that Gypsy camp, I have developed the worst possible opinion of Gypsies. And when I see a Gypsy I make sure to get away quickly. . . . I can't stand to hear Gypsy music." Dr. B. then backdates his disgust. Though he was "deeply interested" in the Gypsy situation, he was also appalled by what he described as scenes of fathers and mothers eating while permitting their children to starve.

The desperate projection of guilt is clear enough; it was of course doctors like Ernst B. who were starving the children—and their parents (the all-orphan barracks were a constant and growing feature of the Gypsy camp). The allegation rings false for other reasons. Family feeling seems to have been stronger than personal survival among the Gypsies. Though it is hard to imagine the SS commandant of Auschwitz being "moved" by Gypsy tears, Rudolf Hoess's recollections nevertheless sound more characteristic:

> In personal relationships they were very aggressive; within the framework of the particular tribes they were united and attached to each other. In camp, when a selection of people for work took place and families had to be separated, there were moving scenes full of

Kalderash Gypsies in Bełżec. Nazi photograph, marked for reduction by the photographer, 1940.

suffering and tears. The Gypsies would calm down and be comforted only when told they would be together later on.

"For a time," Hoess remembers, "the Gypsies fit for work who were in the main Auschwitz camp tried everything so they could see their families, even at a distance. . . . Often, during roll call, we had to search for the younger Gypsies. They would sneak out to the Gypsy camp [3.5 kilometers away], because they missed their families."

That they were allowed to stay together as families at all is a measure of the trouble they caused, or were expected to cause, when they were separated. There were many cases of individual resistance during the final liquidation of the *Zigeunerlager*—especially from the women, it seems. The day before the gassing of all remaining Gypsies, Mengele had one prisoner transferred to the women's camp, perhaps because her husband was a German. However, her children had been left behind to await their death. "You don't even have the guts to kill me," she reportedly shouted at him, seconds before being shot dead. One Sinti camp functionary threw herself on an SS officer, grabbing for his eyes like a wild animal before she too was shot. Was it to reassure these troublesome mothers or to gratify the Nazi sense of humor that a kindergarten was established, complete with merry-go-round, for the frail children of the *Zigeunerlager* just over a month before they were killed?

The Hungarian Jews brought to Auschwitz were briefly lodged in the emptied Gypsy camp; after they were murdered, it was converted into a women's hospital.

When I began my research I had it in mind that the Gypsies were "the new Jews" of Eastern Europe. Here they are, scattered in huge numbers as the Jews were before them, and they have been the first casualties of the nascent democracies. But they are not the new Jews: the Gypsies, alongside the Jews, are ancient scapegoats. The Jews poisoned the wells; the Gypsies brought the plague.

Before the Enlightenment, Gypsies and Jews together represented the migrant poor in the European imagination. Indeed, according to some myths, Gypsies *were* Jews. Collin de Plancy, in his *Dictionnaire Infernal* (1845), tells how the Jews of fourteenth-century France and Germany, blamed for the plagues ravaging those countries, fled into the forests, where they remained for fifty years, living in underground caves. By the time they came out, the story goes, with nothing left of

The Auschwitz survivor Karl Stojka's rendering of the Zigeunerlager, which he signed with his camp number, Z5742. "I saw how they burned . . ." he said of the night of August 2, 1944. "The Gypsy camp stands empty." Stojka's little brother, Ossi, aged seven, died in the camp, and his father, thirty-two, was killed at Mauthausen.

their traditional professions and with no capital, they were forced to make their way by telling fortunes. They said they came from Egypt (a familiar yarn about Gypsies made freshly plausible by the new attribution of a Semitic origin). De Plancy describes their "disguised jargon" as a mixture of "Hebrew and bad German"—which commentators have swiftly identified as Yiddish (though the language of the nomadic Jenische, or the German-influenced dialect of the Sinti, would have fit as well). However stylized this story may be, the desire to establish a

Semitic origin for the Gypsies is easily explained by the compelling similarities of their common destiny in persecution and diaspora.

Jews and Gypsies have their own "national" languages and their own traditional laws and articulated codes of ethics, rituals, and behavior; both have been identified with particular professions, sometimes the same professions (those combining craftsmanship with trade, as would suit migrants). And increasingly, for better or for worse, both have also been alienated from their traditional culture by their dependence on the culture of the "host" society.

Certainly the Nazis were more interested in the Jewish Question than the Gypsy Plague. After all, the Gypsies, already invisible both socially and economically, represented only a tiny fraction of the European population: .05 percent of the 1933 population of Germany. While the Jew was represented as a nefarious and exotic creature—old stereotypes found new life in violent propaganda, such as Julius Streicher's *Der Stürmer*—Gypsies didn't need any further blackening. Inconsequential as they were in numbers, they had remained the quintessential outsiders of the European imagination: sinister, separate, literally dark, and synonymous with sorcery and crime. Their unpopularity could be counted on. ("Never before," a typically ironic Rom leader said to me, as we watched a political meeting disintegrate into a brawl, "has a group been so persecuted *and* so unlovable.")

The Enlightenment brought European Jews opportunities for education and commerce previously closed to them, and they therefore advanced socially in a way that Gypsies did not. For their part the Gypsies rejected assimilation (including education) and kept to themselves. This divergence is reflected in the markedly different responses to the Jewish Holocaust and to the Gypsy *porraimos*.

Forgetfulness about the *porraimos* is sometimes abetted by certain persistent and hopeful cases of *national* amnesia—in the occupied territories, but also in France. (The French still refuse to release wartime documents which relate to Gypsies, presumably to protect French officials.) More generally, documents have been made available, and still the Gypsies appear as a footnote, if at all. Raul Hilberg, in his vast three-volume study of the Holocaust, has fewer than fifteen pages on the fate of Europe's Gypsies; Lucy Davidowicz, in her fascinating book *about* the misappropriation of the Holocaust by historians, deals with them in two paragraphs.

If the ignorance about the fate of Europe's Gypsies under the Nazis sometimes seems willful, perhaps it is because their inclusion undermines what Sybil Milton, the senior historian of the United States Holocaust Memorial Museum, identifies as the fundamental belief of her historian colleagues: "all have continued to focus on the killing of Jews as a unique departure from earlier persecutions, accepting Hitler's antisemitism and that of the Nazi movement as the only motivation for mass murder." As Milton points out, it was the same government, agencies, doctors, anthropologists, and other "racial scientists" who developed and applied the eugenic measures against Jews, Gypsies, blacks, and the handicapped. Starting with marriage laws and sterilization and ending in murder, the methods used to register, to isolate, and finally to eliminate these groups "for the protection of German blood" were similar and sometimes identical.

Whereas Jews were fingered as agents of an international criminal conspiracy, the Gypsies (branded as spies centuries earlier) were now attacked as congenital criminals. The latter libel better stood the test of time.

In war-crimes trials, Nazis attempted to justify—or differentiate—the killing of Gypsies by stating that they had been punished as criminals, not as Gypsies *per se.* And they succeeded: although sufficient documents were available immediately after the war, the mass murder of Roma and Sinti was not addressed at the Nuremberg trials, and no Gypsy witnesses were called. To this day, just one Nazi, Ernst-August König, has received a sentence specifically for crimes against Gypsies. On September 18, 1991, the seventy-one-year-old former Auschwitz guard sentenced to life hanged himself in his German prison cell.

Many "experts" on "Gypsy affairs" during the Nazi period continued to work on the problem in the Federal Republic, making the collapse of the Third Reich a matter of irrelevance to most Gypsies. In 1953 Ritter's files, genealogies, and "racial testimonies" were given to the newly created—or the newly named—Travelers Office of the Bavarian Criminal Police, whose staff included one of his former SS colleagues. Ritter himself, commended by an adviser to the federal government for his "profound appreciation of the situation of Roma," returned to his work as a child psychologist.

A federal court in 1956 chose as the starting point for the racial persecution the year 1943—when the deportations to Auschwitz began—thereby disclaiming responsibility to most Gypsy survivors. Before that date, "police and security" measures against them were legitimized by their alleged "asocial characteristics." This claim was back-dated by the German courts to 1938 only in the 1960s, by which time many survivors were irretrievably dispersed or dead. In the Eastern bloc countries the Gypsies have also been disowned. It has often been convenient for governments to understate the numbers of unwanted people living in their territories; in this way, even for regimes ready to honor the "victims of fascism"—and in Hungary and Czechoslovakia reparations to Jews were made eagerly and early—ludicrously low figures for Gypsies made it politically possible to ignore their legitimate claims. (At the same time, the culture of Gypsies—particularly the contribution of Gypsy musicians in Hungary—has been a prominent feature of the country's folkloric identity.)

The Nazi genocide against Sinti and Roma was officially acknowledged only in 1982, by Helmut Schmidt. But little has changed. The few Gypsy survivors who are able to navigate the bureaucratic obstacles may find that it isn't worth the trouble. For example, all social-security payments received by the successful claimant since 1945 are automatically deducted from any reparations, as if they were the same thing. Nor need the children of victims apply; unlike their Jewish counterparts, Gypsies orphaned by Nazi actions do not qualify. But who is going to complain?

Very few Gypsies know much about their collective history, but none is unaware of its hallmark of persecution. Many (but far from most) Gypsies living in the Balkans have an idea of their fate under the Third Reich and its kindred regimes in Bulgaria and the Czech lands, Croatia, Hungary, Romania, and Slovakia, as well as in occupied Albania, Serbia, and Greece. So was it ironic, or even perverse, that among them now there was such a rush for Germany? (It is hard to imagine that country's exerting magnetic force on today's remaining East European Jews.) Though Romany emancipation movements are working to change this, the instinct to suppress the past remains powerful.

Among Roma, though, "forgetting" does not imply complacency: its tenor is one of—sometimes buoyant—defiance. On a 1993 visit to a miserable Romanian Gypsy settlement which had been razed by a white Romanian mob, I was accompanied by an English Gypsy, Pete Mercer, the head of his community in Peterborough. His reaction to the arson attack, which had left some crippled and hundreds homeless, was spirited—and at the same time characteristically prim in its abbreviation of the swear word. "Hony swacky mally Asbestos," Pete wrote in my notebook, with a translation beneath—not of *Honi soit qui mal y pense,* or "Shame be to him who evil thinks" (the motto of the Most Noble Order of the Garter), but a loose translation of the sense of it: "F. you Jack, I'm fireproof."

The Jews have responded to persecution and dispersal with a monumental industry of remembrance. The Gypsies—with their peculiar mixture of fatalism and the spirit, or wit, to seize the day—have made an art of forgetting.

Historically the Gypsies have not had an idea of, or word for, themselves as a group. In place of a nation, they recognize different tribes and, more locally, extended families or clans. Their European names—like Gypsy or *Zigeuner*—suggest a monolithic whole. This isn't an accurate reflection of how they see themselves: it is a reflection of how they are seen by outsiders.

But things are changing. Just as Eskimos have chosen to call themselves the Inuit—which means "people"—"Roma" is emerging as a common name and signaling the arrival of a new *collective* identity. It is this fledgling recognition that makes the project of remembrance possible. A sense of local and personal misfortune is developing into a broad consciousness of historical wrong. And so for the first time, Gypsies *want* to commemorate the *porraimos.*

On April 14, 1994, the United States Holocaust Memorial Museum held its first commemoration of the Gypsy victims. Among the participants was Ian Hancock, an English Gypsy, now living in Buda, Texas. It was Hancock who coined the term *porraimos;* it was Hancock who more or less single-handedly waged the long battle for inclusion of the Roma in the museum—and on the U.S. Holocaust Memorial Council (founded in 1979), whose sixty-five members already included Poles, Russians, Ukrainians, and more than thirty Jews. It was only after the 1986 resignation of President Elie Wiesel, the survivor and Nobel Peace Prize winner, who had opposed Gypsy representation, that one Gypsy was invited onto the council.

A handful of Gypsies gathered that spring day in the museum's marble Hall of Remembrance. They came from New Jersey, Minneapolis, Los Angeles, Budapest, Bucharest, Bratislava, and Kraków. Hancock (of London and Buda), whom over several years I had rarely seen in anything other than defiant mood, was proudly and solemnly brimming with tears. All the same, he was still fuming about the Gypsy nook upstairs in the museum, decorated like a school play, with a Gypsy caravan and violin. There, under the label "Enemies of the State," his people were as usual lost in a crowd of sundry "undesirables": "communists, Social

Democrats, trade unionists, pacifists, homosexuals, dissenting clergy, Jehovah's Witnesses, freemasons, Roma (Gypsies), Slavs and others." In the museum's permanent exhibition only the Jews are described as racial enemies and therefore uniquely slated for annihilation.

Three Eastern European Roma spoke. Although the very fact of their presence in the Hall of Remembrance was evidence of change—as was their testimony, earlier in the day, before a special congressional hearing on the human-rights abuses of Gypsies—the stories they told mainly suggested that the Holocaust had been a lesson in the usefulness of "forgetting" for their parents, and how richly they felt the role of *baxt*, of luck, chance, or fate. A significant representation of Gypsies would become part of the community of remembrance; but most would remain apart, preoccupied, and vivid to themselves only in the present.

Jan Yoors—the twelve-year-old Belgian boy who in the 1930s had left home to join a passing troupe of Lovara Gypsies—wrote a memoir, many years later, of his adopted people.

> I often wondered at their strange, inexplicable lack of traumatic reactions to their often violent personal persecutions. I observed, and eventually learned to understand, their rejection of hate or personal bitterness as a response to outside pressures. Pulika, my adopted father, said, "Too often the courage about dying is cowardice about living."

During the war, Yoors was contacted by the British Resistance. Gypsies, with their expert knowledge of the forests and byways, the psychology of authorities and of survival, would make natural members of the underground. In addition to the skills developed by an underground *nation*, however, it was the Gypsy instinct to live so responsively in the present which made them valuable to the Resistance, and which also accounts for their "peculiar" lack of interest in the past. In a second book, about the war period, Yoors returns to Pulika and his family with a mission. As an epigraph Yoors offers an example of Pulika's wartime wisdom: "The problem is still one of interpretation, and the response of man is the meaning of his life." Or, as a Welsh Gypsy proverb has it: "The winter will ask what we did in the summer."

EIGHT

The Temptation to Exist

In a 1972 pamphlet called *Romania's Population*, Romanians, Hungarians, and Germans were found to account for 99 percent of the population, the remainder comprising "other nationalities," including "Ukrainians, Ruthenians, Hutsulains, Serbians, Croats, Slovaks, Russians, Tartars, Turks, Jews, etc." Thus the Roma of Romania, long the country's largest minority (and in 1992 accounting for 15 percent of the entire population), were registered simply as "etc."

Nicolae Gheorghe—a scholarly and somehow unlikely activist—was one of those "etc." But after 1989 he emerged as a kind of star, fêted by "the international community," and hailed as one of the new celebrities of ethnic conflict and minority rights (along with, for example, Nobel Peace Prize winner Rigoberta Menchú and the martyred Chico Mendes). To this company, Nicolae Gheorghe brought not only the Gypsies but his own continental flair. Every news story in the foreign press about Gypsies mentioned or quoted him.

Like most celebrities he was also elusive. Under the "G" tab of my address book I have a half-dozen numbers for Gheorghe, none of them his own. Tracking him down required half a dozen conversations: one by one the assistant/wife/sister would tell you (wearily/impatiently/boredly) that Nicolae was at a conference/collecting an award in Helsinki/Warsaw/Geneva/New York. He slalomed from summit to symposium, visiting a score of different capitals a year, and he lived frugally, on expenses. Fittingly for a spokesman for a stateless, notionally nomadic people, even at home in Bucharest Nicolae had no fixed address but only a post-office box. In his carry-on luggage he kept a portable computer, the ring binder in which he logs his life, and a few shirts and ascots. Nicolae was always trying to deflect attention away from himself; such scrutiny illuminated not his cause, but his personal conflict. An academic by inclination, Gheorghe became an activist out of a sense of duty (though he imaginatively combined these roles by being an activist of the intellect, agitating for ideas, picketing for theory). He was also genuinely uninterested in aggrandizement, and donated all his awards to projects benefiting Roma. He had no particular Roma constituency on which he could rely, and other ambitious Gypsies envied the apparently glamorous way he lived, which in truth was the kind of arduous and disconnected regime of a traveling salesman.

The family of Nicolae's childhood was *romanizat*, Romanianized, and they spoke only the national language. His fair-complexioned mother had discouraged identification with *ţigani*. This was hardly a real option, as her husband's side of the family was extremely dark-skinned; but with her son she was adamant. In her own lifetime, passing for a *gadji* had saved her from deportation. At home the Gheorghe family acknowledged that they were Roma, and, long before the advent of political euphemism, they used the term to distinguish themselves from *ţigani*, by which they meant—as did all Romanians— variously corrupted and/or socially inferior Gypsies.

Such taxonomies were not respected at school, though, and Nicolae, who is no darker than many Romanians, has a painful early memory of other boys squawking *Ga!* at him, *Ga! Cioră! Cioră* is the Romanian for "crow"—the black nuisance—and *ga* is the sound the crow makes. (*"Cioră, Cioră,"* goes the schoolyard taunt, *"măta zboară tactu, cintă la vioară"*: "Your mother flies, your father plays the violin.") In the state military academy, where he spent six years, Nicolae became a leader of the Communist Youth League; he went on to university and joined the Party, moving ever further from any *ţigani* identity. Although Gypsies, valued for their particular skills, had once been *integrated* in the Romanian territories, in the sixties large numbers of them were being assimilated for the first time: educated and inducted, for better or worse, into the rank and file. They had less "cultural mobility," as Nicolae would say, but certainly they had more social mobility than ever before or since. Nevertheless, Nicolae does remember being called an African at the military academy.

And then, while doing field work for his sociology degree, Nicolae came into contact with "real" Gypsies. It was a revelation. According to Sam Beck, an American sociologist who met Nicolae during his own field work in Romania in 1979, Gheorghe had by then already been trying to organize what he called "a formal voluntary association of

Roma": a brave venture during a period in which "ethnic politics were understood either as a threat against the state or illegal chauvinism." At the same time, under Ceauşescu, his work and indeed his advice were used to inform policy about which he could only feel ambivalent.

Although Gypsies continued to be a mere "etc." in the official view, secretly the Romanian Communist Party grew anxious to do something about its vast population of a certain dark people who failed to reflect the modern achievements of the Romanian state. And so a committee was formed. Nicolae Gheorghe served the Commission on Demography from 1976 to 1989. He was not deluded about its aims—to disperse and thereby assimilate Gypsies—and cannot have been surprised that the police were the most active element on the project.

In 1983, the Propaganda section of the Central Committee produced a report evaluating the work of the Commission and found that

> a large number of them, persisting in retrograde traditions and mentalities, tend to lead a parasitic way of life, refuse to work, and live in precarious conditions. . . . [They] resist hygienic and sanitary steps . . . and refuse to take part in activities for the welfare of society.

Gypsy "resistance" to hygiene could be explained by the fact that then as now running water and sanitation services did not extend to the Gypsy neighborhoods, not even to those in cities. But garbage collection wasn't among the remedies offered by the committee, which instead included the issuing of police identification cards to all Gypsies and the removal of all private means of transport, such as horses and carts. Vagabonds and beggars should be taken into care, where their education would focus on the moral and the sanitary, as well as "special stress [on] respecting laws, Party decisions and documents."

Following the publication of the commission's report in 1984, Nicolae wrote a report of his own: an article disclosing and denouncing the oppressive new policies, which was smuggled out of Romania and published in a French journal. Soon enough, someone denounced him, and Nicolae was subjected to a campaign of terror which resulted in the loss of his job and the ruin of his family. His children, who are only half Gypsy, not surprisingly have been raised far from the world of Romany emancipation, which is also to say far from him. He seemed to have lost everything.

Ten years later, Gheorghe was still driven to argue from both sides. He maintained his original attraction to the internationalist, humane values of communism; his self-criticism was exemplary. His dilemma derived in part from the fact that he owed his education to that system. Furthermore, like all people from disfranchised groups who enfranchise themselves, his conflict thereafter was over the extent to which he then remained Gypsy—not only in his own mind and in the minds of Gypsies left behind, but also in the view of a state which maintained that a Gypsy was that ineducable thing, innately criminal: a *social* problem.

In truth, Nicolae had been mourning those humane, internationalist values for a long time, well before the Securitate swooped. In the seventies he was a well-assimilated member of the Romanian Communist Party; *he* had changed, and then everything around him changed. After Ceauşescu's famous denunciation of the 1968 Russian tank roll into Prague, Romania moved farther and farther from Moscow and into something known as Socialist Nationalism: the Party became a baldly nationalist organ. Nicolae felt betrayed. The Romanian writer Norman Manea—deported as a (five-year-old) Jew by Antonescu, and an exile from Ceauşescu's regime—puts his finger on it: "The question of the stranger in a society which estranges everybody from it—while forcing everybody to assimilate their own alienation—takes cover under dubious and sinister masks." And so it was only as a *sociologist,* taking testimony from desperate Gypsy survivors of the war deportations, that Gheorghe recognized in them his own history, and possibly his future.

Now I was in Bucharest to meet Nicolae. I tried to telephone him, without success. As late as I dared, I dialed again. A woman picked up on the first ring.

"*Da?*"

"Hello, is Nicolae there?"

"No."

"Oh. Uh, well. My name is . . . Could you please ask him to ring me when he gets in?" Silence.

"No, I'm not sure I can do that."

Oh dear. It was after 11 p.m. "The thing is," I explained, afraid she'd got the wrong impression, "we have a plane to catch first thing in the morning—to go to a village that has been attacked. I was hoping to make a plan. . . ."

"I'm not expecting Nicolae home tonight."

Now what? I paused, hoping she would offer some clue. I was about to give up when finally she spoke.

"Nicolae has been kidnapped."

Her name was Ina. And she was terrified. Like most Romanians she was a skilled dissimulator, but her fright could be measured by the fact that within a few hours she had amassed two American human-rights lawyers, a commentator from French television, a Romanian journalist, and a wire reporter. Outside attention, she believed, might help to galvanize the police. Ina was convinced that Nicolae had been kidnapped by rival Rom leaders Octavian Stoica and the blue-haired Nicolae Bobu. In the course of the night this was confirmed: he had been forced into a car by two men, and the witness, also Rom, recognized the kidnappers.

Early the next morning, Ina heard a rumor that Nicolae had been taken north, to Sibiu, in Transylvania, where Ion Cioaba, the Kalderash racketeer and now self-proclaimed King of the Romanian Gypsies, had his headquarters. By ten o'clock, it emerged that Nicolae had been removed to a small town near Rîmnicu Vîlcea, about four hours northwest of Bucharest, near the monastery where the annual Kalderash festival had been held a month or so before. (This is also Cioaba country. Was he somehow involved?) It seemed likely that Nicolae had been snatched in order to face a *kris*, a Gypsy trial. If true, this was a serious business. A *kris* is outside Romanian law. There is no appeal.

By the time I arrived with the Romanian journalist—the remains of our original squad—at the remote village hall, the trial was in full swing. The defendant, the accusers, and possibly neutral luminaries were seated on the raised stage. There was Cioaba. There were Bobu and Stoica and Cioaba's notorious daughter, Luminitsa. In the gallery were three hundred of the scruffiest and most disorderly Gypsies I had ever seen gathered in one room, all of them jeering. Loyal to her father, Luminitsa later described this meeting to me as a *kris*, but it looked like a kangaroo court. A *kris* would be announced well in advance; it would be public, as this one was, but the accuser and the accused would each be allowed to select a judge. (That judge would in turn select a third, and possibly others, depending on the gravity of the crime.)

First, Nicolae was accused of stealing funds donated to his organization by the World Council of Churches. Over and over he invited anyone at all to examine the books of his Ethnic Federation of Roma, but they talked over him; the accusation itself was the vital thing. Nicolae had no right of reply. Anyway, he would not have been heard through the din. The room was crowded, hot, and angry. It was clear that these Gypsies were mainly Kalderash—among the most traditional, least assimilated Gypsies, who numbered some two hundred thousand in Romania alone. Although Ion Cioaba claimed to be their leader, they didn't appear to recognize any authority. In fact the meeting seemed about to erupt. One rough-looking woman interrupted the proceedings to complain hoarsely that she could not feed her ten children. But it was her face that was evidence of the severity of Gypsy law: the left nostril had been slashed through—traditional punishment inflicted by her husband for adultery.

Stoica, a fiery-tongued evangelical type, accused Nicolae of "anti-Romanian activity." This sounded familiar. Already on the morning of Nicolae's trial a smear article about him had appeared in the violently nationalist (and robustly anti-Semitic and anti-Gypsy) *România Mare,* or Greater Romania. Enough Gypsy leaders were themselves sufficiently "Balkan"—or shortsighted, cynical, and politically perverse—to sacrifice one of their own in favor of a nation that condones attacks on their people. And some, like Stoica, were fanatic patriots, pathetically raging against the stereotype that a Gypsy is by definition disloyal (and probably a spy). But with the support of outsiders Nicolae's Gypsy enemies could do more than beat him up in the woods; they could supply the "proof" that would make it difficult for him to leave Romania, and thereby curtail his alleged efforts to besmirch the reputation of the Romanian nation abroad.

Nicolae was threatened, roughed up, warned, and then released. Still, the so-called *kris* was significant: a dramatic manifestation of the fundamentalist forces that threaten not only individuals but the whole Romany movement.

Much later, when I asked Nicolae what had happened during the night of his kidnap, he coolly replied, "They complained that whenever they spoke to me I looked at my watch. I guess they were trying to get my attention." If Nicolae was cool it was because he had been through versions of this before—many times, since the 1970s, when he'd done his field work and had first properly recognized himself as a Rom. After that experience Nicolae, a confused, thirty-year-old doctoral candidate, sought induction into the "authentic" world of Gypsies, and it was Cioaba he found.

Ion Cioaba never learned to read and write, and in the seventies he took Nicolae on as a kind of secretary. Nicolae wrote hundreds of letters on his patron's behalf, many of them in the cause of recovering confiscated Kalderash gold. When Nicolae told me that as a child he had felt himself to be "lower caste," I had assumed he meant inferior to the white world all around him. But as he talked about his early days with Cioaba, I realized that it was other, "realer" Gypsies whom he had secretly or half-consciously envied. I asked him what someone like Cioaba represented to him. "They are," he said, "what you might call aristocrats."

I first met Cioaba in 1992, at his office in Sibiu, in Transylvania. He was squashed into a swivel chair behind his desk and on his head was perched a tall black astrakhan hat, the very model favored by the late dictator. On the wall was a color election poster of himself as "Senator Cioaba Ion," slightly younger and no slimmer: he is about five feet two and nearly as wide. (Powerful Gypsies tend to be very fat. Heft is suggestive of authority and wealth, as it once was among rich Western Europeans; among Gypsies, a large head is itself regarded as an auspicious feature in any man.) Behind him was the framed desktop diploma of "Doctor Ian Cioaba," from "Texas America University." The only other decor was his jewelry: a solid gold watch and, crammed onto each finger, a chunky gold ring. One of them (which had been sawn off by the time I next saw him) was a signet ring with his initials, I.C., fashioned into a hammer and sickle. All of his front teeth were capped with gold. Normally Cioaba charged journalists for interviews, but this time he waived his fee. He was enjoying himself. "If you were a woman," he said, giving me an illustration of Kalderash life, "you would not be allowed to cross in front of my desk. You walk behind."

His was indeed a traditional household. Across the road from his shopfront office the Cioaba mansion loomed, yet his children were the first of his family to grow up under a roof (and even in cold weather the old women seemed always to be hanging around outside). His diminutive stepmother stood at the gates, with coin-plaited waist-length gray hair and long red skirts, smoking a pipe and fingering a worn deck of cards. As we passed, she tugged at my sleeve and mumbled, attempting to get my business, only to be immediately silenced by the imperious stepson she had raised.

Throughout the Ceauşescu period, Cioaba traveled abroad, which could only mean advanced connections with the security forces. The Cioabas were the first in Sibiu to own a car, then the first to own a Western car (a Mercedes), and they had the first television. Interestingly, these gadgets had made no impact on even their visible culture, and Cioaba's daughter, Luminitsa, showed no sign of the twisted iden-

Kalderash Rom with silver buttons and copper pots, Poland, circa 1865

tity that such swift upward mobility normally entrains. She cheerfully recounts the time her pipe-smoking grandmother ran away shrieking from the television. A Western was on; she thought the horses were real. Among the Kalderash conspicuous wealth guaranteed Cioaba's status. For Nicolae, it was the reverse: he admired the extent to which Cioaba had become a successful settled businessman without relinquishing a single aspect of traditional life. It was those traditions that had kept the family independent.

The Kalderash were metalworkers but like many Gypsies they were also traders. As a child Ion Cioaba had spent two years in the deportation camps in Transdnistria. Even there his father had managed to trade gold. Fifty years on, the Cioabas still made *kazans*, the distillers for home brewing that once were standard items in East European households. Out in a muddy lot behind the house I glimpsed an ancient scene: a brother and several nephews with long, tangled hair lifting heavy hammers and pounding copper on an anvil. But now Cioaba also had an industrial-scale boilermaking concern in town, and, whenever the chance arose, he bought gold. (Did I have any gold I'd like to sell? he asked within minutes—for hard currency of course.)

Cioaba presided over the annual autumn festival of the Kalderash, at the monastery of Bistriţa. To the untrained eye this two-day jamboree looked like a giant car-mart. Hundreds of Mercedes and BMWs were parked any which way, and groups of girls in shiny dresses danced together between the fenders. Families unfurled their elaborate picnics, each one-upping the next with turkeys, lamb, goats, and pigs, spit-roasted right there in the parking lot. Finally it dawned on me: *Love k-o vast, bori k-o grast,* as the saying goes—Money in hand, bride on horse. This was a bride market. Kalderash of course did not marry out, but neither could they wed too close, and so they came from all over, displaying their wealth of motors and daughters and gold, ready to buy and sell.

Although the great majority of (even Kalderash) Gypsies clearly didn't have the resources to attend such an event, this sumptuous display fueled the fantasies of Romanians who insisted that *all* Gypsies were filthy rich—black-market rich. But they didn't care; they answered only to themselves, and they could afford to be contemptuous of the majority.

To be a senator, elected or invented, wasn't much. A "doctorate" was hardly grand. And so, in 1992, Ion Cioaba pronounced himself

*Ion Cioaba, self-proclaimed King of the Romanian Gypsies, with his wife (right)
and daughter, Luminitsa, enjoying a turkey at the annual festival of the Kalderash
at the monastery of Bistriţa, at Costesti, September 1991. This was the first time for
several years that they were allowed to hold the jamboree (which had been banned
under Ceauşescu), where Kalderasha from across the country come to exchange news,
do business, and find brides.*

King of the Romanian Gypsies. He had a gold crown made and rented
Sibiu's Orthodox church for an elaborate coronation. But there was
competition. Cioaba's cousin Iulian Radulescu (with whom he was
also *xanamiki*, or a co-parent-in-law), had returned from a brief but
glamorous stint in Queens, New York. Not to be outdone, Radulescu
countered with a claim to be Emperor of All Gypsies Everywhere. The
two have been bickering and issuing royal—or imperial—denuncia-
tions of each other ever since.

Many Gypsy leaders were infuriated by these antics, which were
attracting the wrong kind of interest. Nicolae also disapproved of the
two Pretenders, but as a sociologist he recognized their shrewdness.
Romania has never been a democratic country; and it has seldom been
so unstable. Into the vacuum of authority, these two stepped up with
their maces, cynically hoping to fill a gap for the country's large Gypsy
population. Mainly, though, they had struck on a commercial hit for

The wedding of the Cioabas' thirteen-year-old granddaughter, with her father (in the hat),
an aunt, her mother (far right), and, in front, Ion Cioaba's stepmother, 1990

export; Gypsy kings after all were the invention of the *gadjo* imagination. Like many instant kings before them, they knew that royalty had
an appeal that secretaries general and co-chairpersons did not.

And sure enough, quality Western papers ran their spreads on the
royal cousins, in features sections but also in the news pages. If every
article appropriately quoted Nicolae Gheorghe, none could resist a
giggling reference to those wacky Gypsy monarchs. And they were
good copy, specializing in insults. While deportation survivor Cioaba
leapt to pay tribute to the wartime fascist dictator, Iulian the First
made headlines with his "regretful" agreement with the incendiary
taunt thrown out by the extremist Russian politician Vladimir Zhiri-
novsky: Romania was an artificial state, populated exclusively by Italian Gypsies.

Gypsies themselves have never recognized kings. Local, brokering
leaders—the *bulibasha*, the *vojvoda*, the *shero rom*, and the *baro rom* (literally "big man")—were the most any group needed or tolerated, and
these men were really judges rather than rulers. Such leaders lasted
only so long as they were respected. But the earliest Gypsy visitors to
Western Europe had also called themselves royals, and captains and

Preparing the wedding feast are the young bride's mother (second from right), all her aunts, and in the center her grandmother, Cioaba's wife, 1990.

counts; the Romanian "monarchs" of the 1990s were merely recovering an old adaptation, a cherished costume, that had been in storage during the communist period.

The Kalderash seemed to have a particular talent for the job. They had attempted to establish a dynasty once before, in the late 1920s, in Poland. Those Kalderash, in particular a family called Kwiek, were in their turn recovering a lost role. In the mid-seventeenth century Gypsy kings were appointed by the Polish Royal Chancery to represent (and to tax) all Gypsies in the territories. They had no traditional or innate authority; they were simply well-dressed bullies with their own police force. And within a single generation these fiefdoms had been subsumed by the Polish gentry. In the 1860s, following the end of slavery, a wave of Gypsies entered the former Polish Commonwealth, and some of them would reclaim the title. These were the aristocrats—Kalderash and Lovara, another dynamic tribe—much resented by the mostly settled Polish Gypsies, who had no comparable form of independent income or self-government, and no such finery (the male visitors wore fur coats and colored waistcoats with egg-size silver buttons). The newcomers managed to establish domination over the long-resident Gypsies. Their fabulous wealth and bravado—and, mainly, their self-belief—were important elements, as they are today. The Kalderash kings also established themselves by making deals with government bodies, thereby securing privileges over the Polish Gypsies, for whom such behavior was unthinkably treacherous. The Kwieks were a family of exceptional ambition, and several members of their *vitsa*, or clan, applied directly to the police, offering services in exchange for recognition as the highest Gypsy authority. Thousands of people, including many foreign diplomats, went in 1937 to watch as Janusz Kwiek in an ermine-trimmed robe (rented from the Warsaw Opera) was crowned by the archbishop.

In the traditional society of even the present-day Kalderash, Luminitsa, the eldest daughter, was an anomalously independent woman, quite unprepared to "walk behind." She had married in her early teens, as Kalderash girls do, but had somehow managed to break away with impunity, even to avoid having children. She was also highly literate. And she had traveled alone—to America, where she rapidly learned English, and sold Gypsy costumes on the street outside the UN in New York's Dag Hammarskjöld Plaza. When she returned to Sibiu, she moved into a studio above her father's office and from there she edited and published a full-color magazine—really a fanzine—with articles, horoscopes, short stories, chapters from a novel, poems, and letters to the editor, mostly about Luminitsa and all written by Luminitsa under various names, published alongside pictures of Luminitsa—in a hat, with a horse, lying on a rug with a carnation between her teeth. Luminitsa, in addition, was always trying transparently to fleece someone—me, for instance (her performance was so enjoyable, say, in telling my fortune, that whatever she came up with it was worth the price and the indignity of the con). Here too there was an echo of the Kalderash past. For the last Kwiek to retain power was Katarzyna Kwiek-Zambiła, the sister of King Janusz; until her death in 1961, she commanded the respect and position normally reserved for men, including, as it had for Luminitsa, the privilege of taking part in a trial—the *kris*.

Luminitsa was a proper princess: she was haughty and ruthless and more than at ease with her own person (which she crop-sprayed with perfumed French talc)—in contrast to such privileged Gypsy women as Antoinette in Bulgaria, who had attended the French Lycée, or even compared to Nicolae, with all his educated, questing intelligence and celebrity. Luminitsa's privilege had not come at the price of

The coronation of Janusz Kwiek, Warsaw, 1937

deracination—she had sold Gypsy costumes, not Romipen, her Gypsiness. In the end it wasn't surprising that Nicolae had attached himself to the Cioaba family. They traded languages. From them Nicolae learned Romani, and in return he taught them the language of *gadjo* politics, of bureaucracy, of the Party. And then, in 1984,

Cioaba traded Nicolae: it was Cioaba who denounced his protégé to the authorities as the author of the article in the French journal.

The years 1984 to 1989 were the worst of Nicolae's life. Like many other Romanians, by the time the revolution came he was ready. That very night—Christmas, 1989, when the Ceauşescus were executed—Nicolae was trapped inside the state television station, where he and others seized the chance to announce the formation of the Ethnic Federation of Roma (this was to be the umbrella group for disparate Romany groups). As I met these nascent organizations, constantly changing and recombining in the next few years, I kept thinking of a phrase of the Romanian writer Emil Cioran, "the temptation to exist": here again was hope for an identity beyond "etc." But Nicolae, unlike many of the hundreds of new organizers, had been taught by experience to reject a nationalist approach. He left the country.

Individual governments had ignored, belittled, or denied the violences committed against their own citizens; the project of capturing the attention, and then the imagination, of the larger world and its august international bodies was therefore that much more difficult. And yet only six months after the revolution, Nicolae Gheorghe brought the plight of Europe's largest and most despised minority to the negotiating table—and even walked away with some commitments.

At Copenhagen (and, later, in more and more clauses and articles, at Moscow, Oslo, Geneva, and Helsinki), the fifty-two nation members of the Conference on Security and Cooperation in Europe (CSCE—now Organization on Security and Cooperation in Europe) "recognized the particular problems of Roma" in Europe, in the context of intolerance, anti-Semitism, and xenophobia in general. The UN Commission on Human Rights followed with a controversial recognition of the Roma minority—controversial because not all its members recognized Gypsies as a people. In the form of the International Romani Union, the Gypsies had already (in 1979) been recognized by the Economic and Social Council of the United Nations, but it was only in 1993, following strenuous lobbying by Gheorghe and Ian Hancock, that this recognition was raised from symbolic "consultative" status to a vote.

Gypsies in the UN! The very presentation of their case in the international *gadjo* arena was going against a millennium of Roma invisibility, ignorance, and indifference. Just as rare, particularly from an Eastern European, was Gheorghe's emphasis on personal responsibil-

ity: "I know these are only paper commitments and not legal obligations," he was quick to say, "but they are our texts, which we ourselves
must realize."

One way the emerging elite was trying to do this "realizing" was in a
different kind of international arena: the gathering of representatives
from their diaspora. At Stupava, in Slovakia in 1992, a large group of
Roma from many countries gathered for the first time since the demise
of communism to discuss their future in the new Europe.

The choice of meeting place itself lent powerful resonance to those
exploratory meetings. The many Gypsy slums of Slovakia are home to
some of the very worst-off. One settlement, at Rudňany, sprawled over
an abandoned arsenic mine, and Gypsy children could be seen playing
among the corroded containers and the little piles of white powder
that leaked from them. They lived in long-abandoned, sagging, and
often roofless mining offices, surrounded by heavy metals: arsenic,
antimony, bismuth, mercury, and iron. It was something worse than
"medieval" squalor: it was post-industrial squalor. These dangers were
well known and ignored. Instead, there in Slovakia the popular Pre-
mier Vladimír Mečiar was able, a year later, to make a speech in which
he claimed it was "necessary to curtail the extended reproduction of
the socially unadaptable and mentally backward population" (the
Gypsies), adding, "If we don't deal with them now, they will deal with
us later." In Prague, Václav Havel countered with a challenging truth—
that the Gypsies are "a litmus test of a civil society"—but his view was
not shared. The squalor of Gypsy life had deepened, and the death toll
had risen. Since the Velvet Revolution, twenty-eight Gypsies have been
murdered in Czechoslovakia. The level of hatred all around could not
be overstated.

In flew the long-serving Gypsy soldiers: Nicolae Gheorghe, Ian
Hancock from Texas, Rajko Djurić from Berlin, Manush Romanov
from Bulgaria. There were also the younger players, newer at least to
the public struggle: Rudko Kawczynski from Hamburg, Klara Orgo-
vanova from here in Slovakia, Emil Sčuka, a Rom lawyer from Prague,
and Aladar Horváth, a Hungarian Rom still in his twenties who had
made a name for himself as a singer and was now a member of the
Hungarian Parliament. And there were the converts from academia:
Andrzej Mirga, and Hristo Kjuchukov, a Bulgarian Rom who had written his country's first Romani ABC. Many academics came too, from

France and the United States; there was Milena Hübschmannová, the linguist from Prague and my guide on an earlier trip in eastern Slovakia, and there was Marcel Courtiade, my guardian in Albania.

Among the Roma every style of politics was represented at Stupava—from black-power militancy and Bible-thumping to quiet accommodation within the *gadjo* political framework. Outside the conference building still other styles were on display. In the drive you'd see conferees lighting up, the blue queries of cigarette smoke floating skywards from each discrete cluster. They didn't mingle, out of shyness (to judge from the awkward glancing and posing); in the case of the Hungarians, though, who moved always in a group of more than a dozen, apparent aloofness could be put down to language. They spoke only Magyar, and so they couldn't talk to anyone who hadn't arrived on their bus. Everyone was turned out in a boxy new suit bought, one sensed, especially for the occasion. These garments also demarcated delegates along national lines, as if they were cut from flags or fashioned from the plumage of national birds: the three Poles appeared in shades of mustard and malt; the Hungarian team wore purple—ranging from mauve to puce. The Bulgarians came in black.

Cigarettes and smoker's coughs, mustaches, hats, and overburdened small frames—these united most of the Roma, but their color-coded allegiances (no doubt merely a reflection of what was available in their countries' sparse shops) could suggest the lack of unity that ignited such meetings and which has thwarted the whole Romany movement.

No self-proclaimed monarch was invited—or dared—to venture into this convention, but there were even more unlikely participants, such as Frank Johnson, a Rom from Los Angeles who had nothing whatever to do with politics or academic life. Like many from within the Eastern bloc, he had never met his brethren from other countries. What would they make of each other? Apart from his dark complexion, Frank was not like an East European Rom. He was big and tall and open and American; he "could not *believe*" the beige meat and jellied potatoes we were being offered. They were all Gypsies, but would they have anything else in common?

The Roma took the opportunity to hold their own private meetings after the scheduled sessions were through. I caught Frank Johnson as he was walking out of one these: from the corridor it sounded like a cockfight. "Gypsies around the world are alike. They can't prioritize," he said. "It's the same back home. They're brain-dead 362 days a year, and then they come to a meeting like this and strut around showing off." Earlier that day Frank had visited a nearby slum and had been consternated by the desperation there. During the sessions Gypsies and their expert friends railed against *gadjo* stereotypes; but at the Gypsy settlement Frank had felt obliged to warn a professor from Duke University to "watch his pockets." Frank was impatient with politicking.

With his square hair-do and black suit, Frank looked like a salesman, and so he was: he sold hope, to women only. "They come and see me, they come in crying and I help them sort out their men troubles. It's always men troubles, you know, and they all want a quick solution. I explain as how men leave them because they've gone and lost their bloom." The next morning, Frank looked a bit wilted himself. The psychic (as he called himself) was staring at his salami-and-gherkin breakfast. I wondered what had brought him from L.A. to a political meeting in Slovakia. "I've had two wives, thirty-six years gone between the two of them, one Gypsy, one American. I thought I'd come to Europe and try to find a woman with traditional values, one who'll appreciate what I can give her, which ain't much what with mortgage payments and whatnot, not that I pay mortgage when I'm renting. When I was growing up we owned our house. I hate renting."

Marriage and politics were of course linked in traditional Gypsy life, and Frank could be forgiven for thinking that a political meeting such as this might turn up another kind of candidate. But it wasn't wives or rent or even the Slovakian slum that had really got Frank down. It was what he had seen of the new Gypsy leadership. Scattered, vain, egomaniacal, ignorant, power-mad, back-stabbing. ("Though they don't even stab each other in the back," an American woman observed, half impressed, "they stab each other in the front.") The florid infighting was depressingly familiar even to an American Rom, but to new non-Gypsy observers it was frankly alarming. I too had been shocked the first time I saw a Gypsy leader get down on his knees and cry to make a point. Far from being embarrassed or worried by his behavior, both he and his audience duly returned to the business at hand. These were conventions—like the ritual wailing at a funeral— and they were understood by everyone in the group. It made sense to keep non-Gypsies out of their "real" meetings because things could be so easily misunderstood (and ridiculed). If Gypsy lamentation was mainly a matter of style, something like a living counterpart to the bold colors they liked, the keynote here was unembellished despair.

Ian Hancock was one of the few leaders with a keen sense of the honorable and much-thwarted evolution of Romany nationalism, which began in the 1930s, in Romania. And he was proudly aware of the astonishing proliferation of new groups formed in the Eastern bloc since 1989: in Hungary alone, there were already 140 registered Rom organizations. Nevertheless, here Hancock spoke most evocatively of Rom fatalism (and, like Frank Johnson, he used the third person). "They are so skeptical. Some don't even believe they have a language. They deny their identity." Dispersal and the imposition of varieties of white culture, Hancock believed, had caused the Gypsies to lose their language, their sense of belonging, and their ability even to recognize each other.

Writing for a Gypsy readership in a 1988 issue of the magazine *Roma* (published in India and one of the enduring Gypsy publications), Hancock pointed to a different cause:

> It has been said more than once that our main problem is lack of enough educated people among us to organize things. This is not true; there are certainly enough educated and concerned Roma to do the job. The problem is, instead, an old one: our national disease, *hamishagos* [to meddle or to disturb]. This for some reason, makes us want to hinder, instead of help, our own who are getting ahead. *Sar laci and'ekh vadra* ("like crabs in a bucket"), when one tries to climb out, the others hang on to him and pull him back down.

He offered the example of the first appointment of a Gypsy by a president (the president was Ronald Reagan, as it happened) to a federal position—the direct result of Hancock's years of pushing and pestering. When Bill Duna, a Gypsy of Hungarian origin living in Minneapolis, was appointed as the single Rom member of the U.S. Holocaust Memorial Council, "the very next day," Hancock told the readers of *Roma*, "other Gypsies sought to wreck things. They sent cables and telegrams to the Council saying that they were more qualified than he. The Holocaust Memorial Council's response was to make fun of the situation. Individuals unable to read or write, knowing nothing of the history of the Holocaust . . ."

At Stupava, though, Hancock did not want to discuss these internal problems. Among his publications is a book called *The Pariah Syndrome*, and the title is an indication of what he believes to be the cause of Gypsy fatalism. "For example, the newspapers. Whenever there is a story about Gypsies it's always about crime. And only when Gypsies are implicated is ethnicity mentioned: 'the Gypsy mother,' 'the Gypsy home.' Imagine substituting the word 'Jew.' " He was talking about the *Western* press, about *The New York Times*. Some of his most useful work has been in his role as a one-man watchdog, patiently correcting the stereotypes that crop up everywhere, from editorials and police reports to greeting cards, which in the U.S.A. in the 1990s could still feature thieving hook-nosed Gypsy crones. Hancock is offended, and he has a point. "But we are never identified when there are serious rights issues involved. For example, no one mentions the fact that most children in Romanian orphanages are Roma, like most refugees in Germany."

One of those refugees was Rajko Djurić, the poet and president of the International Romani Union, who had been threatened with death and forced to flee his native Yugoslavia after enraging authorities with his call to the disintegrating country's eight hundred thousand Gypsies to refuse to fight. Gypsies lived in every part of the country, he'd pointed out; their name was a term of insult; what interest or duty could they find in a nationalist scramble for land? A year before Stupava (when a full-blown Balkan war still seemed unimaginable to most observers) I went to meet Rajko Djurić in Belgrade, and I found him in the middle of the Serbian capital's first mass protest. That day in March 1991, over the din of the crowd, Rajko reminded me that few Gypsies had survived the terror once the Ustasha (the Croatian fascists in the Second World War) came to power in the north. And in occupied Serbia, he continued (in the relative calm of the packed bus we had boarded), Gypsies fell to firing squads at a rate of one hundred for each German killed by partisans, and fifty for each German wounded. Rajko correctly predicted that in the coming years of war the Gypsies would again be used as cannon fodder. A year later, at Stupava, he again rightly promised that the Gypsies of the former Yugoslavia, with no patch of ground to bargain with, would also be excluded from all the negotiations which would dramatically affect their lives. Every discussion at Stupava pointed to an emerging theme: that Gypsies must redefine themselves as an ethnic problem—rather than a social one, with the deathless implications of parasitism and criminality (and, perhaps worse, of invisibility).

To that end, the three American experts lectured the Gypsies on the management of ethnic crisis. They knew about Mexican Americans, about blacks and whites in America, and about ethnic conflict in general. Well-meaning though they were, none of them knew anything about Gypsies, and this was noticed. Still, their immediate credibility had already been more comically undermined by scratchy radio dispatches announcing the ethnic riots back home in L.A. The radio belonged to a Serbian political scientist sitting in the back row, who had been tuning in for news of his own ethnic crisis.

It was my impression that most of the Roma were not listening to anything, though none was more theatrically indifferent than Rudko Kawczynski, the militant leader from Hamburg. In Germany he had organized sit-ins and hunger strikes—new directions in Gypsy protest; and he had established an international parliament called Eurorom, as well as a Roma National Congress. It was impossible to ignore him at Stupava. He arrived ostentatiously late at each session, preceded always by two leather-jacketed henchpersons who would lean cross-armed against the wall rather than sit at the school desks like everyone else. His manner of speaking—with elaborate pauses and the intentionally soft voice of a Mafia *capo*—was as pompous as his carefully tilted widebrimmed hat. Kawczynski was the Eldridge Cleaver of the Romany emancipation movement; and he could barely contain himself.

Donald Horowitz, the professor from Duke, stood at the podium describing how the negative image of Roma was shared by other "subordinate ethnic groups" formed through slavery and conquest. He cited American blacks, some low castes of India and Africa, and, perhaps unintriguingly and even insultingly to his present audience, the Burakamin of Japan. "The Burakamin had also been characterized as dirty, lazy, sexually promiscuous, and akin to four-legged animals." But such images could be changed, he was going on to say, when Kawczynski cut him off.

"Roma are sitting, *gadje* are speaking. They are telling us what to do, which language to speak. They want to teach us how to speak our own language. What are they *doing* here? . . . Ten miles from here Gypsies are starving. This is not a concern of the *gadje*. It is our problem. They don't want to help us. They want to quell us, or else expel us or maybe to kill us. Europeans try to make our life so difficult that we will leave voluntarily. They drive us to think that they are all alike. Brothers, don't think that the *gadjo* is more clever than you are. You must help yourselves. We cannot expect any kind of help from anyone."

Manush Romanov, the diminutive leader from Bulgaria, was twenty years older than Kawczynski and, though a separatist himself, he was not convinced. "They are stronger than us!" he shouted out during Kawczynski's tirade, to which the Polish-born panther replied:

"No." (Deep pause.) "Only in seminars, not in the street. We must take back the streets." Manush Romanov was more poetic. "We have problems," he replied, "like leaves in the forest." Many, I supposed he meant, and here he had some authority.

If among Gypsies the act of survival, even identity itself, is a kind of victory, in the case of Manush it was a three-part triumph. His name, which he took for himself in 1989, means "Gypsy Man" in Romani, or "Man Man." He used to be Mustapha Alia, and then, after the first campaign of forced name-changing in Bulgaria, Lyubomir Aliev. In his former life, before Sofia's once-thriving Gypsy Theater had been shut down, Manush had been a playwright and a puppeteer. He was one of three Gypsies to be elected to Bulgaria's first free Parliament, and the only one to admit to being a Gypsy. Like many of the new figures (and despite such glamorous political credentials as a stint in prison), he seemed an unlikely leader. But there were very few "likely" leaders, mainly because, as Hancock had pointed out, there were very few likely followers among the Roma. Some sixty distinct tribal groups existed among Bulgaria's population of eight hundred thousand Gypsies—and there was Manush's lone cultural association (ethnically based political parties were illegal in Bulgaria). Some of the proudest groups, such as Bulgaria's Grastari, or Lovara, an elegant population of horse-dealers—who had remained nomadic until it became a punishable offense in 1958, expressly forbade defiling involvement in *gadjo* politics, and they thought Manush should be lynched.

An unlikely leader. And yet, apart from an unpopular obsession with a Gypsy homeland, on paper he was not so different from the more charismatic black-power brokers: "We want separate schools, our own languages taught in those schools, and our own villages. We must build houses for our people, new houses in new neighborhoods, not mixed in with the Bulgarians with whom we cannot get along. We must have our own homes for our own way of life. One day we will have our own country—Romanistan. Now we don't even have our own places. To have a home, to have a *house*, is, after all, more important even than to have a country."

I asked Manush if there wasn't a danger of creating an even bigger Gypsy ghetto. "The greater danger," he replied, "is to disappear."

The need for a homeland must be most acute in those whose right to belong anywhere at all has been most stridently questioned. (Norman

Manea has called it "the psychosis of the provisory.") But if the idea of Romanistan has not in general tempted the Roma, perhaps it is because they have experienced enough encampment on various reservations: as slaves on the estates of noblemen, as deportees to the colonies, in the death camps, or just at the bottom of the heap.

The Gypsies were—and are—a people on the brink. They have begun to taste the power of the idea of knowing that they are Roma; at the same time, they are in danger of becoming just another "language" (in their case, little-understood dialect) of ethnic self-assertion and victimhood. "The greater danger is to disappear," Manush had said; but there was more than one direction for the Gypsies to disappear in.

Over the several years since Stupava I had been a spectator at many conferences. I admired the speed and apparent ease with which the Gypsy participants took up this form of politicking. I was impressed by how well they spoke and how much they had to say. But I kept wondering: Is this really it? *Konferença, kongresso, parliamento?* At meeting after meeting the most promising men and women, decked out in their conference clothes, increasingly retreated into the phony language of consensus and euphemism. Was their future to be like everyone else's, after all? What kind of "existence" was this, if not another version of "etc."? *Konferença, kongresso, parliamento . . .*

The world of Papusza—the silhouette of traveling Gypsies—was of course long gone. No more caravans and bears, and, please, no more kings. You didn't have to romanticize the past to feel a real loss, and an ambivalence about the new: the enclosed, and incurably sedentary, world of the conference-goer.

Often at these events I found that I had to escape for a while, to stop listening and clear my head. I'd walk around, fanatically inhaling, and wonder how Gypsies would ever breathe the fresh air *and* be the insiders they now also clearly wanted to be and had to become. It was in such a mood that Nicolae once found me, pacing another conference-center parking lot. He was always rushing between a podium and a working group at these meetings, but here he paused to say hello and to give me news from Romania. He seemed to intuit my concerns; and what he described to me made me want to cry with vicarious pride.

The Gypsies had experienced centuries of strategic chaos, of elaborate social fragmentation and epic instability, and now they were making their case, and making it publicly. In politics, but also in work. Nicolae's report of new Gypsy initiatives didn't sound like much just to

list them: an all-Rom brick-making enterprise here, a farming cooperative there. But the farming cooperative of forty Roma families was in
Palazu Mare, just by *Kogălniceanu*, the Black Sea town razed by a mob,
the home of the rhomboid Discobar and the little girl whose legs had
been melted by an arsonist's smoldering beam. And Nicolae had news
from Hădăreni, in the heart of Transylvania, where two Gypsies had
been lynched and a third burned in his bed. In Hădăreni the church
bells tolled in warning whenever a dispossessed Gypsy dared approach
the town. Now those same outsiders were setting up shop—indeed,
setting up a factory, in a *synagogue*—to make fur hats. They were not
going to be kept out. They were not going to disappear. As he told me
of these endeavors I thought of Luciano, the seven-year-old Gypsy boy
who had died before any Romanian doctor would treat him, and who
had been buried in his new panama hat. Nicolae's news of Rom grass-
roots projects were, I thought, a proper tribute to Luciano.

In the international arena Gheorghe always emphasized what
Gypsies had to offer—not the specter of the desperate Rom, the eternal
victim, dependent and discriminated against. I knew it would have
been easier the other way around. It was expected; human rights
always describes human wrongs. And I knew he was right. They were
good at everything—more enterprising and energetic, more imagina-
tive and more good-humored, than most of the people around them—
when they got the chance. They were good at everything. Everything
except representing themselves.

Nicolae Gheorghe saw ethnic politics as a fool's paradise, a new
ghetto or margin or lay-by for Gypsies. But most Roma were skeptical of
an international identity (Andrzej Mirga called it "self-stigmatization"
and an invitation to governments to disown their least-loved citizens).
Vulnerability, however dignified, ensured that for the time being Gypsies were concerned mainly with survival in the places they lived. Few
shared the idealism of Gheorghe, and even fewer recognized the pragmatism at its core.

On his travels, Nicolae had discovered that without land or a parent
country, without the special claims of an indigenous population, "the
Roma" in international law "have the status of trade unions, environmental lobbies, or professional associations." He had noticed that the
foreigners most interested in the Roma were immigration authorities.
He got the idea that Gypsy poverty, illiteracy, unemployment, ill health,
early death, and stupendous birthrates—all record-breaking for a European population—were not the real subject. And the Roma are the

largest minority in Europe. It was just their existence, their *being there*, and being everywhere, that stirred people, and so he too made this his theme. Gheorghe promoted an alternative—and to many a sacrilegious—identity in which people could be seen and discussed independent of property. He believed that the separation between citizenship and nationality, which in Eastern Europe neatly divides territorial and cultural allegiances, could be stretched to accommodate a transnational population made up of loyal citizens from different countries.

Transnationalism appealed to others as well, though, and it could mean many things. To Kawczynski, for example, it meant that Roma should have a special right of passage—and to this end he had even produced a beige, passportlike document complete with fake stamps and available, through him, for one thousand deutschemarks a pop. Ian Hancock imagined a transnational identity in the form of "reunification," which he sought through a web of organizations across the diaspora and through the standardization of the Romani language. "We came out of India as one people, sharing one language and one history. We only fragmented since we've been in Europe," Hancock told the congregation. "We must be one people again." The stressing of Indianness has never amounted to a call to mass repatriation; any Gypsy, wherever he or she lives, has had enough experience of the stranger to need no confirmation in the subcontinent. Rather, Hancock's insistence on "reunification," like Gheorghe's case for a "transnational identity," expressed the idea that a people could themselves act as a country. The use of the term "nation" to describe what were once known as tribes already widely acknowledges that possibility and that need.

Rudko wanted to "take back the streets"; Hancock wanted to take back the narrative. Like many who champion the cause of the powerless against the abusers of power, against the usual writers of history, Hancock was entirely engaged in the redressing of wrongs, wrongs flagrant and invisible. For thirty years, his aim had been to correct the history of the victors—and thereby to reroute the destiny of the victims—and sometimes this justified what others, mainly *gadjo* historians, rejected as exaggerations. Hancock's theory of a single-tribe, mass exodus out of India was not much endorsed, nor was his claim of 1.5 million Roma Holocaust victims. But who would doubt the *gist* of his history? And who would deny his propriety in telling it? Was it pos-

On the panel from left to right: Dr. Mirga, Dr. Hancock, Dr. Gheorghe, Dr. Orgovanová.
On April 14, 1994, these four Rom intellectuals gave testimony before the first-ever congres-
sional hearing in Washington, D.C., on the human-rights abuses of Roma.

sible to exaggerate the wrongs committed against Gypsies? Victims'
versions certainly had spiritual and moral truth. Among Roma, "talking back" (in Hancock's phrase) was a particularly radical development. Frank from Los Angeles was wrong to despair.

The governments of the formerly communist countries regard the
plight of Gypsies mainly as an occasionally useful gambit in their bids
for foreign aid. Minorities are a test case for democracy, or, as Havel
had properly refined it, for a civil society. In theory. Nicolae Gheorghe
understood that minorities, and particularly Gypsies, might at least be
a showcase. And so he sought—and got—government sponsorship for
a follow-up meeting in Stupava a year later, at the large summer palace
of Ceauşescu on Lake Snagov. (*This* venue had a different resonance:
Romanian Gypsies in particular seemed to enjoy occupying the dictator's garish residence; better still, on the lake was an island, and in the
middle and far from his Transylvanian home, Vlad Ţepeş, the Impaler
himself, was buried—presumably by some of his hundreds of Gypsy
slaves.) And then, only a few weeks after an apparent breakthrough,

Nicolae was publicly denounced by his own sponsors at a high-level international congress on minorities. The Romanian representatives complained that "Mr. Gheorghe was introduced as a 'representative of the Romany people,' " whereas "this seminar is about minorities, not about 'peoples.' There is no question of self-determination. Minorities remain under the jurisdiction of sovereign national states. Anyway, Nicolae Gheorghe is not the representative of the Romany people; where is his 'King'? Where is his *Emperor*?" For once, and understandably, Nicolae was speechless.

Elsewhere, Manush Romanov always had something memorable to say, especially, and sweetly, in farewell. (Comings and goings also always entailed his courtly kissing of all the ladies' hands.) Once, at the end of a visit in Sofia in which he was practically in tears for his Gypsies, he dramatically called after me, *"Prohasar man opre pirende—sa muro djiben semas opre chengende"*—"Bury me standing. I've been on my knees all my life."

Within the crusading Roma community every step forward also entrained a half-step back, as a reactionary and growing Roma movement sought to thwart any organization in the public eye. *Sar laci and'ekh vadra*, like crabs in a bucket. Violent attacks from fundamentalist, anti-intellectual Gypsies, or just from some envious, frustrated individual, were a feature of all meetings and they would not be understood by most *gadjo* observers, who would walk away with their prejudices confirmed. These Romany "crabs" didn't see how far and how fast their own elite had come. *They* weren't impressed that Andrzej Mirga, whose mother was an illiterate fortune-teller, was now publishing scholarly books and running for the Polish Parliament. On principle, they would identify less with the Hancock they knew than with his beloved grandfather Marko, a rat-catcher, or his great-grandmother Granny Bench, who was born in a wagon off London's Vauxhall Bridge Road. No, the crabs wouldn't see any progress in the move from kidnap to Capitol Hill, from *kris* to congressional hearing.

Long before 1989, a French Rom called Mateo Maximoff used the journey of his own family to illustrate the dilemma which is central to the future of Romany emancipation. In 1947 he published his first novel, *Le Prix de la liberté;* its hero, Ioan, is based on Maximoff's own grandfather, who was born a slave. The novel is set in the last period of slavery in Romania, after the revolutions of 1848, which had given some of the captives the courage to revolt. In the novel, a group of them escape from their estate and flee to the mountains and the Resistance. Ioan is left with a problem. He has been educated along with his master's children and now must decide: Will he join the mutiny or stay in the library? Is he one of us or one of them? It is of course Ioan's knowledge of "the library," of the *gadjo* world, which will decide the outcome of the uprising, but despite or because of this he is called a traitor—as was Nicolae, as were others, and as was Papusza, who had so inspired Mirga. The new leaders were indeed "career Gypsies," as accused. They were also the only hope for millions of Roma who had never heard of them, the ones who live in the Black Towns, the toxic slums and townships across Eastern Europe with no names, or with names like Take-It-or-Leave-It, Like-It-or-Not, No-Man's-Land, Cambodia, and Bangladesh.

Simione Mihai, a Kalderash boy, in his camp at Sintesti, Romania, 1992

SELECTED AND ANNOTATED
BIBLIOGRAPHY

An asterisk indicates that the source is not specifically about Gypsies.

General Studies

Balić, S., et al., eds. *Romani Language and Culture*. Sarajevo: Institut za Proučavanje Nacionalnih Odnosa, 1989. A large collection of papers produced for a conference of the same name held in Sarajevo in 1986.

Clebert, J-P. *Les Tziganes*. Paris: B. Arthaud, 1961; English translation, *The Gypsies*. London: Vista Books, 1963. Dated and unreliable, this is nevertheless a source of Gypsy lore.

Fraser, A. *The Gypsies*. Oxford: Blackwell, 1992; revised edition, 1995. The most thorough, reliable, and readable general history, with detailed accounts of origins, migrations, and the linguistic arguments, along with extensive documentation of European persecutions.

Grellmann, H. M: G. *Die Zigeuner*; English translation, *Dissertation on the Gipsies*. London: William Ballantine, second edition, 1807.

Hancock, I. *The Pariah Syndrome: An Account of Gypsy Slavery and Persecution*. Ann Arbor: Karoma, 1987. The prominent Rom activist and linguist draws on many sources in his account of persecution through the ages.

Kenrick, D., and Puxon, G. *The Destiny of Europe's Gypsies*. London: Sussex University Press and Chatto-Heinemann, 1972. See the Holocaust section for notes.

Kogălniceanu, M. *Esquisse sur l'histoire, les moeurs et la langue des Cigains*. Berlin: Behr Verlag, 1837.

Liegeois, J-P. *Tsiganes*. Paris: La Decouverte, 1983; abridged English translation, *Gypsies: An Illustrated History*. London: Al Saqi Books, 1986.

———. *Gypsies and Travellers*. Strasbourg: Council of Europe, 1987; revised edition, 1994. Reliable and useful overviews. Liegeois includes less documentation than does Fraser and more sociological analysis of, for example, official policies and prevalent attitudes towards Gypsies.

Rehfisch, F., ed. *Gypsies, Tinkers and Other Travellers*. London: Academic, 1975. An excellent selection of essays.

Vaux de Foletier, F. de. *Milles ans d'histoire des Tsiganes*. Paris: Fayard, 1970.

On the Asian background and the linguistic arguments see also:

Goeje, M. J. de. *Accounts of the Gypsies in India*. Delhi: New Society, 1976. Contribution to the proceedings of the Koninklijke Akademie van Wetenschappen of Amsterdam in 1875.

Hancock, I. "On the Migration and Affiliation of the Domba: Iranian Words in Rom, Lom, and Dom Gypsy." *International Romani Union Occasional Papers*, series F, no. 8 (1993). Looks, through linguistics, at whether Middle Eastern and European Gypsies are related.

Kenrick, D. *Gypsies from India to the Mediterranean*. Toulouse: CRDP, 1993.

Rishi, W. R. "History of Romano Movement, Their Language and Culture." In *Romani Language and Culture*, edited by S. Balić et al. Sarajevo: Institut za Proučavanje Nacionalnih Odnosa, 1989).

Sampson, J. *The Dialect of the Gypsies of Wales*. Oxford: Clarendon Press, 1926.

Turner, R. L. "The Position of Romani in Indo-Aryan." *Journal of the Gypsy Lore Society* (third series) 5 (1926): 145–89. Sampson's comments on this article and Turner's reply can both be found in *Journal of the Gypsy Lore Society* (third series) 6 (1927).

Social Anthropology/Sociology

Okely, J. M. *The Traveller-Gypsies*. Cambridge: Cambridge University Press, 1983. The result of field work on the campsites of British Travelers in the 1970s, this study offers insights into the maintenance of symbolic boundaries (she explores, for example, how Gypsy notions of cleanliness inform their attitudes towards animals), economic survival, and the lives of Gypsy women. It is considered controversial because Okely rejects the widely accepted theory of (and the linguistic arguments for) the Gypsies' Indian origins, suggesting instead that the Gypsies were indigenous folk who became outsiders with the collapse of feudal society.

Sutherland, A. *The Hidden Americans*. Prospect Heights, Illinois: Waveland, 1975. A model study of the Gypsies' internal social organization and their complex relations with non-Gypsies based on the author's field work among a group of Vlach Roma in California.

Sway, M. *Familiar Strangers: Gypsy Life in America*. Urbana and Chicago: University of Illinois Press, 1988. Particularly interesting on the Gypsies' economic adaptability.

Despite their regional focus, all of the above studies offer insights into Gypsies in general.

Folktales, Folklore, and Memoir

Bercovici, K. *The Story of the Gypsies*. London: Jonathan Cape, 1929. A ludicrously romantic account ("Where do the [Gypsies] come from? Where do swallows come from?"), this book nevertheless contains some intriguing legends.

Borrow, G. *The Zincali* [or, an account of the Gypsies of Spain]. London: John Murray, 1841.

———. *The Bible in Spain*. London: John Murray, 1843.

———. *Lavengro*. London: John Murray, 1851.

———. *The Romany Rye*. London: John Murray, 1857.

———. *Wild Wales*. London: John Murray, 1862.

———. *Romano Lavo-lil: Word Book of the Romany*. London: John Murray, 1874. As an agent of the British and Foreign Bible Society and a gifted linguist, Borrow traveled to St. Petersburg, and then to Portugal and Spain. He did translate the Gospel of St. Luke into Spanish Romani, but, more important, his travels, and his adventures, inspired some of the richest and most enjoyable books ever written about Gypsies. *The Bible in Spain* was the most popular during Borrow's lifetime and it is perhaps the most brilliant.

Boswell, S. G. *The Book of Boswell*. Edited by J. Seymour. London: Gollancz, 1970. Memoir of an English Gypsy.

Gorog-Karady, V., and Lebarbier, M., eds. *Oralité Tsigane: Cahiers de Littérature Orale*, no. 30. Paris: Publications Langues'O, 1991. Essays on Romany oral traditions and culture.

Groome, F. H. *Gypsy Folk-tales*. London: Hurst and Blackett, 1899.

Hancock, I. "Marko: Stories of My Grandfather." *Lacio Drom* supplement to no. 6 (December 1985): 53–60. Lively memoir of the activist's differently active ancestors in London. This issue of *Lacio Drom* is dedicated to folklore, folk-tales, and traditions—including essays about Greek, Bulgarian, Hungarian, Slovak, Kosovan, and English Gypsies.

Hübschmanová, M., Šebková, H., and Žlnayová, E. *Fragments Tsiganes: Comme en haut, ainsi en bas*. Paris: Lierre et Coudrier, 1991. Personal histories (including songs, recipes, and wartime terrors) of Slovak Roma told by them in the first person. Their Czech amanuenses, all Romani speakers, have done an admirable job of retaining in translation the tone and flavor of Romany speech.

Marushiakova, E., and Popov, V., eds. *Studii Romani, vol. 1*. Sofia, Bulgaria: Club '90 Publishers, 1994. A collection of legends, myths, and songs of Bulgarian Gypsies.

Starkie, W. *Raggle-Taggle, Adventures with a Fiddle in Hungary and Roumania*. London: Readers Union, 1949.

———. *In Sara's Tents*. London: John Murray, 1953. More adventures, this time in Spain.

Tong, D. *Gypsy Folktales*. New York: Harvest, 1991.

Vesey-Fitzgerald, B. "Gypsy Medicine." *Journal of the Gypsy Lore Society* (third series) vol. 23 (1944): 21–50.

Yates, D., ed. *A Book of Gypsy Folk-tales*. London: Phoenix House, 1948.

Yoors, J. *The Gypsies*. London: George Allen & Unwin, 1967. At the age of twelve, Jan Yoors left his home in Antwerp to join a passing band of Lovara Roma. The result of a boy's dream adventure, his memoir is one of the most valuable accounts of Gypsy life. Years later, during the Second World War, Yoors rejoined his adopted family, with a mission. In a second book, *Crossing* (New York: Simon & Schuster, 1971; reissued, Prospect Heights, Illinois: Waveland, 1988), he tells a story of Gypsies in the Resistance and his own role in their involvement.

Eastern Europe

Ascherson, N. *Black Sea*. London: Jonathan Cape, 1995.*

Cioran, E. M. from the French, *The Temptation to Exist*. New York: Quadrangle, 1968, with an introduction by Susan Sontag; London: Quartet, 1987. This collection of essays, along with most of the rest of the late Romanian aphorist and essayist's *oeuvre*, is not *about* Eastern Europe; but one might argue that only a Mitteleuropean (or perhaps a Latin American) could have written it.*

Crowe, D. *A History of the Gypsies of Eastern Europe and Russia*. New York: St. Martin's Press, 1994.

Crowe, D., and Kolsti, J., eds. *The Gypsies of Eastern Europe*. Armonk, N.Y.: M. E. Sharpe, 1991.

Havel, V. *Living in Truth*. London: Faber & Faber, 1987.*

Bibliography

Huttenbach, H. R., ed. *Nationalities Papers* 19: 3 (1991). Special issue: "The Gypsies in Eastern Europe."

Kiš, D. *A Tomb for Boris Davidovich*. London: Faber & Faber, 1985.*

Jelavich, B. *History of the Balkans*. Vol. 1: *Eighteenth and Nineteenth Centuries*. Cambridge: Cambridge University Press, 1983.* *History of the Balkans*. Vol. 2: *Twentieth Century*. Cambridge: Cambridge University Press, 1988.*

Kundera, M. *The Book of Laughter and Forgetting*. London: Faber & Faber, 1982.*

Lockwood, W. G. "Balkan Gypsies: An Introduction." In *Papers from the Fourth and Fifth Annual Meetings*, Gypsy Lore Society, North American Chapter, New York, 1985.

Magocsi, P. R. *Historical Atlas of East Central Europe*. Seattle: University of Washington Press, 1993.*

Magris, C. *Danube*. London: Collins Harvill, 1990.*

Manea, N. *On Clowns: the Dictator and the Artist*. London: Faber & Faber, 1994.*

Miłosz, C. *The Captive Mind*. New York: Alfred A. Knopf, 1953.*

Poulton, H. *The Balkans: Minorities and States in Conflict*. London: Minority Rights Publications, 1991.

Silverman, C. "Rom (Gypsy) Music." *Garland Encyclopedia of World Music*, European volume. Eds. James Porter and Timothy Rice (forthcoming in 1996).

Soulis, G. C. "The Gypsies in the Byzantine Empire and the Balkans in the Late Middle Ages." *Dumbarton Oaks Papers* 15 (1961): 143–65.

Particular Countries

Albania

Courtiade, M. "I Rom in Albania. Un profilo storico-sociale." *Lacio Drom* 28 (gennaio-aprile 1992): 3–14.

Bulgaria

Marushiakova, E. "Ethnic Identity Among Gypsy Groups in Bulgaria." *Journal of the Gypsy Lore Society* (fifth series), 2 (1992): 95–115.

———. "Gruppi e organizzazioni zingare in Bulgaria e il loro atteggiamento verso l'impegno politico." *Lacio Drom* 28 (gennaio-aprile 1992): 51–63.

Popov, V. "Il problema zingaro in Bulgaria nel contesto attuale." *Lacio Drom* 28 (gennaio-aprile 1992): 41–50.

Silverman, C. "Bulgarian Gypsies: Adaptation in a Socialist Context." *Nomadic Peoples*, nos. 21/22 (1986): 51–60.

Zang, T. *Destroying Ethnic Identity: The Gypsies of Bulgaria*. New York: Human Rights Watch, 1991.

Czechoslovakia

Davidová, E. "The Gypsies in Czechoslovakia." *Journal of the Gypsy Lore Society* (third series), 50 (1971): 40–54.

Erich, R. "Roma in Slovakia: Experiments with an Ethnic Minority," draft report. Vienna: International Helsinki Federation for Human Rights, 1992–93.

Gross, T. "The Czech Republic: Citizenship Research Project," an unpublished report on how the new citizenship law affects Roma. See also Ina Zoon's report (1994), both written for The Tolerance Foundation, Senovazne Nam. 1, Prague 1, Czech Republic.

Guy, W. "Ways of Looking at Roms: The Case of Czechoslovakia." In Rehfisch, *Gypsies, Tinkers and Other Travellers*, pp. 201–29.

Hübschmanová, M. "What Can Sociology Suggest About the Origin of Roms?" *Archiv Orientalni* (Prague) 4 (1972): 51–64.

———. "Economic Stratification and Interaction: Roma, an Ethnic Jati in East Slovakia." *Giessener Hefte für Tsiganologie,* 3/4, 1984/1985, 3–25.

Kamm, H. A particularly good series of reports on the plight of Roma in the Czech Republic, Slovakia, and Hungary. See *The New York Times,* November 7, 1993, p. A9; November 17, 1993, p. A6; November 28, 1993, p. A4; December 8, 1993, p. A7; December 10, 1993, p. A4.

Kólvada, J. "The Gypsies of Czechoslovakia." *Nationalities Papers* 19:3 (1991): 269–96.

McCagg, W. D. "Gypsy Policy in Socialist Hungary and Czechoslovakia, 1945–1989." *Nationalities Papers* 19:3 (1991): 313–36.

Mann, A. "The Roma—An Ethnic Minority in Slovakia," unpublished paper presented at a Project on Ethnic Relations conference, Stupava, Slovakia, 1992.

Orgovanová, K. "Human Rights Abuses of the Roma (Gypsies)." Testimony before the Subcommittee on International Organizations and Human Rights of the House Committee on Foreign Affairs, House of Representatives, 103rd Cong., 2nd sess., April 14, 1994. Washington, D.C.: U.S. Government Printing Office, 1994, 26–28.

Tritt, R. *Struggling for Ethnic Identity: Czechoslovakia's Endangered Gypsies.* New York: Human Rights Watch, 1992.

Zoon, I. "Equal Rights Project." Prague: Tolerance Foundation Report, 1994. An unpublished report on the dangers to Roma posed by new citizenship laws in the Czech Republic.

Germany

Buruma, I. *The Wages of Guilt.* London: Jonathan Cape, 1993.*

———. "Outsiders." In *The New York Review of Books,* April 9, 1992. A particularly good analysis of antiforeigner violence.*

Cartner, H. *Foreigners Out: Xenophobia and Right-Wing Violence in Germany.* New York: Human Rights Watch Report, October 1992. A particularly good work of documentation.

Enzensberger, H. M. "The Great Migration." *Granta* 42 (1992): 17–64.*

Grass, G. "Losses." *Granta* 42 (1992): 99–108.

Heuss, H. "Die Migration von Roma aus Osteuropa im 19 und 20 Jahrhundert: Historische Anlässe und staatliche Reaktion." Unpublished paper.

Ignatieff, M. *Blood and Belonging: Journeys into the New Nationalism.* London: BBC Books and Chatto & Windus, 1993, 57–102.*

Macfie, R. A. S. "Gypsy Persecutions: A Survey of a Black Chapter in European History," *Journal of the Gypsy Lore Society* (third series), 22 (1943): 64–78.

Survey of the Policy and Law Regarding Aliens in the Federal Republic of Germany. Bonn: Federal Ministry of the Interior, 1991; *Daten und Fakten zur Ausländersituation.* Bonn: Federal Ministry of the Interior, 1992.*

See the Holocaust and Nationalism sections for other sources on Germany and the Roma.

Hungary

Féher, G. *Struggling for Ethnic Identity: The Gypsies of Hungary.* New York: Human Rights Watch, Helsinki, 1993.

Stewart, M. S. "Brothers in Song: The Persistence of (Vlach) Gypsy Identity and Community in Socialist Hungary." Doctoral thesis submitted to the London

School of Economic and Political Science, Faculty of Economics, 1987. Based on fourteen months of field work in Hungary. Stewart takes as his thesis the Rom reaction to compulsory wage labor, though his study also includes, for example, an investigation into Roma notions of community and sharing.

Macedonia

Puxon, G. "Roma in Macedonia," *Journal of the Gypsy Lore Society* (fourth series), 1:2 (1976): 128–33.

Tassy, M. "La poésie des Roms de Macédoine," *Etudes Tsiganes*, no. 4 (1991): 20–29.

Poland

Ficowski, J. *The Gypsies in Poland.* Warsaw: Interpress, 1990.

———. "The Gypsies in the Polish People's Republic," *Journal of the Gypsy Lore Society* (third series), 35 (1956): 28–38.

Kowalski, G. *The Story of a Gypsy Woman*, a documentary film about Papusza. Ul Brogi 19/4, 31-431, Kraków, Poland.

Mirga, A. "The Effects of State Assimilation Policy on Polish Gypsies," *Journal of the Gypsy Lore Society* (fifth series), 3 (1993): 69–76.

———. "Human Rights Abuses of the Roma (Gypsies)." Testimony before the subcommittee on International Organizations and Human Rights of the House Committee on Foreign Affairs, House of Representatives, 103rd Cong., 2nd sess., April 14, 1994. Washington, D.C.: GPO, 1994, 29–32.

Romania

Cartner, H. *Ethnic Conflict in Tîrgu Mureş.* New York: Human Rights Watch Helsinki, 1990, May newsletter.

———. *News from Romania.* New York: Human Rights Watch Helsinki, 1990. July newsletter.

———. *Destroying Ethnic Identity: The Persecution of Gypsies in Romania.* New York: Human Rights Watch Helsinki, 1991.

———. *Romania Lynch Law: Violence Against Roma in Romania.* New York: Human Rights Watch Helsinki, 1994. November newsletter.

Deak, I. "Survivors," *The New York Review of Books*, March 5, 1992, 43–51.

Florescu, R., and McNally, R. T. *Dracula Prince of Many Faces: His Life and Times.* Boston: Little, Brown, 1989.

Gheorghe, N. "Origin of Roma's Slavery in the Rumanian Principalities," *Roma* 7: (1983): 12–27.

Gilberg, T. *Nationalism and Communism in Romania: The Rise and Fall of Ceauşescu's Personal Dictatorship.* Boulder, Colo.: Westview, 1990.*

Maximoff, M. *La Prix de la liberté.* Paris: Flammarion, 1947. Rom novelist's fictional version of his ancestor's experience of slavery in the Romanian principalities.

Panaitescu, P. N. "The Gypsies in Wallachia and Moldavia: A Chapter of Economic History," *Journal of the Gypsy Lore Society* (third series) 20 (1941): 58–72.

Potra, G. *Contribuțiuni la istoricul Țiganilor din România.* Bucharest: Fundatia Regele Carol I, 1939.

Holocaust

Bandy, A. "European Gypsies Forgotten Victims in Story of Nazi Genocide," *Los Angeles Times*, June 26, 1994, p. A6.

Berenbaum, M. *The World Must Know: The History of the Holocaust as Told in the United States Holocaust Memorial Museum.* Boston: Little, Brown, 1993.

Berenbaum, M., ed. *A Mosaic of Victims: Non-Jews Persecuted and Murdered by the Nazis.* New York: New York University Press, 1990.

Bernadec, C. *L'Holocauste oublié: Le Massacre des Tsiganes.* Paris: France-Empire, 1979.

Braun, H. "A Sinto Survivor Speaks." In *Papers from the Sixth and Seventh Annual Meetings,* Gypsy Lore Society, North American Chapter, Cheverly, Md., pub. no. 3, edited by Joanne Grumet and translated by H. Silver, 165–71.

Burleigh, M., and Wippermann, W. *The Racial State: Germany 1933–1945.* Cambridge: Cambridge University Press, 1991.

Czerniakow, A. *The Warsaw Diary of Adam Czerniakow: Prelude to Doom.* Edited by R. Hilberg, S. Staron, J. Kermisz. New York: Stein and Day, 1982.

Dawidowicz, L. S. *The Holocaust and the Historians.* Cambridge: Harvard University Press, 1981.

Djurić, R. "Il calvaio dei Roma nel campo di concentramento di Jasenovac," *Lacio Drom* 4 (1992): 14–42.

Ficowski, J. *Cyganie na polskich drogach.* Kraków-Wrocław: Wydawnictwo Literackie, 1985. *Gypsies on Polish Roads,* translated by Regina Gelb, 129–51.

Friedman, I. *The Other Victims: First-Person Stories of Non-Jews Persecuted by the Nazis.* Boston: Houghton Mifflin, 1990, pp. 7–28.

Gilbert, M. *The Holocaust: The Jewish Tragedy.* London: Collins, 1986.

Gutman, I., ed. *Encyclopedia of the Holocaust.* 4 vols. New York: Macmillan, 1990.

Hancock, I. " 'Uniqueness' of the Victims: Gypsies, Jews and the Holocaust." In *Without Prejudice* 1:2 (1988): 45–67.

Hilberg, R. *The Destruction of the European Jews.* Chicago: Quadrangle Press, 1961.

Hoess, R. *Commandant of Auschwitz: The Autobiography of R. Hoess.* London: Pan, 1961.

Huttenbach, H. "The Romani Porajmos: The Nazi Genocide of Europe's Gypsies," in *Nationalities Papers* 19:3 (1991): 373–94.

Kenrick, D., and Puxon, G. *The Destiny of Europe's Gypsies.* London: Sussex University Press and Chatto-Heinemann, 1972. Revised and updated edition forthcoming from University of Hertfordshire Press in 1995 and retitled *Gypsies Under the Swastika,* with greater focus on the war period. This study is still the only work that deals with all the occupied and satellite countries.

Levi, P. *The Drowned and the Saved.* London: Michael Joseph, 1988.

———. *If This Is a Man.* London: Orion, 1960; published in the United States as *Survival in Auschwitz.* New York: Collier Books, 1993.

———. *If This Is a Man/The Truce.* London: Sphere, 1958, 1963.

Wiesenthal, S. *Justice Not Vengeance.* London: Weidenfeld & Nicolson, 1989.

Lifton, R. J. *The Nazi Doctors: Medical Killing and the Psychology of Genocide.* New York: Basic Books, 1986.

Michalewicz, B. "The Gypsy Holocaust in Poland." In *Papers from the Sixth and Seventh Annual Meetings,* Gypsy Lore Society, North American Chapter, Cheverly, Md., edited by Joanne Grumet, 73–83.

Milton, S. "The Context of the Holocaust," *German Studies Review* 13:2 (1990): 269–83.

———. "Gypsies and the Holocaust," *The History Teacher* 24:4 (1991): 375–87.

———. "The Racial Context of the Holocaust." *Social Education,* February 1991: 106–10.

———. "Nazi Policies Towards Roma and Sinti, 1933–1945," *Journal of the Gypsy Lore Society* (fifth series), 2:1 (1992): 1–18.

———. "Holocaust: The Gypsies," *Genocide in the Twentieth Century: Critical Essays and Eye-witness Accounts.* William S. Parsons, Israel W. Charny, and Samuel Totten, eds. New York and London: Garland Publishing, 1995, pp. 209–64.

Müller-Hill, B. *Murderous Science: Elimination by Scientific Selection of Jews, Gypsies and Others, 1933–1945.* Oxford: Oxford University Press, 1988.

Piper, F. *Auschwitz: How Many Jews, Poles, Gypsies . . .* Kraków: Poligrafia, 1992.

Wytwycky, B. *The Other Holocaust: Many Circles of Hell.* Washington: Novak Report, 1980: 30–39.

Yoors, J. *Crossing.* New York: Simon & Schuster, 1971; Prospect Heights, Illinois: Waveland, 1988.

Zimmermann, M. "From Discrimination to the 'Family Camp' at Auschwitz: National Socialist Persecution of the Gypsies," *Dachau Review,* no. 2. (1990): 87–113.

Nationalism, Ethnopolitics, etc.*

Anderson, B. *Imagined Communities: Reflections on the Spread and Origins of Nationalism.* London: Verso, 1983; revised edition, 1991.

Berlin, I. *The Crooked Timber of Humanity: Chapters in the History of Ideas.* London: John Murray, 1990.

———. "Two Concepts of Nationalism: An Interview with Isaiah Berlin," *The New York Review of Books,* November 21, 1991.

Breilly, J. *Nationalism and the State.* Manchester: Manchester University Press, 1982.

Brubaker, R. *Citizenship and Nationhood in France and Germany.* Cambridge: Harvard University Press, 1992.

Gellner, E. *Nations and Nationalism.* Oxford: Blackwell, 1983.

Gottlieb, G. *Nation Against State: A New Approach to Ethnic Conflicts and the Decline of Sovereignty.* New York: Council on Foreign Relations, 1993.

Greenfeld, L. *Nationalism: Five Roads to Modernity.* Cambridge: Harvard University Press, 1993.

Hertzberg, S. *Strangers Within the Gate City: The Jews of Atlanta, 1845–1915.* Philadelphia: The Jewish Publication Society of America, 1978.

Hobsbawm, E. J. *Nations and Nationalism Since 1870.* Cambridge: Cambridge University Press, 1990. A masterly and essential guide to the subject.

Horowitz, D. *Ethnic Groups in Conflict.* Berkeley: University of California Press, 1985.

Ignatieff, M. *Blood and Belonging: Journeys into the New Nationalism.* London: BBC Books and Chatto & Windus, 1993.

Moynihan, D. P. *Pandaemonium: Ethnicity in International Politics.* Oxford: Oxford University Press, 1993.

Rothschild, J. *Ethnopolitics: A Conceptual Framework.* New York: Columbia University Press, 1981.

Smith, A. D. *Nationalism: Theories of Nationalism.* New York: Harper & Row, 1983.

———. *The Ethnic Origins of Nations.* Oxford: Oxford University Press, 1986.

Romany Emancipation

Acton, T. *Gypsy Politics and Social Change: The Development of Ethnic Ideology and Pressure Politics Among British Gypsies from Victorian Reformism to Romani Nationalism.* London and Boston: Routledge and Kegan Paul, 1974.

Beck, S. "Racism and the Formation of a Romani Ethnic Leader." In *Perilous States, Conversations on Culture, Politics, and Nation,* edited by G. E. Marcus. Chicago:

University of Chicago Press, 1993, pp. 165–91. A portrait of Nicolae Gheorghe
by a fellow sociologist.

Gheorghe, N. "The Social Construction of Romani Identity," paper given at ESRC
Romani Studies Seminar, University of Greenwich, London, March 1993.

——. "Roma-Gypsy Ethnicity in Eastern Europe." *Social Research*, 58:4 (Winter
1991), 829–44.

——. "Romanies in the CSCE Process: A Case Study for the Rights of National
Minorities with Dispersed Settlement Patterns." A report on the debates at the
CSCE Human Dimension Seminar, Warsaw, 1993. (Romani Criss: Rom
Center for Social Prevention and Studies, P.O. Box 22-68, 70.100, Bucharest,
Romania.)

Hancock, I. "Talking Back," *Roma* 6:1 (1980): 13–20.

——. "Reunification and the Role of the International Romani Union." *Roma*, no.
29 (July 1988): 9–18.

——. "The East European Roots of Romani Nationalism." *Nationalities Papers*, 19:3
(1991): 251–68.

Liegois, J-P. *Mutation Tsiganes, la révolution bohémienne.* Brussels: Complexe, 1976.
The historical and cultural context within which to understand Romany adap-
tations and emancipation is laid out in this intelligent and influential book.

Project on Ethnic Relations. This organization hosted two conferences that yielded
two impressively succinct reports, both by Larry Watts: "The Romanies in Central and Eastern Europe: Illusions and Reality," May 1992, and "Countering
Anti-Roma Violence in Eastern Europe: The Snagov Conference and Related
Efforts," May 1993. PER, 1 Palmer Square, Suite 435, Princeton, New Jersey
08542-3718.

Puxon, G. "Romani Chib—The Romani Language Movement," in *Compass Points*, a
selection from the first hundred issues of *Planet,* ed. J. Davies; introduction by
J. Morris. Cardiff: University of Wales Press, 1993, 192–98. Though this essay is
now out of date (it was published in 1980), Puxon gives an idea of how "the
Romani language, a living link with India, has through its suppression become
the symbol of national liberation."

Periodicals

Etudes Tsiganes (since 1955), 2 rue d'Hautpol, 75019, Paris, France.

Journal of the Gypsy Lore Society (since 1888, with interruptions). Now in its fifth
series, this venerable journal is invaluable to anyone interested in Gypsy studies. The Society, founded in Britain but now run by what was its American
chapter, also publishes a *Newsletter of the Gypsy Lore Society,* 5607 Greenleaf
Road, Cheverly, Maryland 20785.

Lacio Drom (since 1965). Centro Studi Zingari, Via dei Barbieri 22, 00186, Rome,
Italy.

Patrin. Written mainly by Roma and published in bilingual editions (English-
Romani), *Patrin* has covered issues such as education, anti-Roma violence, and
language standardization. Founder-editor, Orhan Galjus, Nevipe Press Room
News Agency, PO Box 166, 080 01 Prešov, Slovakia.

Roma (since 1974). 3290/15-D, 160015, Chandigarh, India. Founder-editor,
W. R. Rishi.

INDEX

Page numbers in italics indicate illustrations.

PHOTOGRAPHIC CREDITS

Courtesy of Austria Presse Agentur/Scharr (photo by Agence France-Presse): 222
Courtesy of the United States Holocaust Memorial Museum (photos from
  Bundesarchiv, Koblenz): 260
Courtesy of Jerzy Ficowski (reproduction by Kazimierz Czapiński): 10
Courtesy of Jerzy Ficowski (photo by Jerzy Dorożyński): ii–iii, 11
Courtesy of Jerzy Ficowski (photo by Jerzy Ficowski): 6
Courtesy of Jerzy Ficowski (photos from the United States Holocaust Memorial
  Museum): 269, 270
(photos by Isabel Fonseca): 25, 41, 55, 61, 69, 86, 102, 105, 117, 119, 121, 132, 135, 144, 149,
  170, 175, 183, 184, 195, 246, 251, 287
Courtesy of Tobias Goulden (photo by Tobias Goulden): 114
Courtesy of Network Photographers Ltd. (photos by Witold Krassowski): 201, 203
Courtesy of Jerzy Ficowski (photo by Ignacy Krieger, Historical Museum of Kraków): 285
Courtesy of Elena Marushiakova (photo by Elena Marushiakova): 125
Courtesy of Luminitsa Mihai: 288, 289
Courtesy of Magnum Photos (photo by James Nachtway): 95
(photos by Polish Information Agency): 99, 291
Courtesy of Jeremy Sutton-Hibbert (photos by Jeremy Sutton-Hibbert): 105, 169, 226,
  306
(photo by Mary Thomas): 303

Illustration Credits
(illustration from I. Hancock, *The Pariah Syndrome*, 1987): 181
(illustration from Nördlingen Museum, Bavaria): 238
(illustration by Karl Stojka): 272

Map Credits
Isabel Fonseca: 84
(map by Tadeusz Kinowski, reproduced from the State Museum in Oświeçim,
  Auschwitz-Birkenau Guidebook, Oświeçim, 1992): 256